URBAN TERRORISM

URBAN
TERRORISM

Theory, Practice & Response

ANTHONY M. BURTON

The Free Press
A Division of Macmillan Publishing Co., Inc.
NEW YORK

The Free Press
A Division of Macmillan Publishing Co., Inc.
866 Third Avenue, New York, N.Y. 10022

Library of Congress Catalog Card Number: 75-21937

Printed in Great Britain

printing number
1   2   3   4   5   6   7   8   9   10

CONTENTS

ILLUSTRATIONS

The author and publishers would like to thank the following for permission to reproduce copyright illustrations: John Moss /Colorific!, no 1, United Press, nos 2, 8 and 11, Camera Press Ltd, no 3, the *Aldershot News*, no 4, *The Times*, no 5, Keystone Press Agency, no 6 and the Ministry of Defence, no 14.

Turning and turning in the widening gyre
The falcon cannot hear the falconer;
Things fall apart; the centre cannot hold;
Mere anarchy is loosed upon the world,
The blood-dimmed tide is loosed, and everywhere
The ceremony of innocence is drowned;
The best lack all conviction, while the worst
Are full of passionate intensity.

W. B. YEATS
The Second Coming

PREFACE

The purpose of this book is to give something of the background to the contemporary phenomenon of urban terrorism. It is concerned with the use of violence on the streets which is aimed at the overthrow of governments or which, in the colonial/separatist context is designed to pressure 'foreign' governments into acceding to demands for independence.

Acknowledgement is due to Messrs Constable for permission to quote from *Rule of Terror* by Helmut Andics; to Robert Hale and Co for *Grivas and the Story of EOKA* by W. Byford-Jones; Macmillan & Co for *Revolution* by Peter Calvert; Routledge for *Rape of the Masses* by S. Chakhotin; MR Press for *Revolution in the Revolution* by Régis Debray; Thomas Nelson and Sons for *Guerrilla Movements in Latin America* by Richard Gott; Foreign Affairs Publishing House for *Today's Revolutionaries* by Ian Grieg; Longmans for the *Memoirs of General Grivas*; Jonathan Cape for the *Essential T. E. Lawrence* ed. Garnett, for *Post Prison Writings and Speeches* by Eldridge Cleaver and, together with the Seven Pillars Trust, for *Seven Pillars of Wisdom* by T. E. Lawrence; Prentice Hall for *On Revolution* ed. Lutz and Brent; William Heinemann for *Hermann Goering* by Manvell and Frankel; Sage Publications for *Riots and Rebellions* by Masotti; Secker and Warburg and Mrs Sonia Brownell Orwell for *Homage to Catalonia* by George Orwell; to the Chilton Book Company for the *Ku Klux Klan* by W. P. Randel; to Faber and Faber for *Collected Poems* by Herbert Read; to Penguin Books (UK) for *Anarchism* by George Woodcock; M. B. Yeats and Macmillan & Co for *Collected Poems* of W. B. Yeats; the *Daily Telegraph* for the report on Black Power; the extract from Robert Fisk's report

ix

on 'Bloody Friday' is reproduced from *The Times* by permission.

To all my recent colleagues (who do not of course necessarily agree with the views expressed in this book) I wish to express my thanks for argument, discussion and encouragement, and especially to Jim Bradley, Peter Brushwood, David Hawkins, Cliff Kinvig and Robin Usher.

May 1974   ANTHONY M. BURTON

CHAPTER 1

An Outline of Terror

*'Unfortunately only those who have themselves risen by
violence know how dangerous it is to tolerate its appearance.
While those who have risen by legitimate means are puzzled
by the inception of violent politics, and hesitate to deal with
the peril in time'.*

BERTRAND DE JOUVENAL

We are, we are told, in an age of deterrence, not of war—not
of 'brinkmanship' but of 'crisis management'. Yet below and
to an extent guaranteed by this strategic stalemate lies an under-
world of politically motivated violence—sometimes organized,
often encouraged by states which, in their official pronounce-
ments, proclaim adherence to peaceful co-existence and the
principle of non-intervention in the internal affairs of others.

Numbered among its practitioners are the contemporary
folk heroes, Mao Tse-tung, Ho Chi-minh and Che Guevara.
Intellectuals who view war between nation states—and the
'diplomacy of force' short of it—as an obscenity, sometimes
regard terrorism as legitimate since, in their view, it is not
'imposed from above' but 'springs from the people'. People
die, of course, as irrevocably in the latter case as in the former.
Yet the contemporary preoccupation with revolutionary violence has tended to obscure its long history and many antecedents. We may, for example, recognize the face of terror in
the papyri of ancient Egypt and in the party feuds which
characterized the Greek city states. 'Blood is everywhere',
writes the Egyptian chronicler, 'the mummycloth speaks, before
ever one comes near it . . . the stream is a sepulchre and the
place of embalmment has become a stream'.[1]

1

Thucydides records the physical and psychological accompaniments throughout Greece to the upheavals which followed the battles between oligarchy and democracy in Corcyra; he speaks in words which might today be applied to Northern Ireland, of 'Cities harassed with seditions . . . Even words now lost their former significance, since to palliate actions they were quite distorted; for, truly, what before was a brutal courage became to be esteemed that fortitude which becomes a human and sociable creature, prudent consideration to be specious cowardice; modesty, the disguise of effeminacy; and being wise in everything, to be good for nothing: the hot temper was adjudged the exertion of true manly valour: cautious and calm deliberation to be a plausible pretext for intended knavery: he who boiled with indignation was undoubtedly trusty; who presumed to contradict, was ever suspected: he who succeeded in a roguish scheme was wise . . . associations were not formed for such mutual advantage as is consistent with, but for the executions of such rapines as are contrary to, human laws. In mutual trust they persisted, not out of any regard to religious obligation, but from the bond of communicated guilt . . . Revenge on another was a more valued possession than never to have suffered injury . . . revenge was not limited by justice or the public welfare; it aimed at more ample satisfaction . . . all this while the moderate members of such communities, either hated because they would not meddle, or envied for such obnoxious conduct, fell victims to both (sides)'.[2]

The historian also records how the citizens of Plataea, finding Theban soldiers in their city streets, broke down the partition walls between their houses in order to move secretly and concentrate their numbers; ox carts were then used as barricades to isolate Theban parties one from another. Modern street fighters have used similar methods by, for example, knocking holes in the dividing walls in the attics of terraced houses.

Men have been fighting in the streets ever since the latter were built; it was not, however, until the nineteenth century that physical and political conditions coincided to produce a theory of urban insurrection still relevant today.

A turning-point in the story of urban warfare came with the failure of the Paris Commune rising of 1870, for it constituted the last act in the drama of the classic barricade revolution when a population could, by seizing a few key buildings and throwing up street defences, hope to inspire a revolution. The most compelling actor in this saga was Auguste Blanqui[3] whose life is of particular interest, spanning as it does an era which saw the end of the insurrectionary techniques associated with the French Revolution and the rise of those which were to find their most successful exponent in the person of Lenin.

After the defeat of the Paris Commune, the physical planning of cities and the increasing gap between the resources available to the citizen and those of the professional soldier rendered street warfare on Blanquist lines a quite hopeless, indeed suicidal, technique. Narrow, medieval streets of tall, huddled buildings gradually gave way to wide, straight prospects and cobblestones to tarmacadam. While the removal of paving stones deprived insurrectionaries of their building materials, the regular patterns of the new streets gave an excellent field of fire to the weapons placed in the hands of the soldier by the armaments industries of the late nineteenth century. The advent of more accurate repeater rifles and, in particular, the machine-gun rendered the city population a helpless mass quickly dispersed or, if need be, slaughtered. The result was, on the one hand, to increase the popularity of individual assassination as a revolutionary technique and, on the other, further to professionalize the art of insurrection.

If the urban insurgent was, in these new conditions, to harass the troops sent against him he would have to utilize the mobility which knowledge of the terrain (and ideally the support of the people) gave him in order to move both laterally and vertically through the buildings, firing down on the troops who would, in such circumstances, find it difficult to bring their superior fire-power to bear. Barricades would be used, not for shelter but to tempt the troops sent to dismantle them into a killing zone overlooked by small trained bands of insurgents.

These changed conditions also placed a premium on the

3

infiltration and subversion of the armed forces opposing the insurrectionaries; only by persuading a significant number of them to change sides could the insurgent get his hands on the weaponry which would enable him to outface his enemy. Hence the efforts to divide the men from their officers and the infantry from the cavalry made by the Bolsheviks in Russia in 1905 and 1917. After the 1917 Revolution the Comintern continued to propagate the techniques of armed insurrection which had been perfected by Lenin.[4] Today new technological and ideological dimensions have been added to these traditions to create a potent blend of history, myth and technical expertise.

Contemporary violence ignores national frontiers and involves states which are geographically and politically indifferent to the issues at stake. The maverick behaviour of the modern terrorist makes prediction and counter-measure difficult; the terrorists are few in number and, as their co-operation increases, their individual backgrounds may bear no foreseeable relation to their actions.[5]

On 30 May, 1972, North-Korean-trained Japanese terrorists of the so-called *Red Army*, armed with Czech-made automatic weapons, killed, among others, sixteen Christian pilgrims from Puerto Rico at Lod Airport, Tel Aviv, Israel. They acted ostensibly in the cause of 'Palestine Liberation'. A month later (26 June) Croatian separatists of a very different ideological persuasion belonging to the *Ustashe* organization crossed the Austrian border into Yugoslavia. Shortly thereafter, according to the Yugoslav Federal Secretariat of the Interior, they were reported to the authorities and tracked down by Security Forces. In the ensuing engagement six intruders were killed. This same organization hi-jacked a Swedish airliner (15 September) and forced it to fly to Spain. The following day there were bomb attacks in several Australian cities. These incidents alone involved ten countries.

There were in 1971 more than thirty groups throughout the world actively pursuing urban terrorist activities. They were motivated by a variety of ideologies—Anarchist, Castroite, Leninist, Maoist, Nationalist and Trotskyist—and ranged in

4

size and influence from the Uruguayan Tupamaros with, at the height of their power, a cadre estimated at nearly 1,000 to the 100-strong Iranian group (which hopefully adopted the same Uruguayan name) down to the small splinter groups of unknown strength probably involving only a few hard-core adherents such as the Nicaraguan *Frente Sandinista de Liberacion Nacional* (named after Augusto Sandino, a guerrilla leader who fought the US Marines in the 1920s) and the Castroite *Moviemento Popular* in Dominica. Some countries have had the doubtful distinction of playing host to several such groups; in Guatemala there have been at times two Left Wing and three Right Wing counter-movements; in 1971 Argentina boasted five Leftist organizations, three of them Castroite, one Trotskyist and one owing allegiance to the ideas of the late President Peron.

The activities of such groups do not involve merely policemen, soldiers, diplomats and officials. On the contrary they are designed to kill ordinary people. The purpose of terrorism is to terrorize. When a child is caught in their cross-fire or a worker killed by a bomb their deaths represent not 'mistakes' but an integral part of the business of terror. When technicians like the Britons, Banner and Turner—killed by Turkish terrorists some two hours before the Security Forces stormed the farm in which they were being held—or innocent citizens who died in the Official IRA bomb blast in Aldershot become victims of violence the incident is 'regrettable' only in the eyes of the Governments concerned; to the terrorist it is part of his trade. Just as the terrorist aims to kill the innocent so he seeks to justify what he does by opposing his ideology to the 'violence of the system'; for the sanctity of the individual life he substitutes the 'truth' of his own global concepts. In a liberal democracy he, not the Government, is the Inquisition, the Cheka, the Gestapo; intellectually calculating or merely nihilist, he remains emotionally stunted. His object is to shake the faith of the man in the street in the Government and in its local representatives, especially the police, so that in the end a desperate population will seek security, not from the authorities, but from the terrorist and his political allies. Terrorism is a protection racket on a national scale.

Technology which, in the strategic dimension, has led to the need for conflict avoidance, has in the modern internal environment, provided both weapons and targets. The complexity of the industrial state and the comparative ease with which explosives and arms may be acquired together provide the opportunity for a small group of terrorists to achieve an economic and psychological effect vastly disproportionate to its numbers or support among the population. Nor is it difficult for such groups to learn the techniques of bomb manufacture. In the United States identical army handbooks were used by extreme Right and extreme Left. Target selection is comparatively simple:

> 'Extensive sabotage is possible. Gas tanks on public vehicles can be choked up with sand. Sugar is also highly effective in gasoline lines . . . phosphorus matches (kitchen matches) placed in air-conditioning systems will destroy expensive buildings'.[6]

Statistics show the ease with which bombs can be made. In 1969 there were 93 explosions in New York City, 62 in San Francisco and 32 in Seattle. In 1972 bombs went off in Italy at the rate of about one a day. The underground Press has produced an abundance of advice, verbal and diagrammatic, on bombs and bombing—but one does not have to go to clandestine sources. General Grivas' book on Guerrilla Warfare, published in Britain in 1964, contains explicit bomb-making instructions.[7] No one thought it worth while at the time to suppress such information; it is certainly too late now.

In general the more sophisticated the technology, the more vulnerable it is to the urban terrorist's attack. The technology of response, on the other hand—at least in democratic societies —can normally only be developed after terrorism has occurred. Thus when the British Army first went to Northern Ireland to face urban violence and terrorism the only specialized riot

6

equipment they possessed were old wire-mesh shields previously used in Cyprus. Pre-emptive measures, while widely practised in totalitarian régimes, are unacceptable in a democracy. The initiative lies therefore with the terrorist and Governments are from the start thrown on to the defensive.

Industrial states, whether established or still going through the experience of rapid economic change, not only have a sensitively complex technical structure and the means for sabotaging it, they also possess vast conurbations. The New York metropolitan area has a population of some eleven millions, Greater London over seven and a half millions, São Paulo, Brazil, five millions and Montreal over two millions. Within such cities are yet more densely populated enclaves based on the economic, racial, cultural or religious affinities of their inhabitants. In Newark, New Jersey, scene in July, 1967, of some of America's worst racial riots, twenty-three square miles holds a population of four hundred and five thousand, the third highest density in the United States. Within this area some two hundred thousand Negroes and forty thousand Puerto Ricans are even more closely packed together in their ghettoes. In 1967, at the time of the riots, the Negro unemployment rate was running at 11·5%.

In Latin America there is a pattern of movement from rural to urban areas; between 1940 and 1970 the number of cities in that sub-continent with a population of a million or more rose from five to sixteen, and the number of their inhabitants from about ten to about forty millions. Of these up to 40% may at any time be unemployed (or underemployed on 'jobs' which amount to the same thing—like rag-picking or selling lottery tickets). In Uruguay, home of the Tupamaros, one of the most successful of the urban guerrilla groups, some one and a half million people—about half the country's total population— live in the capital city, Montevideo. Most Latin-American cities are ringed by the shanty towns of their immigrant inhabitants —*favelas* in Brazil, *villas miseria* in Argentina, *barriadas* in Peru and *ranchitos* in Venezuela.

People in such areas are able to observe the relatively better

7

economic and social conditions of many of their countrymen. It is the consciousness of deprivation and a belief that this condition is no longer inevitable that changes a passive acceptance into an active and exploitable discontent.

Poverty and misery are not, however, necessary or sufficient conditions for the operation of groups using terror tactics. Such conditions may be regarded as constituting a 'demand' for violence but this does not necessarily become politically significant until leadership emerges—or is provided from outside. Even then it is generally only when the authorities grant concessions in what appears to be a response to violence that it becomes clearly politically instrumental and more than a sporadic outburst of frustration and hatred. If it is seen that the system can after all be made to yield, that struggle is no longer hopeless, then, having gained a little, the population will agitate for more. It may, in these circumstances, be possible for the various parties involved to imagine that, on this occasion, violence, endemic in their historical experience, may succeed in stimulating what it has never produced in the recent past—real social revolution rather than simply the replacement of one élite by another. An administration which equates good government with weak government cannot survive in such an environment. It will either fall to the revolutionaries or, as is more likely, will be succeeded by a military régime. Preceding this change will often be a 'war of all against all' as factions organize terror and counter-terror in a running-dog fight for supremacy. The difficulty with granting concessions once violence has begun is that, whatever is conceded, popular agitation and expectation will always outrun it. Demands will escalate until they reach a point where the authorities are physically unable to meet them. It is in such a situation, which he has helped to bring about, where 'acceptable' violence has been for a time successful, that the urban terrorist may find the disappointed expectations and resentment upon which he may batten.

This phenomenon is not confined to the disappointment of expectations which are rising, for a similar effect may be observed where a relatively prosperous community, which

8

naturally expects its standard of living to continue to rise, faces a sudden and psychologically inexplicable drop in its affluence. Middle-class consumers—or those who aspire to that status—mortgage their future in emotional as well as in financial terms. The disappointment of these expectations—which they have come to regard as the job of the Government to fulfil—produces in them a bewilderment and disorientation at least equal to that experienced by their poorer counterparts. The non-appearance of a presently expected bonus may be as traumatic as the failure of reality to measure up to the images of a newly discovered hope.

Modern communications can serve both to initiate and to spread violence. The North American dream materialized on to the communal TV screens of Latin America may remain a world of fantasy (unless allied to a perception of a real possibility of attainment) but news of violence elsewhere is another matter. While totalitarian régimes may deny access to such news, censorship is not generally open to more or less democratic societies which are thus vulnerable to the 'monkey see, monkey do' effect. Urban rioting in the United States spread as the initial examples were shown on TV and reported on the Radio networks. The example of the Tupamaros in Montevideo or the Provisional IRA on the streets of Belfast is instantly available to those elsewhere who feel that they, or the population they seek to influence, may plausibly be presented as suffering from similar deprivations. Nor is it only the contemporary example which provides a model; for those groups with a traditional role in their host societies there remain the legends of the past or the historical example of others. Thus the EOKA campaign in Cyprus[8] could be regarded by the Provisional IRA as a paradigm of the neo-colonial war they saw themselves waging, and they have both personal contact and literature to reinforce this view. In Uruguay the Tupamaros, before entering on their urban campaign, studied the Algerian War and the activities of the *Irgun* Jewish terrorists against the British.[9]

The perpetrator of violence is assured of wide and efficient Press, TV and Radio coverage, however minute his organization and marginal his support among the population. It is therefore possible for fringe groups such as the Weathermen in the USA, the Angry Brigade in Britain and the Baader-Meinhof Gang in Germany[10] to gain both national and international notoriety. The global character of modern communications systems enables the more politically sophisticated terrorist to aim his propaganda campaign not merely at his host population but at wider audiences—foreign Governments, sympathetic groups in other countries and world opinion. In order to give both a superficial legitimacy and an impression of strength, organization and purpose, such groups usually call themselves 'Armies' or 'Fronts' and refer to their operations as 'guerrilla' attacks. Commentators have tended to fall in with this nomenclature.

'Urban guerrilla' is a phrase, however, which can only be loosely applied to groups who use terror in cities; in many cases it is a misnomer. Only those who utilize terror as a stage or tactic complementary to a campaign of strikes, riots and political front activity aimed to lead eventually to a 'revolutionary war' are properly described as 'guerrillas'. To give this name to other groups is to suggest a degree of planning, political sophistication and revolutionary intent which they only infrequently possess. An urban guerrilla is one who is fighting a 'little war'—a 'war', moreover, which is conceived as the pursuit of political objectives by armed struggle. Such groups are conscious of the primacy of the political aim. Their view is traceable to that of the nineteenth-century philosopher of war, Carl Maria von Clausewitz (Lenin was to become one of his most ardent admirers), who wrote, 'The political object . . . will be the standard for determining both the aim of military force and the amount of effort to be made.'[11] These movements are characterized by ideological commitment and political awareness. They are as much guerrillas as were the Viet Cong. They have departed from the classical guerrilla pattern only in their use of the slum and the ghetto instead of or in addition to the jungle and the peasant village.

'The city is the area of complementary struggle and the

whole urban struggle whether on the guerrilla or mass movement front, must always be seen as a tactical struggle', wrote
the Brazilian urban guerrilla, Carlos Marighela.[12] The Tupamaros of Uruguay hold similar views. They are conscious that
increasing urbanization is making irrelevant nonsense of much
of the detail of the revolutionary war theories of Mao Tse-tung
and Che Guevara—an irrelevance confirmed by the latter's
failure and death in Bolivia in 1967. To talk in Maoist terms of
the villages surrounding the towns becomes progressively less
meaningful, at least in the physical sense, as the population
desert the former and migrate to the fringes of the cities. Many
urban movements are today eclectic as regards doctrine. The
Maoist dogma that political power grows out of the barrel of a
gun is a much-quoted text. Most are also aware that the text
goes on to insist that the Party must control the gun—yet this
has rarely been the case in contemporary movements.

There is a difference between such urban guerrillas and
those who use terror in very different political contexts.
Separatist movements such as the *Euzkadi Ta Azkatazuna*
(ETA–Freedom for the Basque Homeland) in Spain, the
Croatian Ustashe or the Provisional IRA do not necessarily
seek social revolution. Their concern is not primarily to overthrow the existing Government or to alter the social structure
but to coerce the authorities into acceding to their demands.
They are motivated by a sense of frustrated nationalism and
their programme, far from being revolutionary, may in fact be
politically reactionary. Such groups may find themselves in
competition with those who seek revolution. Thus the EOKA
terrorists received no support from AKEL, the Cypriot Communist Party, and in Eire the IRA split into a Marxist-
oriented Official Wing and the Provisionals. The latter's
ideological base was Irish nationalism with religious connota-
tions rather than godless international proletarianism. They
were attempting in an urban environment to continue the
legends of national rebellion created in the pre-industrial age.
They wished to remember and celebrate the past as a base for
national self-determination, not seek some eventual evolution

to a classless society. In their rejection of 'class' and the emphasis on the 'organic State' they lent some credibility to the views of the Yugoslav Government which, for its own internal purposes, described them as 'clerical Fascists'. It was ex-IRA men who formed the nucleus of the Irish Fascist Blueshirt movement of the 1930s.

All such separatist groups are concerned with particular not general characteristics, with a sense of individual uniqueness not of socialist international solidarity. These movements may have links with other groups (some of them Communist or Trotskyist) since they tend to see themselves as taking part in an anti-colonial struggle. They are also susceptible to infiltration from Communist or Trotskyist elements, especially when under pressure from Security Forces.

The use of terror by such groups is indeed analogous with that waged in colonies to affect public opinion in the 'home' country and thus pressure its Government into a precipitate withdrawal. The success of such campaigns would result in governments in the 'ex-colonial' territories which would of course be different—but not necessarily revolutionary. While the withdrawal of the British from Aden resulted in a so-called 'Peoples' Republic' a similar success for EOKA in Cyprus would in all probability have led to that island becoming part of Greece.

Other groups receive their ideological impetus from racism, whatever the semantic trappings with which they may seek to disguise it—for example, the branch of the Ku Klux Klan responsible for a series of bombings of Negro and Jewish properties in Meridien, Mississippi in 1968 and, on the other side of the racial divide, the Black Panthers and their various competitors and offshoots.[13]

Some urban terrorists are motivated neither by revolution in any conventional sense nor by 'sectional chauvinism'. They are the heirs, not of Lenin nor of the mystique of a historic nationalism, but lie instead within the Anarchist tradition. Anarchism does not necessarily imply violence. Historically, however, anarchists have always been more specific about the evils of present authority and the need to expose and destroy it than about what is to follow its destruction; necessarily so, since they would argue that what follows the removal of authority will be decided by those thus freed and so cannot be foreseen. The implication of such a view is clear. What must be done is to proceed with the destruction of 'what is'—'what ought to be' automatically following. Anarchists are further concerned with the assertion of the individual against what they see as an evil system. Authority to them is institutionalized violence and in attacking it they see themselves defending the individual against the de-humanizing categorization and anonymity of the industrial state. Some may further assert that violence is the only means open to people who eke out a wretched existence on the margins of a society to find their dignity and become 'men'. Many of the self-styled 'guerrillas of the New Left', who like to describe themselves as 'post-Communist revolutionaries', in fact fit most comfortably into this anarchist image—since they too are considerably more eloquent about present vice than about future virtue; a naïvely Utopian view of tomorrow is allied with a belief in the cathartic value of violence, both for the individual and for society. 'Revolution' is seen not as a process nor an event but essentially as a 'way of life'.

Within all such movements will be found some whose motivation is less political and less subtle. There are those who find release in the projection of their own aberrations onto society and expiation in then attacking that society, which seems to them to bear the responsibility for their sense of inadequacy or guilt. Psychiatrists are currently investigating the indications of mental abnormality in captured terrorists. In Germany proposals to study Meinhof (who underwent an operation for the removal of a brain tumour before she embarked on her terrorist career) produced an outcry. Hiroko Nagata, of the Japanese 'Red Army' terrorist group suffered from goitre and was sexually disturbed. On the margins of such groups will be found more political exotica—nihilists, 'liberation' sub-cultures representing minority interests and a large and constantly changing variety of 'front organizations' to provide some cover for the terrorist and a propaganda machine and apologia for his acts. Beyond them lie the hooligans indulging in an apparently pointless violence characterized by sociologists as 'anomic'—lashing out at a fate which has arbitrarily cast them in the role of social victims. Such petty criminals and rioters may in time of crisis be drawn into, or find their gangs changed into, politically orientated organizations.

Occasionally, and particularly in societies with a tradition of rebellion, the young may join what are essentially terrorist groups—though they may try to dignify themselves by more grandiose titles—because it is expected of them. It is regarded as part of the process of attaining and being initiated into manhood. In Latin America there exists what has been called the 'unsheathed drive of the Latin-American male to be "macho" or manly'.[14] In such societies rebel bands have a recognized social function and the young who join them are accorded some degree of indulgence by the class from which they spring. Historically this background exists also in Ireland where duelling and internecine strife were endemic when effectively outlawed in most other countries. A young man was not considered fit for marriage, he had not reached adult status, unless he had 'blazed'—taken part in a duel or armed group confrontation—though these rarely had any political significance.

Criminal elements are, not unnaturally, attracted by the chances of easy pickings apparently afforded by the tactic of 'expropriation' as a means of raising funds for terrorist groups. Lenin in the early days of the Bolshevik movement was well aware of this danger and was at pains to try to screen out such elements from his 'exactivities'. The line between bank robbery and 'expropriation' is thin indeed; while the activities of an anarchist such as Francisco Sabati Llopart fall into the latter category since he lived simply, had no personal wealth and robbed only for 'the cause', the Sicilian Salvatore Guiliano was by contrast merely a bandit, for all his stated dislike of Communism and belief in the cause of Sicilian separatism.[15]

Psychopathic killings, rape, arson and sheer nihilistic destruction flourish in the atmosphere induced by the urban terrorist—developments which at first he welcomes, then often attempts to stem as he belatedly realizes that he has unleashed a tiger which he cannot control and which may well turn on him. In such an environment psychopaths may indeed become leaders instead of outcasts.

If conditions conducive to urban unrest exist[16] then we must expect one or more of the types of movement considered to attempt to capitalize on them. Most of the countries of Western Europe have already experienced some degree of urban terror. With the increasing population pressures of the late nineteen-seventies it would be as irresponsible to dismiss the possibility of further politically motivated violence in the years ahead as it would be to panic and exaggerate its dangers.

For those who seek to foment unrest and use terrorism as a tactic, the ideologies and historical examples are to hand.

NOTES

1 Leiden Papyrus 344, quoted Peter Calvert, *Revolution*, Macmillan, 1970, p. 21.
2 Thucydides, Peloponnesian War, Dr Smith's translation, Routledge, pp. 206, 207, 110.
3 See Chapter 3.
4 Notably in *Armed Insurrection* by A. Neuberg, see Chapter 3.
5 See Segre and Adler, *Encounter*, February, 1973.
6 *Crusader*, journal of the Progressive Labour Party, 1964.
7 General George Grivas-Dighenis, *Guerrilla Warfare and EOKA's Struggle*, Longmans, Green, 1964, p. 101.
8 See Chapter 10.
9 See Chapter 10.
10 See Chapter 7.
11 Leonard, *A Short Guide to Clausewitz on War*, Wiedenfeld & Nicolson, 1967, p. 48.
12 Carlos Marighela, *For the Liberation of Brazil*, translated by John Butt and Rosemary Sheed, Pelican, 1971, p. 47.
13 See Chapter 8.

14 Jack Davis, *Political Violence in Latin America*, IISS, 1972, p. 6.
15 See E. J. Hobsbawm, *Bandits*, Pelican, 1972, pp. 113–26.
16 See Appendix B.

CHAPTER 2

'Creative Violence'

'Our task is terrible, total, universal and merciless destruction'.
NECHAYEV, *Revolutionary Catechism*

On Wednesday 6 December, 1972, sentences were pronounced in what became popularly known as the 'Angry Brigade' trial. The Judge, Mr Justice James, referred when sentencing to a 'warped understanding of sociology'; subsequently academic psychologists and psychiatrists were recruited by the media to discuss and categorize the individuals involved. The defendants were thus docketed and despatched to jail. A bunch of 'two-penny-halfpenny kids', as the *Wood Green, Southgate and Palmer's Green Weekly Herald* called student protesters,[1] had apparently tried to upset a political and social system and had been properly dealt with. Yet perhaps the effort to interpret and explain their actions might first be made in terms of their own categories and in the light of the examples of history. For here were some of the classic preoccupations of anarchism—the 'propaganda of the deed', the logic of self-sacrifice as constituting a further increment, however small, to the furtherance of 'revolutionary consciousness'. Here was the traditionally anarchist tactic of trying to wear away the fabric of authority by a continuous process of attrition rather than by a sudden attack.

Anarchism may be seen as a set of ideas, as descriptive of a certain naturally oppositional character or as an insurrectionary technique;[2] it is with the last of these that we are principally concerned.

The word 'anarchos' literally means 'without a ruler' and

thus may be applied to anyone who denies that there is a 'right to rule' conferred by a social order. It may alternatively be used by the guardians of that order to describe someone who is in fact 'lawless'. The vagueness and confusion surrounding the use of the word has spread to those movements described as or claiming to be 'anarchist'.

The popular image of the anarchist, fostered by innumerable cartoons, is that of a man of the shadows, furtive and simian of feature, about to hurl a large and spluttering bomb. This picture has emerged partly because from time to time it receives empirical confirmation but mainly due to the interests (of both Right and Left) which find its propagation advantageous. Journalistically moreover such a portrayal is attractively dramatic. Thus both the popular Press and political parties have been ready to label any maverick bomb-thrower (be he unknown to them or a politically embarrassing, if undeniably enthusiastic, adherent) as an 'anarchist'. The population will be disposed to accept the explanation since it accords with the expectations fostered by folk myth and memory. The legendary Siege of Sidney Street is an example of the process which follows such stereotyping. In December, 1910, a jeweller's shop was attacked and police fired upon. A number of emigré anarchists were at that time in London and 'foreign terrorists' were swiftly blamed. One of the men involved had a lady friend who had attended anarchist meetings which was enough to explain the affair to the popular satisfaction. Troops were ordered in by Winston Churchill and the robbers, who had taken refuge in a house in Houndsditch, were killed. Anarchism has been saddled with the affair ever since, although the connection was peripheral. Anarchists have themselves compounded the error with characteristic perverseness by adopting the incident; in July, 1969, a Spanish Bank in London was bombed by one reportedly belonging to the 'Sidney Street Appreciation Society of Anarchists'.

Anarchists have done little, however, to counter the more conspiratorial interpretations of their activities. Since they reject 'organization' as de-personalizing it is natural that they have failed to present any coherent face to the world. Always they have given the impression of a series of temporary coalitions of freelance revolutionaries, squabbling among themselves, forming alliances, splitting into mutually suspicious factions and generally seeming as much intent on self-destruction as on the smashing of the apparatus of the State which they detest.

Yet physical destruction is not necessarily a part of the anarchist creed and represents but one thread in the eccentricities of its history. To feel that society is evil does not lead inevitably to a desire to smash it physically. One may equally wish for reform or simply shrug one's shoulders and 'drop out'. Nor is 'destruction' only to be achieved by attacking people and property; it may perhaps more speedily be accomplished by intellectual or moral assaults on the credibility of the contemporary order.

The evolution of anarchist thought may be traced from the great upsurge of nonconformity of all descriptions which characterized the seventeenth-century English Civil War period. Among the sects which at that time flourished both 'Levellers' and 'Diggers' appeared to possess anarchist ideas but it was the latter and in particular Gerrard Winstanley, suggests Woodcock, who articulated them.[3] Winstanley's identification of property relationships, 'mine and thine', as the source of conflict and his attempt to have all things genuinely in common rather than to substitute one order for another has a truly anarchist ring to it. Far from being violent Winstanley and his followers were pacifist, rejecting violence and even refusing to defend themselves when attacked.

It was in the nineteenth century, however, that such ideas and an impatience for change coincided to produce a more violent version of anarchism. In that century the concentration of population and the revolution in communications reached a point where one man could touch millions by a single act of terror. Only then could the denial and destruction of self be at the same time plainly and publicly a contribution to the destruction of authority. In general the prophets whose words were to inflame men to acts of terror were themselves peaceful; those who talked most wildly of bloody revolution rarely took part in it.

Ideas of the uses of terror may be traced to the writings of Max Stirner who, by proclaiming the supremacy of the individual will and the sovereign necessity of selfishness (in his work *The Ego and His Own*, published in 1843), helped to overcome the psychological barriers against violent action. In Stirner's work one may also observe that belief in the cathartic utility of violence for the individual which was to take hold so tragically later in his own century and which is fashionable in some quarters today. Only in conflict, argued Stirner, does the individual become truly himself; by rebellion alone may man 'rise or exalt' himself.

Up until the mid-nineteenth century anarchism existed as a philosophy; in the 1860s it emerged as a movement. Its captain, who was to provide for a time a centre and subsequently a point of departure for anarchism was Mikhail Bakhunin. It is Bakhunin who is regarded as a main influence by activist elements in today's New Left; student-leader Daniel Cohn Bendit proclaimed that he was a Marxist in the sense that Bakhunin was a Marxist.

The contrast between huge words and small action which had been all too clear with Stirner was less marked in Bakhunin. Where Stirner lives only through his writing Bakhunin, who wrote little, comes across the pages of history by sheer force of personality. To his identification of the authoritarianism inherent in Marxism is owed both the split which developed in working-class movements and the hatred with which anarchism is regarded by Marxist-Leninists to this day—a hatred which is likely to spill over into repression and murder, as it did after 1917 in Russia.

Bakhunin turned to ideas of socialism after leaving Russia to study in Germany. In the euphoria following his conversion he uncharacteristically wrote an essay which contained what was to become the most famous anarchist cry of all:

'Let us put our trust in the eternal spirit which destroys and annihilates only because it is the unsearchable and eternally creative source of all life. The urge to destroy is also a creative urge.'

After moving to Paris Bakhunin joined that city's emigré society of apprentice revolutionaries, yet he remained an aristocrat and a Russian. There was in him, for all his new-found socialism, a streak of romantic Slavism just as in other revolutionaries of the nineteenth century (notably Blanqui) there was a similar inability to break with nationalist or separatist tendencies. Bakhunin decided that a Union of all the Slav peoples could constitute the vanguard of revolution, with the Russians, naturally, in the leading role. This Slavic cataclysm was to be brought about by the complete destruction of the existing order. He urged this thesis, with little success, first on the Poles and then at a Slav Congress in Prague. He is said to have taken part in an uprising in Prague—even to have started it by loosing off a few rounds from his hotel window.

In 1863, by now internationally known, he arrived in Italy and dedicated the remainder of his life to the organization of anarchist secret societies, conspiratorial 'Brotherhoods' whose size and influence he optimistically, rather than mendaciously, exaggerated. At this point there arrived on the scene the Svengali-like figure of Sergei Nechayev who, though much younger, succeeded in fascinating and manipulating Bakhunin. He it was who created that blood-stained reputation which remains associated with the name of Bakhunin.

Nechayev was in truth a nihilist, a destroyer; he was, as Dostoievsky portrayed him, 'possessed'. His was a daemonic influence on the ageing Bakhunin and their collaboration in the production of literature for dissemination in Russia seems almost entirely to have been the work of Nechayev. It remains true, however, that Bakhunin lent his prestige to all the publications and his name to at least one. In Nechayev Bakhunin perhaps thought he had found the completely dedicated revolutionary, possessed of a ruthlessness that he himself could not quite summon up. Nechayev's exaggerated tales of his own insurrectionary prowess and the largely mythical organizations he claimed to have created in Russia may have impressed Bakhunin, always prone to optimistic self-delusion. Nechayev proved later to be a thief and a murderer—not of the authorities but of his own comrades. Too late Bakhunin denounced him. The damage had then been done, particularly by Nechayev's *Revolutionary Catechism*, whose apocalyptic flavour ensured it a ready circulation among both revolutionaries and reactionaries. It was guaranteed to curdle the blood of the bourgeoisie and thus made more effective propaganda for Governments than it did for their enemies.

The revolutionary, wrote Nechayev, has 'torn himself free from the bonds of the social order and the civilized world . . . If he continues to co-exist' with that world 'it is only so that he may more speedily destroy'. Nechayev is dedicated to the 'merciless destruction' of this 'filthy order'. The revolutionary must be ready to lie, steal, betray, kill, dissemble and cynically manipulate others to the end that the common workers, inflamed by the oppression provoked by such measures, will 'rise up in a *levée en masse*'. To Nechayev the masses were sunk in ignorance and apathy; they were not aware of the animal conditions in which they existed. The revolutionary must demonstrate to the peasantry that someone was ready to risk all for them. He must by the very dramatic intensity of his actions break through to them and, since intellectual argument was beyond the capacity of their understanding, that breakthrough must be achieved by the 'propaganda of the deed'.

Thus the nakedness of authoritarian power would be revealed and the peasantry, at last socially aware, could realize each his own individuality in an orgy of destruction. Thus the intellectual might cleanse himself by going to the people and seeking a more natural and primitive system through the accompanying renunciation of the artificialities of the contemporary social order.

Nechayev sees the bandit, rootless and murderous, yet often idolized by the poor, as the true revolutionary. In him the anarchist tendency to see the marginal elements of society, especially the peasantry, led by a dedicated intelligentsia as the revolutionary base, find its most fanatical expression.

As for Bakhunin, his remaining life was a tragi-comedy; anathematized by the Marxists and with all his enterprises failing he made one last attempt to achieve success, or at least martyrdom. The insurrection he sought to lead in Bologna failed even to begin. He died in 1876.

Bakhunin's death marked a new beginning for anarchism. Over the next fifty years it was to spread across Europe and into the Americas. His ideas and example became more powerful after his death than they had been in his lifetime. The name of Bakhunin, who had fired few shots in anger and had probably killed no one, was to become synonymous with the age of the bomb, the bullet and the knife.

During the period of 1885–1914 one Head of State or leading Minister fell every eighteen months—and most of them by the hand of anarchists.

After Bakhunin's death the anarchists formed the so-called 'Black International' which contained among its members a number who favoured the use of terrorism. Wild statements were bandied about, many of the most extreme by Government spies and *agents provocateurs* who quickly infiltrated the movement. Soon words were succeeded by action.

One of the earliest successes of the terror campaign was the assassination of Tsar Alexander II by the Russian terrorist organization *Narodnaya Volya* (People's Will) in 1881. Elsewhere a pattern of violence was soon established. Individual anarchists, having committed acts of terror, would be apprehended, tried and executed—whereupon their deaths would be avenged by others. Action and reaction followed, for a time seemingly almost mechanically. Some contemporary intellectuals initially felt that these acts were romantic but ended by seeing them as merely sordid, especially when plainly criminal elements began to justify their excesses in terms of social justice.

In France the cycle of violence began in earnest in the 1890s and was then associated with the archetypal anarchist figure of Ravachol. Ravachol was a criminal who sought some psychological justification for his activities by proclaiming himself as a revolutionary Robin Hood, robbing the present in order to liberate the future. He was a tomb robber and a miser killer. On the other hand he does seem to have contributed some of his loot to 'revolutionary' funds and he certainly blew up the houses of officials who had previously been instrumental in punishing anarchists. Eventually caught and convicted (for killing the miser) he died bravely, warning that vengeance would follow. He was correct in his forecast; the restaurant where he had been arrested was duly blown up. Later four policemen were killed by a bomb, the Serbian Minister was knifed and a bomb was thrown into the Chamber of Deputies. The culprit, Auguste Vaillant, was executed. Once more revenge bombings followed; this time the target was a café and one person was killed. The intellectual élite, hitherto titillated by the sensationalism of the events and the 'nobility' of the anarchists now felt that the game had gone far enough. Things were becoming serious. There was a veritable outcry as explosions continued and after the climactic blow when President Carnot, who had refused clemency to Vaillant, was stabbed to death by an Italian anarchist, came a vigorous suppression of anarchism. For their part most anarchists turned to a more peaceful pursuit of their social and political objectives. It was their misfortune however to be the subjects of a famous quasi-scientific study of 'criminal types' carried out by Lombroso, an Italian. Phrenology enjoyed a considerable vogue at the turn of the century and Lombroso's typology, which used anarchists as prime examples of the 'typically criminal physiognomy' achieved considerable notoriety. There thus seemed a 'scientific' basis for the popular horror, as Lombroso was held to have demonstrated a causal connection between physical and social characteristics—in this case skull-shape and a propensity to throw bombs.

The French pattern of violence was repeated elsewhere. In **Italy anarchists made two unsuccessful** attempts on the life of

King Umberto before the third, made in 1900 on a 'contract' put out by the Paterson, New Jersey, anarchists eventually succeeded. Anarchist traditions of violence in Italy have not died. In 1921 bombs in a Milan theatre killed twenty people and a good proportion of those that have been going off regularly over the past few years have been of anarchist origin. Sixteen people were killed when a bank in Milan was attacked in 1969; the device was allegedly planted by an anarchist, Pietro Valpreda, although it was subsequently decided that Fascists may have been responsible. A Police Inspector investigating the case was shot dead in 1972 and shortly after a memorial to him had been unveiled a further bomb was thrown at the Central Police Station in Milan, killing one and wounding fifty-seven. The perpetrator of the deed, one Gianfranco Bertoli, claimed to be avenging Pinelli, an anarchist who was supposed to have 'fallen from a window' during interrogation. In keeping with the confused nature of the affair the anarchists in Italy disclaimed all knowledge of him.

Anarchism in Spain has been interwoven with the anti-clericalism of the Left in general and also with those separatist tendencies today observable in the Basque 'Freedom for the Homeland' movement (ETA).[4] Spain has been notable for the ritual extremes to which both terror and counter-terror have been carried. Spanish anarchists made an attempt on the life of King Alfonso in 1878 and the movement reached the apogee of its influence during the Spanish Civil War, when it ended up fighting as much against the Republican Government as against the Fascists.

In Spain there arose the most powerful expression of the anarcho-syndicalist belief in the strike as the weapon to destroy the old and herald the new age of liberated man. The CNT,[5] formed in 1910, grew out of the bitter experience of the failure of spontaneous insurrection. What became the CNT in arms, the *Federation Anarquista Iberica*, aimed to liberate areas from government control and then to allow the people to organize themselves. Subsequent anarchist involvement in the Spanish Civil War revealed both the strengths and weaknesses

25

of the movement. The anarchists fought well in the Civil War and produced, in Durruti, an outstanding leader. Yet the CNT-FAI was unable to adapt to the political manoeuvrings and betrayals which bedevilled the Republican side, especially after Russia began to send advisers and *materiel*. The disparate groups forced into a temporary alliance by Franco's rebellion included Basque and Catalan separatists as well as anarchists, Communists and the indigenous Marxist POUM.[6] The Basque Nationalists were Catholics, concerned with the preservation of their language and culture, while at the same time others in the coalition were busily engaged in the physical destruction of Church property and the murder of its clergy. In Fraga, for example, the Durruti column executed thirty-eight 'Fascists'. The list is representative of the normal procedure on such occasions—the priest, leading landowner, the lawyer and 'all the rich peasants'.[7] Towards the end of the war the Basques had forcibly to prevent the anarchists from laying waste their country before the advancing Franco armies. Anarchist armies, quite apart from internal problems of authority and discipline, feel not unnaturally uncomfortable when called upon to order people about and even more so when the ultimate ideological idiocy is reached—anarchist policemen.

Spanish anarchism continued to operate, even after the triumph of Franco, and produced one of the most extraordinary figures of the twentieth-century movement in Francisco Sabati Llopart, known as 'El Quico'. Llopart completed a career of outstanding individual initiative by hi-jacking a train before inevitably falling before the bullets of the police.

Nor is contemporary Spanish anarchism a spent force; the Spanish-inspired 'First of May' group, founded by Octavio Alberda, claimed to have been active against buildings in Britain, including the US Embassy. The choice of the US Embassy was presumably dictated by conventional current political categorization rather than by the fact that the United States had itself harboured in its time a number of fanatical anarchists. At the turn of the century there existed a parti-cularly active American anarchist movement, centred mainly on immigrant groups. In that continent too there occurred one of the last anarchist dramas to catch the attention of the world. North America already possessed a violent history of class strife and rioting on a massive scale when, in 1882, Johann Most arrived from Europe. He was an anarchist of German extraction who had spent some years in England, where he had been imprisoned for eighteen months for writing an article congratulating the assassins of the Tsar and recommending that some emulation might not be misplaced. He found a situation of some promise. 'Revolutionary Clubs' already existed and the variety of America's immigrant population meant that any economic disaster could also be presented as having an ethnic dimension. Johann Most was regarded with some awe as an experienced and accomplished European revolutionary and he swiftly established an ascendancy, especially in Chicago. There was plenty of relevant literature on insurrection in circulation in the 1880s.[8] The example of the Paris Commune was fresh in everyone's minds; the authorities called the 1877 Chicago rioters 'the ragged Commune wretches'. Johann set about adding more provocative verbiage; relevant chapters of his comprehensively entitled book, *Science of Revolutionary Warfare; a Manual of Instruction in the Use and Preparation of Nitro-glycerine, Dynamite, Gun Cotton, Fulminating Mercury, Bombs, Fuses, Poisons*, were freely circulated in anarchist clubs and, together with the newspaper he controlled, *Die Arbeiter Zeitung*, constituted a standing invitation to bloodshed. His cry, 'Extirpate the Miserable Brood', was backed by the wide availability of dynamite and the technical expertise in its use which he made available. The atmosphere of extremism he fostered was reflected throughout the labour movement and especially in Chicago. The anarchist movement, though in fact quite small, was seen by the authorities as a serious threat—a threat which the popular Press played up in language as extreme as that of the anarchists themselves. Nor was the atmosphere unreceptive to such provocation; depression and unemployment had produced crowds of hungry, idle and desperate men. The Red and Black Flags, symbols of revolution and anarchy, flew side by side at rallies organized to agitate for an eight-hour working day. Confrontation between Unions and employers became increasingly bitter as the latter hired Pinkerton men to protect non-Union labour. *Die Arbeiter Zeitung* advised its readers to clean their guns.

On 4 May, 1886, a demonstration to protest at the deaths of some workers in an industrial dispute assembled in Haymarket Square, Chicago. Just at the moment when the crowds, after an order from the police, were about to disperse, a bomb was thrown from a side street. Both sides began firing in an indiscriminate panic and a number of people were killed. Several of the demonstration's leaders were sentenced to die; two were subsequently reprieved after public pressure from both sides of the Atlantic. The remainder went to their executions bravely; one was said to have cried, 'Hurrah for Anarchy', another, 'This is the happiest day of my life'.

The idealism of those early American anarchists did not long survive the increasing scale of union and employer violence. Alexander Berkman, later to write a standard anarchist text[9] made a typically individualistic gesture when he attempted to kill Henry Fiske of the Carnegie Steel Corporation. The opening meeting of the Industrial Workers of the World (I.W.W. or 'Wobblies') payed homage to the graves of the Chicago Anarchists as to a shrine; but in general it was the Red Flag rather than the Black which was the dominant force. Thereafter there was plenty of slugging and dynamiting with the dramatis personae of Pinkerton agents, scabs, bully boys, *agents provocateurs* and militia men which culminated in the spectacular blowing-up of the *Los Angeles Times* building; the newspaper was published by the pugnacious, bad-tempered and primitively American figure of Colonel Harrison Gray Otis. The figures on the Trade Union side were equally colourful—but far from being anarchist. After the explosion, however, Otis, never one to reject the use of an emotive word on grounds of inaccuracy, pronounced the perpetrators 'anarchist scum'.

Anarchism thus seemed to have been swallowed up in the widespread violence characteristic of the age; yet it was to depart the American stage with an incident which is remembered for its pathos (and propaganda value) rather than its violence.

The post-1919 era in America produced a kind of early 'McCarthyism' due to fears of Bolshevism spreading from Russia. In this panic all the 'Left' were lumped together as 'part of the threat' and especially if they were of foreign origin. It was in this atmosphere that two Italians, Sacco and Vanzetti, allegedly connected with a group of Boston anarchists, were convicted. They had, with some success, organized rope workers; when arrested they were charged with armed hold-up. After trials so casual in their approach and so perfunctory in their attendance to the rights of the accused as to render their guilt or innocence from the anti-Government propaganda point of view quite superfluous they were convicted and, eventually, executed in 1927. The two became famous and Vanzetti's statement, frequently quoted, a symbol of martyred dignity in the face of an 'oppressive' Government:

'If it had not been for this case, I might have lived out my life, talking on street corners to scorning men. I might have died, unmarked, unknown, a failure . . . Our words, our lives, our pains—nothing! The taking of our lives—lives of a good shoemaker and a poor fish peddler—all. The last moment belongs to us—that agony is our triumph.'

Whether or not the two were in fact guilty, the manner of their trial and sentence and the delay in settling their fate represented a propaganda defeat of global proportions for the US Government.

If in the USA anarchism was suppressed, in the USSR it was wiped out. After the November Revolution anarchism in Russia was ruthlessly and entirely crushed. The successors of the Tsars killed not only militant anarchists but even the pacifist followers of the teachings of Tolstoy. Only in the Ukraine did anarchism flicker briefly into life in the medieval figure of Nestor Makhno. This bibulous and eccentric peasant ruled, or rather prevented anyone else from ruling, a large area of southern Russia for six months until about mid-1919. He was, with the possible exception of the Mexican peasant, Emiliano Zapata, the only outstanding guerrilla leader who can plausibly be claimed as an anarchist. Although prepared to use terror freely enough, he never succeeded in dominating the cities, which he hated; therein lay the weakness of his movement which was in essence based on rural brigandage and lacked any political sophistication.

Compared with all the sound and fury in America and Russia, anarchism in Britain has until recently been a quiet and intellectual affair. Emigré anarchists from the Continent added their voluble extremism to the more reticent British tradition and, in 1894, one of them blew himself up with his own bomb. The much-travelled Johann Most began, in 1879, the anarchist newspaper in which he was to write the inflammatory article on the assassination of the Tsar which resulted in his imprisonment. Peter Kropotkin was involved in the foundation of another journal, *Freedom*, in 1886. Numbers of late-nineteenth-century intellectuals flirted with anarchist ideas; Woodcock mentions Willam Morris, Oscar Wilde and the formidable Charlotte Wilson, 'a Girton girl who wore aesthetic gowns and had gone to live in a cottage on Hampstead Heath rather than accept the earnings of her stockbroker husband'.[10]

The sympathies and passions aroused by the Spanish Civil War revivified anarchism in Britain, especially among intellectuals. Herbert Read celebrated the halcyon period when rural anarchism achieved for a time that success which it had never before enjoyed:

'The oxen pass under the yoke
and the blind are led at will:
But a man born free has a path of his own
and a house on the hill.

And men are men who till the land
and women are women who weave:

30

Fifty men own the lemon grove
and no man is a slave.'[11]

It is still to Spain that British anarchists appear most instinc-
tively to relate—but the tradition that anarchist violence was
imported has of course recently been broken.

If the terrorist version of anarchism is now to appear significantly in the United Kingdom it will be by way of the student
sub-culture rather than in any real historical continuity with
traditional anarchism—though the latter may afford example
and inspiration.

Contemporary middle-class youth who find a need to destroy
the system that created them may find a satisfactory political
excuse for their actions in anarchist doctrine. A condition for
self-liberation is that one should first of all be oppressed.
Bourgeois youth tends actively to court persecution in order to
undergo this personally satisfying catharsis. To pretend anarchist views provides one way to 'de-class' oneself and thus, as
Nechayev expressed it, 'to wrench free from the ties of the
social order and the civilized world'.

It is unlikely that anarchism will make much headway with
the modern industrial proletariat; this despite the efforts of
such organizations as Solidarity for Workers' Power, which
claims to see in the Paris student riots of 1968 proof that revolution is possible under conditions of modern bureaucratic
capitalism. All the evidence on such questions as race, nationalism and wages suggests that the West European industrial
worker today is materialistically orientated and politically
reactionary. Hence the only short term means open to the
anarchist of propagating revolution is through direct and
dramatic action—and to this the historical examples of anarchist violence constitute a clear temptation. The attitude of the
anarchist journal, *Freedom*, has been ambivalent:

'Inasmuch as *Freedom* has a policy on violence, it may be
said that a majority of us who work on the paper accept
that there have been times, and will be times again, when

31

violence is unavoidable. But we don't like it, don't want to be involved in it if there is a better way of reaching our goal, and don't think it has anything whatsoever to do with the idea of anarchism. It may have something to do with achieving an anarchist society, but that's all.'[12]

Since the anarchist tendency to organizational proliferation is as rife as ever there is always the danger of maverick splinter groups attempting to force the issue by bomb or bullet. That the opportunities afforded by the modern urban environment and communications system are understood by anarchists is evidenced by the publication, *Anarchy Magazine Number 9*, published in 1972, which devotes its pages to an exposition of the principles of urban guerrilla warfare.

'The reality of the present', it declares, 'is that bombing is here to stay.' It goes on to repeat the familiar anarchist cry that 'the criminal fraternity' has 'within it possibilities of developing a closer relationship with the Revolutionary Left'. It further suggests what is in fact a kind of 'urban Debrayism',[13] asserting that small armed groups can themselves constitute the vanguard of revolution and it shows the influence of the Tupamaros' campaign, which it extols, in its insistence on, 'mastery of the technical means that the system appropriates to itself to destroy others'.

The Anarchist Federation of Britain has also been peripherally involved in the Northern Ireland situation, particularly in the formation of the student-based People's Democracy in 1969 and the demonstrations of that year. Propaganda in schools and universities is a continuing preoccupation of anarchist groups—and the background of the Angry Brigade bears witness to some success in that context.

On the other hand it is all too easy to exaggerate the importance of these groups; they are romantically self-indulgent or are out to 'psyche' the extreme Right into over-reacting by way of some suitably provocative verbiage. They are susceptible to infiltration and manipulation by others more professionally organized and externally disciplined than themselves.

The indirect influence of anarchist thought and example is much more pervasive and significant than any direct and specifically 'anarchist' organization. Anarchism in a vague and vulgarized form is now part of the untidy welter of influences which go to make up the 'New Left' orientation of the young intelligentsia. It is one component, together with 'pop Marxism' and ersatz Eastern mysticism in the staple student intellectual diet. The conventional ideological repetitions of 'anarchist' categories and slogans are part of the 'conditioning of people throughout the world to accept subversive ideas so that they will act on them when the time is ripe'.[14] It is in this context that contemporary anarchism may be a motivating factor in urban violence since any, even superficial, analysis would reveal that such violence, unless used in a far more politically sophisticated manner than has been the case in the examples in recent history, will be counter-productive. The impact of such violence, though individually distressing, is likely to have little political significance since it is articulated with no clear strategy adapted to contemporary conditions. The idealism which may characterize some of the individuals involved will be used by others to achieve ends far more totalitarian than those of the system the protester is seeking to destroy. When Anna Mendleson, one of the members of the Angry Brigade, was asked if she thought that it had influence on the British scene she replied, 'It hasn't changed anything at all'. It is in this confused area of New Left thinking therefore that the traditions of anarchism may be of relevance to and influence the perpetration of acts of urban terror; both the Angry Brigade, and the Weathermen in the United States of America were so influenced. (Yet while the use of the modern time-bomb may appear to fit the anarchist tradition it in fact involves a kind of betrayal; the resort to technology de-personalizes the protest and effectively removes the terrorist from the acceptance of individual responsibility historically characteristic of anarchist actions.)

Apart from the malign if indirect influence of historical example, the contemporary anarchist is in practical terms a piece of political Victoriana. Heir to a tradition that contains figures of nobility and tragedy as well as some more sinister (and occasionally plainly murderous) ones he remains at the same time that tradition's prisoner. Today he is more than ever alone. The archetypal heroes of the past fill his life with more meaning than can be offered by the present. The Paris Commune and its defeat, the act of individual protest by anarchists and the manner of their deaths, frequently bravely borne, may appear closer to his personal needs than today's constant and continuing compromises. Anarchism is a cry for a brighter, cleaner world where the problems are clearly dichotomized and the confusion and complexity of modern existence can be forgotten. For the young anarchist violence thus becomes less a currently relevant social protest and more a communion with the past and a plea to be noticed.

NOTES

1 Quoted Clutterbuck, *Protest and the Urban Guerrilla*, Cassell, 1973, p. 249.
2 See James Joll, *Anarchism—a Living Tradition* in Apter and Joll *Anarchism Today*, Macmillan, 1971.
3 George Woodcock, *Anarchism* (indispensable for those interested in this subject), Pelican, 1963, pp. 42–6.
4 See Chapter 9.
5 Confederacion Nacional de Trabajo.
6 Partido Obrero de Unificacion Marxista.
7 Broué and Témine, *The Revolution and Civil War in Spain*, Faber and Faber, 1972, p. 125.
8 e.g. Olin, *Suggestions Upon the Strategy of Street Fighting*, 1886; Ragnar Redbeard, *Might is Right*, 1895; Most, *The Beast of Property—Total Annihilation Proposed as the Only Infallible Remedy*, 1885.
9 Berkman, *The A.B.C. of Anarchist Communism*, 1942.
10 George Woodcock, op cit, p. 420.
11 Read, 'A Song for the Spanish Anarchists' in *Thirty Five Poems*, Faber and Faber, p. 41.
12 *Freedom*, 20 December, 1969.
13 See Chapter 5.
14 Kitson, *Low Intensity Operations*, Faber and Faber, 1971, p. 17.

CHAPTER 3

'The Spark'—the Re-Discovery of Lenin

'We can see that with Iskra *was born a Terror which no longer had anything in common with Anarchism, a Mass Terror which would not merely destroy, but would aim to set up by force a Utopian paradise on earth.'*

HELMUT ANDICS

Russia, we are told, has mellowed; her actions reflect neither a Tsarist-style Imperialism nor any real revolutionary fervour. The KGB,[1] although involved in espionage and the support of subversive elements in other countries, is similar to the security services of any other country.

Russia's intentions and attitudes have been changed, not by any ideological revision so much as by the logic of internal industrial and technical development and, externally, by the situation of nuclear 'mutual and assured destruction' which exists between her and the United States of America—so runs the argument.

The villain of the piece, it is concluded, was all along Dzhugashvili, alias Stalin. Since that gentleman had developed into a Byzantine tyrant his successors must regard him as having deviated from a correctly Marxist-Leninist line. The 'un-personing' of Stalin by Khruschev led inevitably to a re-discovery of Lenin who, now that his acolyte was revealed as more closely comparable to Ivan the Terrible than to the 'Uncle Joe' of wartime euphoria, stood out all the more clearly as the founder and source of orthodoxy. Hence the 'new line' of peaceful co-existence was presented as in fact a reversion to a Leninism which had been warped by Stalin. Nor did Russia's actions, except in Eastern Europe (which was anyway admitted by other powers to be within the Soviet sphere of influence), apparently belie her words. *Détente* between East and West got under way. The bad days of Stalinism were relegated to the past.

Yet a reversion to Leninism, both by the USSR and by fellow travellers elsewhere, should hardly have been a cause of rejoicing to the West. If the mad logic of nuclear escalation in fact ruled out war as a sensibly Clausewitzian 'continuation of politics by other means', then, given the dichotomous view of the world held by Lenin, the historically necessary antithesis between socialism and capitalism would have to be resolved differently. Instead of war, conflict short of it and, in place of strife, clandestine subversion—these would be the new priorities. Precisely because 'war' was unthinkable subversion became more attractive and appeared likely to be remarkably cost-effective.

Stalin, for all his terrorism at home, was in foreign policy generally both careful and skilful. World revolution was, in his view, firmly to be discouraged unless it clearly contributed to the security of the Soviet state. An internationalist, he blandly argued, was one who unreservedly, without hesitation, without conditions was ready to defend the Soviet Union.

Such an attitude lent a degree of consistency and predictability to his external policies. Stalinist 'socialism in one country'—the granting of priority to the internal requirements of the USSR over the requirements of world revolution—was, from the point of view of the world of sovereign states, infinitely to be preferred, even if it was only a temporary expedient, to a process of comprehensive global subversion. The removal of the iron hand of Stalin from the central control of world communism was by no means necessarily an advantage to the West. Local initiative was likely to be potentially more successful than the adulation of Stalin which had all too frequently previously passed for intelligent thought.

Lenin remains a more potent revolutionary model than the

nervous Stalinist apparatchiks could ever hope to be. If Russia were to aim primarily to weaken the West rather than to extend her own control in an immediately imperialist sense she might the more plausibly do so via financial and military support for sympathetic domestic governments or movements rather than by a doctrinaire insistence on an outmoded set of ideological rigidities.

To the extent that Lenin is studied and his precepts observed, to that extent will the tactical approach of guerrilla groups and the use or non-use of terrorist tactics be likely to make political sense.

Lenin was the completely professional revolutionary. To him the business of revolution required a lifetime's dedication—it was not a dilettante exercise for free evenings. To a mastery of technique he added a grasp of the strategic dimension of violent action. Clausewitz, a particular intellectual hero of Lenin's, wrote that war had its own grammar but not its own logic; Lenin was to apply this reasoning to the use of violence in the civil context. Violence, be it used in strikes or terrorism, in assassination or guerrilla war, is irrelevant personally and socially unless it constitutes an integral part of a political logic aimed at the seizure of power. The insurrectionary operated under no moral constraints; morality was only relevant insofar as other people's possession of it constituted a weakness which might be exploited. Political logic was not enough; to it must be added the mastery of the 'grammar' of insurrection—the techniques which would result in the out-manoeuvring of the opposition and the defeat of police and soldiery by a professionalism greater than theirs.

In order to encompass the destruction of the existing order Lenin was able to use the experience of a number of revolutionary traditions to which he was heir; from among them he chose his tactics, always subordinating them to his aim—the taking and holding of political power.

By the end of the nineteenth century there was available an impressive array of ideological and technical tools for insurrection. The mistakes and small triumphs of revolutionary endeavour provided a fund of experience on which he could draw. Contemporary theories of revolution were not, however, consistent; in particular there was disagreement on the vexed question of the role of the revolutionary élite as opposed to the more mechanistic view of the less imaginative Marxists who placed their trust in the inevitability of eventual capitalist breakdown.

A stubborn belief in the efficacy of action by an élite group of dedicated conspirators had characterized the tactics of Louis Auguste Blanqui, who was born in 1805. He formed numerous societies which sought to foment rebellion by clandestine activity. These displayed the standard trappings of early 'combinations' of workers. To a ritual of initiation with blind-fold and the swearing of oaths was added a cellular organization in which each sub-group was kept in ignorance of the existence of the others; responsibility was to the centre.

Blanqui was never successful and spent thirty-six years of his life in prison. Yet his influence was considerable. His cynicism about voting, (The ballot, he said, was, 'in the absence of freedom', a means for misleading the people.) his belief in the revolutionary potential of a few alienated intellectuals and in the necessity for violence became, reinforced by the mystique which surrounded him in old age, widely accepted doctrines in revolutionary circles. 'Arms and organization', he wrote in his *Warning to the People* (addressed to emigré groups in London) 'these are the decisive elements of progress. He who has lead has bread. France bristling with bayonets, that means the advent of Socialism.'

The Blanquist tradition emphasized the necessity for organization, discipline, hierarchy and secrecy. Technically Blanqui's ideas for insurrection were sensible enough; particularly sound was his advice to the Government in the Franco-Prussian war. By using the citizenry as soldiers, he argued, the costs of fighting and occupation to the invading Prussians could be raised to the point where they might be persuaded to modify their demands. Like Bakhunin, however, he tended to see revolution in national, almost parochial terms. France, and in particular its capital, was the hub of civilization; he believed therefore that to win Paris was to win the world. The Prussians he considered a 'people of brutes'.

By the year of his death (1881) Blanquism was evolving into yet another political party, gaining a certain cloak and dagger aura by its association with his name but eventually merging with the French Socialist Party. Although revered, as the Russian Tkachev said at Blanqui's funeral, as 'our inspiration and model', he left a legacy essentially of failure, neither politically nor philosophically sufficiently substantial to provide a basis for the future. Blanquism became in fact an accusation of heterodoxy—sometimes levelled at Bolsheviks in general and at Lenin in particular—suggesting a belief in the ability of the conspiratorial élite to make a revolution without the pre-existence of a 'Class conscious proletariat'.

Lenin was also influenced by the specifically Russian movements for social reform which began in 1825 with an insurrection attempted by a group of young aristocrats known as the *Decembrists*. The tendency for noblemen to be the leaders in such movements was maintained later in the century by Bakhunin and Kropotkin. Subsequently attempts were made to preserve what was felt to be the essential 'Russianism' of society from the inroads of that oppressive and alienating industrialization whose effects were observable in Western Europe. At the heart of such ideas lay the concept (rather than the frequently sordid reality) of the peasant commune, from which it was hoped that a truly 'Russian' style of socialism might be evolved. A romantic attachment to the rural was allied to a realization that the peasants' intellectual backwardness and filial loyalty to the Tsar made necessary a preliminary period of education and inspiration. These beliefs were articulated by the Populist movement associated with Alexander Herzen.

In practical terms the consequences of the populist idea were less than impressive. Although thousands of idealistic young Russians 'went to the people' in 1874 they found a blank and crushing hostility. Many were arrested; the rest, their bright hopes disappointed, crept back to the cities. Since messianic expectations of a peasant Utopia had been destroyed the young revolutionaries canvassed the remaining options. Land and Liberty, the organization which grew out of this debate, soon went over to terrorist tactics with the object of eradicating persons in positions of political power. They succeeded in wounding a particularly unpopular Chief of Police and his assailant was acquitted by a sympathetic jury. Peoples' Will (as the group was later called) anticipated Bolshevik organization in two respects—the emphasis on the primacy of the political aim and the firm control imposed by a Central Committee. An apparent success was the assassination of the Tsar in 1881; tactically, however, this was an error since it brought about the full force of a reaction which the movement was unable to withstand.

By this time some of the erstwhile populists had discovered Marxism; a discovery they were to utilize in the formulation of a new revolutionary strategy adapted to conditions inside Russia.

Marx provided little direct guide to revolutionary tactics; at the same time he and Engels had perforce to pass some judgement on contemporary insurrections and guerrilla warfare. They did not want to encourage ill-considered and unplanned adventures which under existing conditions could lead only to repression, not only of the conspirators but also of the people they were aiming to liberate; on the other hand they had no wish to forego any possibility of hastening the collapse of capitalism by the bomb, the riot or the progression to guerrilla warfare. Engels, while he was opposed to Tkachev's 'Blanquist' views, commented that insurrection was an art quite as much as any other and subject to certain rules of proceeding. The problem of adapting Marxism to Russian conditions was debated during the years of exile in Switzerland. Marxism gave the assurance of ultimate success since the logic of developing property relationships under capitalism would produce that politically conscious industrial class which would be at once numerous and educated enough to provide the basis for revolution; it provided a philosophical foundation and a guide to

40

action. Applying it to conditions in Russia was, however, difficult. So backward was that country that the prospect of a
sufficiently large and politically literate industrial class seemed
Utopian. It was indeed arguable whether Russia had gone
beyond feudalism. An alliance with the bourgeoisie looked
unlikely since the latter possessed no political organization.
Nor did Marxism give any clear guide to the vexed question of
the peasantry whose hunger for land was being met, gradually
if reluctantly, by the Tsars who were deliberately creating a
class of minor landowners dedicated to the maintenance of the
existing system and inimical to any social change which might
threaten their new-found patrimony.

In these circumstances the possible revolutionary strategies
appeared to be:

(a) To attempt revolution via a small band of professionals,
     assassinating Ministers and seizing on any economic or
     political breakdowns in order to foment unrest.
(b) To attempt to seize the leadership of revolution from
     the class next expected, according to the Marxist thesis,
     to possess it—the bourgeoisie (This involved abbreviat-
     ing the full cycle of Marxist evolution by collapsing the
     bourgeois stages together.) with the working class swiftly
     taking the lead and 'having the hegemony'.
(c) To work for and through democratic machinery,
     attempting to achieve desired social reforms and even-
     tually accede to power through the ballot. This view,
     eventually anathematized by orthodox Communists,
     was put forward by the German, Bernstein, and became
     known as 'revisionism'.

It was contained most notably in his book, *The Assumptions
of Socialism and the Tasks of Social Democracy*, published in
1899. On this interpretation no period of proletarian dictatorship was required; once the proletariat was sufficiently influen-
tial such a drastic step would be unnecessary. A concomitant
heresy was that of 'Economism'—the concentration on attempts
to improve the workers' conditions rather than using these
conditions as a lever to political action.

41

The first alternative was that embraced by the Socialist Revolutionaries—a party in the intellectual and organizational traditions of Populism. This group was socialist without being Marxist. Loyal to its populist antecedents it concentrated on the issue of land and aimed its main appeal at the peasants. It possessed a separate terrorist arm which was headed by one Azef. Azef had one peculiarly damaging characteristic—he was a police agent. The Socialist Revolutionaries' programme of terror, apart from being designed as much by *agents provocateurs* as by the Party itself, was in any case politically inept. They succeeded in assassinating Prime Minister Stolypin (though the executor of this deed, Bogrov, was also in the pay of the police). As is often the case in such affairs the quick promotions brought about by bomb and bullet left the revolutionaries in a worse case than before. The state is hydra-headed and the new appointees are frequently more oppressive and more efficient than those so bloodily removed. Indeed they have the justification of recent example and the motives of personal survival to urge them to adopt draconian measures.

Lenin would have none of such tactics; terrorism *simpliciter* was no answer—its employment had cost him his elder brother, executed in 1887 for his part in a plot to assassinate Tsar Alexander III. The question to be faced was whether such actions contributed to the political triumph of the cause?

His tactical plan is conventionally held to be found in *What Is To Be Done?* (1902) and its postscript, *Letter to a Comrade on Our Organizational Tasks. What Is To Be Done?* was written when Lenin was editor of *Iskra (The Spark)* and head of a small group of inner party colleagues known by the same name. Already he had, therefore, a miniature of the organization for which he was to argue in print.

The orthodox few who truly understood Marxism (that is, agreed with Lenin) should be at the head of the movement; their task was to direct the activities of those below them in a strictly ordered and disciplined manner. What was required was not 'spontaneity' but a conscious strategy for the seizure of power. The chosen handful should be protected and nurtured; below them the followers must be prepared to fight and die for the cause. This élite needed a Nechayevan dedication and, as Lenin wrote to Gorky, it was 'not the time to stroke peoples' heads, today hands are raised to split skulls open'. Lenin admitted that intellectuals might not enjoy the necessarily tight discipline and central direction of such an organization. The workers, on the other hand, slaves of industrialism, were already used to doing as they were told; Lenin would replace those capitalist processes by political manipulation and the captains of industry with revolutionary activists. Nor should revolutionary zeal be diluted by any other consideration; those who were not for the revolution were against it. The bourgeoisie were to be hated. Liberals on the other hand should in no way be disdained—they should be used. Bolshevik Deputies in the Russian Assembly were ordered to utilize their parliamentary immunity in order to agitate for an uprising.

Lenin's amoral approach to insurrection places him in the Nechayevan tradition; individual populist terrorists were by contrast eager to sacrifice themselves and at pains to justify what they did. They criticized the assassination of the American President Garfield since they felt that in the United States people had a legitimate means of political expression which had not been utilized. Populist morality thus remained within the main stream of European thought; to this Nechayev and Lenin opposed a total commitment to any means—lies, deception, murder, and the abandonment of all human feeling and loyalty in order to gain power.

Tactically it was necessary to exaggerate and generalize small and separate grievances and relate them to vague but sweeping complaints against the Government. While spontaneous terrorism was to be avoided it was to be used mercilessly once an uprising had begun. Lenin was to maintain this position when the abortive 1905 insurrection, at its most severe in Moscow in December of that year, was bloodily suppressed. The failure of this insurrection stimulated an even more than usually heated argument among Russian exiles. Plekhanov argued that 'They should not have taken up arms'; Lenin replied in *Lessons of the Moscow Uprising* that, on the contrary, arms should have been taken up more vigorously and aggressively! Once insurrection had commenced all means should be used to propagate it. A professional study of the tactics and counter-tactics of urban warfare must be undertaken. Lenin himself read the memoirs of General Cluseret who had been involved in suppressing the French uprisings in 1848. What was important, said Lenin, was not victory in any narrowly military sense, but the act of insurrection in which every squad could learn, if only by beating up policemen. Bolshevik duty was in such circumstances ruthlessly to exterminate civil and military chiefs by using small killer squads. Once the battle was on the streets the Party should eradicate its opponents by unleashing a full-scale terror. 'Terror', as Dzerzhinsky, the first head of the Cheka, Lenin's Secret Police, was later to remark, 'is an absolute necessity during times of revolution.' From the outset guerrilla-style warfare was seen as eventually inevitable and thus insurrectionary tactics must be kept strictly under Party control. Expropriations such as the bank robberies carried out under Stalin's orders in Tiflis in 1907 might, Lenin realized, attract criminal elements ('drunken riff-raff'). Such activities should not necessarily be avoided but should be 'ennobled' by the 'enlightening influence of socialism'.

If 1905 caused heart-searching among the exiles it produced near panic at the court of the Tsar. To demands for a *Duma* (Parliament) with real powers and for amnesty for the prisoners of 1905 the Tsar replied with reforms which gave the shadow but not the substance of power. At the same time the Secret Police organization, the *Okhrana*, redoubled its 'counter-terrorist' activities. A front organization, the Union of Russian Men, was formed with Tsarist approval to combat revolutionary tendencies. Police Unionism—the setting up of bogus Trade Unions—flourished. Infiltration of genuinely Left wing movements was increased. *Okhrana* became a State within the State. Its operatives organized the murders of Ministers and officials so that they could arrest the assassins—thus justifying the existence and the financial demands of their organization.

It soon became clear that the Duma had no power; its pleas were ignored by the Tsar—or failed to reach him. Counter-terror continued to the point where *Duma* Deputy Tcheidze remarked sardonically in 1909 that, 'Civic freedom in Russia is now confined to the hangman.'[2]

The success of the *Okhrana* in infiltrating revolutionary organizations reinforced Lenin's argument for a tight-knit and élite group directing operations—although, ironically enough, the *Okhrana* had their man at Lenin's elbow also (Roman Malinovsky). To many people Lenin's organizational theories sounded suspiciously like Blanquism. Throughout his career Lenin was at great pains to refute this charge. There is a reference to such an accusation in a letter to the Central Committee of the Party as late as September, 1917, in which he calls the charge 'an opportunist lie'. Lenin insisted that his propositions for a small professional revolutionary caucus were not like those of Blanqui for the latter had no real contact with and did not agitate among the proletariat. In the Leninist model the moment for action is to be decided by an analysis of the 'class situation' and will be accompanied by mass disturbances.

The 1905 uprisings contained another lesson which Lenin was later (1916) to find confirmed in his reading of Clausewitz. War (in 1905, the Russo-Japanese War) seemed to him the great opportunity for revolution. For by then war was being waged not by professionals who marched and counter-marched, 'won' or 'lost' according to predetermined 'rules'; it was being waged by peoples. Defeat was thus not a matter of a few minor territorial adjustments but an experience which tore at a nation's very heart—its wives, sons and brothers. As resource commitment to the war effort rose towards totality so did the scale of political disillusionment and economic disruption, should victory not swiftly be forthcoming.

In *What Is To Be Done?* Lenin had spoken of 'decisive links' which, once identified in a situation, led on to others in a kind of causal chain toward revolution. War might be one of them—another might be the question of national minorities. Already in the eighteen-nineties some attempt had been made to appeal to such sentiments. Traditional Russian anti-Semitism, with pogroms being used by the Tsars to divert attention from domestic problems, had ensured a heavy Jewish representation in revolutionary circles. While within the Party Lenin opposed attempts at de-centralization he was only too willing outside it to utilize such tensions within the Tsarist Empire. Ethnic divisions in the USSR had led to a number of regional movements—in the Ukraine, in Siberia, in Georgia and Turkestan. Lenin was willing to promise autonomy and to support the principle of 'national self-determination'; politically it suited him to do so at the time, and in any case he perhaps felt that such differences would wither away once the, to him, deeper distinctions of class were revealed. The oppression of ethnic minorities in the name of Great Russia is associated with Stalin, Commissar for Nationalities under Lenin. Lenin died before the hard choices in this area had to be made. Everything in his background, however, points to a belief in centralism; whether the 'democratic discussion' which was supposed to precede central decisions would have been any more real under Lenin than it turned out to be under Stalin can only be conjectured. It would seem unlikely that any real autonomy would have been granted, certainly not to the point of secession. The fact remains that Lenin can be represented as favouring such measures; a reversion to Leninism thus looks a much better stance for the USSR to adopt in the contemporary world than the Great Bolshevik Nationalism which was adopted by Stalin.

Lenin's use of these tactics provided a number of still currently relevant techniques. The shooting of a number of supplicants who had come to the Tsar's winter palace in 1905 was a staggering moral defeat for the Government. The authorities proceeded to compound their error (The affair was known as 'Bloody Sunday'.) by setting up an Enquiry. The Bolsheviks used the proceedings to present demands amounting to the total enactment of their programme. The 'Enquiry' merely succeeded in picking at the sore; it achieved nothing except to hand the Bolsheviks some extra propaganda.

Of such stuff are myths made; nine years later Russian workers were still going on strike on the anniversary of 'Bloody Sunday'. In 'progressive circles' throughout the world articles were written on 22 January every year celebrating that year when 'the whole of Russia was one sea of blood'—'in memory of a beginning, the end of which is not yet'.[3]

Lenin's characteristic flexibility and use of popular grievances, whether or not ideologically consistent, was further demonstrated during 1917. He saw that the main desire of the war-weary Russians was for 'peace'—and at any price. He understood that the main ambition of the peasant was for 'land'. It did not matter whether tactical expedients squared with conventional Marxist analysis. If the Socialist Revolutionaries had the most effective slogans then Lenin would steal them. Power, not consistent or elegant analysis, was the prize for which he fought. Weakness, not strength, led to the decision to seize power and carried with it the penalties of haste and improvization so that later, as Rosa Luxemburg was to point out, there was a tendency to set up as a model 'all the distortions prescribed in Russia by necessity and compulsion'.[4]

Lenin was also master of the propaganda of written communication, as the Nazis were to be of the wireless. The favoured verbal tactic was to impose a terrorism of the word. Language is used not to convince an opponent but to destroy him; one does not discuss, one denounces. The mark of ideological heresy must be branded on the adversary's brow in letters of fire. Words are to be judged on their degree of efficiency as politically damaging invective. The objective is not to correct the other's mistake but to annihilate the enemy's organization and wipe it off the face of the earth.

Perhaps the essential extra factor which led to Lenin's success when others failed and which, despite the theoretical polemics, most clearly distinguished Leninism from Blanquism, was his closeness to his countrymen, not in his writings, but in his person. 'Lenin evoked Russia', as his compatriot Radek put it; he had about him the presence of his native land. He was clearly of his time and place when so many contemporary, and subsequent, self-styled 'revolutionaries' seemed alien to the environments in which they operated.

Lenin as revolutionary strategist left a legacy which was of importance to Russia, and thus may have relevance to that nation's contemporary behaviour towards other countries and movements, and as 'Leninism' may influence approaches to insurrection in general.

After 1917 it soon became apparent that Russian-style revolution needed modification before it could be successfully exported. Attempts in Hungary, Bavaria and Berlin at carbon copies of the November Revolution all failed. Utopian hopes of an immediately ensuing world revolution were disappointed. Experience in Poland dimmed them still further. Polish workers, far from supporting the invading Red Army in the war of 1920, fought tenaciously against it.

'Socialism in one country', the essentially 'Russian' policy associated with Stalin, was a product of the logic of events. Western European failure to display any revolutionary enthusiasm necessitated the speedy construction of an industrialized state on the ruins of the Civil War. Interest was therefore deflected away from any faith in European revolutionary immediacy toward the colonial countries. Insurrectionary techniques in Europe were to concentrate on methods by which the minority Communist Parties might weaken their host régimes in the interests of the security of the Soviet Union.

Theoretical arguments for the colonial option were already to hand. In 1916, in his book of the same name, Lenin had stated that 'Imperialism' was a characteristic of the death throes of capitalism. A 'labour aristocracy' had been created in the home countries which was being bribed by capitalism with the profits made from sweated colonial labour. Attention should therefore be switched to those colonies and the patron régimes attacked through their material resources and markets. Lenin had seen Russia, though backward, as lighting the lamp of revolution in Europe and passing on the flame to Germany, France and Britain. The lamp, after a brief flickering, had gone out in the West—in the exploited East, however, it might catch fire with a double strength and eventually turn to engulf the whole world. By 1919 Lenin was suggesting that perhaps the revolution in Asia would precede that in Europe. Interviewed by a Japanese journalist in 1920 he grimly observed that the imperialists were giving weapons to their colonials and teaching them how to use them—the West was digging its own grave in the East.

After Lenin's death the failure of the Stalin-inspired urban-based insurrections in China reinforced some of the former's observations that the colonial countries would have to find specific forms adapted to their particular conditions for carrying on the revolutionary struggle. The tactic recommended was an alliance between workers and middle class against the landlords and 'colonial lackeys'. The principal weakness of the Russian model as developed by Stalin was precisely its failure to give due weight to these separate conditions. In particular the peasantry was thought of in Russian terms as being a reactionary class, blocking the necessary industrialization of backward countries and, though useful as an ally, lacking in any ability to take a revolutionary initiative. As a guide to action Marxist-Leninism, in the then only orthodox interpretation, that of the Stalin-dominated Communist International (*Comintern*), remained a mainly urban operation. Revolution was held to come, in effect if not always in apparent intention, 'from above'—that is from the industrial proletariat, led by the Party élite. As the *Comintern* became more and more clearly a tool of Russian foreign policy, with Stalinist apparatchiks in key positions, so this view grew more rigid and doctrinaire; the fears previously expressed by Rosa Luxemburg were amply borne out in practice. Asian Communists such as Mao Tse-tung and Ho Chi-minh had thus to fight not only against colonialism but also against the myopic views of their patron state, which claimed the ideological as well as the practical leadership of world revolutionary forces.

Ho Chi-minh contributed to a work on armed insurrection,[5] published under the name A. Neuberg in 1928, but in fact compiled by an expert panel of the 'Agitation and Propaganda' section of the Comintern. Their 'programme for insurrection' envisaged a progression from the sporadic strike and demonstration via an increasing polarization of class feeling to a culmination in the General Strike and simultaneous armed uprising. The bulk of the book, despite Ho's relatively modest contribution on revolutionary guerrilla methods among the peasantry, is concerned with tactics in the advanced industrial countries. Previous uprisings are analysed and tactical conclusions drawn. Surprise attacks by small groups are ruled out as 'petty bourgeois adventurism'. Most importantly, the technology and military tactics of insurrection are discussed and certain positive conclusions drawn.

It was pointed out that the authorities are in no position effectively to oppose a resolute group of marksmen who operate in a complex urban environment and who enjoy the support of the population to facilitate their movements and hinder those of the police. Provided the insurgents occupy the 'high ground' —rooftops and balconies—they have the fields of vision and fire which those same buildings deny to the police. In Hamburg the Prefect of Police had acknowledged the powerlessness of his men, faced with such tactics. Similar conclusions had previously been drawn from a study of the 1905 Russian uprising by the Irish Republican Socialist, James Connolly. Connolly wrote articles in *Workers' Republic* in 1915[6] in which he likened the cities to areas of mountainous country where, for the military, communications are restricted and terrorist positions notoriously difficult to locate. *Armed Insurrection* also emphasizes the importance of subverting the régime's police and army. The principles on which this should be based were known already. In the Moscow disturbances of 1905 posters had appeared advising the population not to attack the infantry soldiers who were 'children of the people'. The cavalry (in that case Cossacks) were of course another matter and to them no quarter should be offered. Bolsheviks should identify and subvert particularly sensitive parts of the Army—for example ethnic or linguistic sub-groups who might be cold-shouldered or even victimized by their fellows. Common 'fronts' should be organized against 'reactionary' Commanding Officers. Once arms had been taken up terror should be used in order to 'decapitate the counter-revolution'—a point stressed in particular by Marshal Tukhachevsky.

In general, insurrectionary technology and organization should be in a constant state of readiness; the political situation, a matter for Party decision, would be the crucial factor in determining the timing and the direction of the attack.

Spain (1936–9) soon provided an environment for the further testing of some of these hypotheses. At the beginning of the Civil War the Spanish Communist Party was in a minority position; during its course it expanded, with Russian support, to become the most powerful force both militarily and politically on the Republican side. The Communist Fifth Regiment (later Corps) abandoned revolutionary fraternity in favour of a traditionally hierarchical rank structure. Political agents from the Comintern used the Spanish situation to impose a Stalinist uniformity on the Party. They were not disposed to allow military or political requirements for an anti-Fascist coalition to obstruct the liquidation of ideological heretics. Antonov-Ovseyenko, the USSR's Consul General, had no compunction about interfering in the internal aspects of Republican policy. The allegedly neo-Trotskyist POUM[7] was swiftly anathematized. 'In Catalonia', observed *Pravda*, 'the elimination of Trotskyists and anarcho-syndicalists has already begun; it will be carried out', it added darkly, 'with the same energy as in the USSR.' Since at that time the Stalinist purges were under way in Russia the implication was clear enough.

While the defence of Madrid was conducted in a passion for revolution inspired by the memory of 1917 its aftermath was less than glorious. When the euphoria of apparent victory had died away and the immediate threat was over, the commissars proceeded to carry out their unlovely work of smear and vilification. In the babel of factional propaganda the voice of the Communist Press was always the most strident and its *apparat* the most efficiently organized. Accusations of Trotskyism, German and Italian Fascism, collaboration and betrayal were

51

widely made and ruthlessly hammered home. POUM was suppressed and its leaders imprisoned or, where they were of outstanding calibre, murdered. Its leader, Nin, was eradicated by the Russian secret police. The anarchist CNT/FAI was similarly dealt with. A secret police was set up. In this situation the underlying divisions between the Republican Government and its Basque and Catalan separatist supporters became yet more evident, and the possibility that the latter, sickened by the tyranny which they saw would eventually engulf them too, would come to terms with the Fascists was enhanced.

Stalin's iron hand succeeded in divesting the anti-Fascist coalition of its revolutionary character at the same time and by the same means as it made it from a technical military viewpoint more efficient. The camaradarie to which both Spaniards and members of the International Brigade have testified gave way, under the ministrations of men like the Hungarian Gero, and the head of the Russian secret police, Orlov, to the terror described by George Orwell:

> 'There was a peculiarly evil feeling in the air—an atmosphere of suspicion, fear, uncertainty and veiled hatred.'[8]

The preferred Stalinist procedure in infiltrating and taking over an existing Government rather than by supporting revolution as such was clearly demonstrated in Spain; far from decapitating the counter-revolution, however, the apparat's terror tactics had done the 'reactionaries' work for them. The Fascist garotte had been replaced by the Communist shot in the back of the head.

In the years following the Second World War the pattern of infiltration and subsequent terror refined in the Spanish Civil War was adapted with success in Eastern Europe. The Russians capitalized on the desire for reform, the anti-German sentiments of the population and the weakness of opposing political elements to help their local allies to power. In Poland, of the leaders of the (non-Communist) Polish Socialist Party alive at the beginning of the war, two had, by its end, perished in Nazi concentration camps, two had died in Stalin's prisons, two had been shot by the secret police and one was in exile in London. The Katyn massacres[9] had already decimated the Polish élite and the tacit acceptance by the West of the Soviet hegemony over Eastern Europe made armed opposition pointless. In Poland it nevertheless occurred, only to be crushed by the Soviet Red Army and its local supporters.

Western Europe, despite large Communist Parties in Italy and France, came under the economic and military domination of the United States of America. The role of insurrection in the armoury of the Soviet Union received a further reappraisal. Post-Stalin analysis made it clear that Europe remained at the bottom of the league for revolutionary potential. On the periphery of capitalism the situation appeared on the other hand encouraging and the correctness of the original Leninist analysis vindicated.

Khruschev and his successors have sought to distinguish 'local wars' (with their attendant dangers of an escalation into confrontation with the United States of America) from 'wars of national liberation'. The latter will be supported by the USSR. The export of revolution by overtly military means is regarded as an incorrect response at this time to the world situation. To attempt to do so would in Soviet eyes be to threaten the existence of socialism in their country and thus the main achievement of revolutionary activity to date. Today the use of military force to start revolutions in other countries is regarded as 'Trotskyist'.

If, however, a country should display some internal revolutionary initiative then the USSR may be prepared to support those involved. Should such a movement appear likely to be successful then steps will be taken to infiltrate it. Khruschev pointed out[10] that the 'CPSU and the Soviet people' (avoiding any State commitment) 'consider it their international duty to give all-round political and economic support, and if necessary, armed help too, to the national liberation struggle of the people'. Russian activity in Cuba, where the Revolution became officially Marxist-Leninist at a comparatively late stage, demonstrates the presently favoured pattern.

The Official IRA

The only currently active 'revolutionary' movement which concerns the United Kingdom and which has Marxist-Leninist antecedents is the Irish Republican Army.

Marx had seen in the exploitation of Ireland a reason why his confident expectation of a radicalization of British politics in the year of suffrage reform (1868) had been so thoroughly disappointed at the polls.

Both the Official and the Provisional Wings of the IRA have tended to talk in the language of Left Wing revolution, although one of the causes of the original split between them was the Marxist views and projected common front tactics of those who were to become known as the Officials. Infiltration of the Provisionals from the Left has been mainly Trotskyist while the Officials remain ideologically a more orthodox Moscow-line Marxist-Leninist organization. For all the jargon, however, the Provisionals remain essentially Irish Nationalists, their motivation springing from tribal memories, not proletarian internationalism.

In the opinion of one expert, 'The IRA . . . of all revolutionary movements in Europe, would be the most vulnerable to a Communist takeover.'[11] This might seem unlikely in so Catholic a country as Ireland. The embattled position of the Church in contemporary societies, together with the influence of foreign revolutionaries, via books and personal contacts, has, however, produced a certain weakening of the traditional religious elements in nationalism. Flirtations with Marxism on the part of clerics and a certain naivety about Communist intentions have reduced the 'devil content' of dealings with the Left. Gone are the days when Jesuit sermons in Dublin could produce broken windows in Communist or Socialist Party buildings. Contemporary problems appear to find no clear answers in a

1. The battlefield of the future: the cardboard jungle and the concrete jungle, São Paolo city, Brazil

2. A demonstrating crowd in the Steamer point area of Aden is dispersed by tear gas in 1967

3. A civilian victim of the unrest in Algiers c. 1956

Church which seems to have lost its confidence. This failure of Vatican nerve has left an ideological vacuum and Marxism is well equipped to fill it. Nobody can hope to influence Irish Republican politics unless he boasts a suitably dramatic history. The Left has, apart from its Marxist faith, a goodly number of heroes who sacrificed themselves for the cause in which they believed. James Connolly, martyred for his part in the 1916 uprising, provided with his citizen army a Socialist element in Republicanism. The Connolly Association swiftly became and has remained a Communist-front organization.

Attempts have been made throughout its history to politicize the IRA away from a policy of blind force, usually in a Marxist-Leninist direction, and the movement has been split and split again as a result. The antithesis between the bullet and the ballot has never been resolved. In one of the more bizarre episodes in IRA history emissaries were sent to Stalin. He seems to have been unimpressed. However IRA contacts with the Comintern were maintained.

During the thirties the IRA was much occupied—as were similar movements elsewhere—in fisticuffs with the militant Right. Their opponents were the Irish Blueshirts, a movement which in part represented a reaction to the Leftward trend of Republicanism. The effect was to push the IRA itself further to the Left.

In recent years the old dichotomy between armed force and political action has reappeared. Attacks were made in the 1960s on foreign capital interests in Ireland and a rapprochement with the Communists seemed in the offing. The tactic which led to the Provisionals leaving the IRA (though dissatisfaction with the 'Left' line went deeper, especially in the American support organizations) was the recommendation (March, 1969) that parliamentary institutions should be used— even if the aim was eventually to destroy them. The IRA was attempting to go over to a National Liberation Front strategy with the newly-united Irish Communist Party (i.e. of both North and South).

The Officials have continued to adopt a Marxist-Leninist line while the Provisionals, insofar as it is possible to identify a coherent political platform, have tended to seek the best of all possible worlds, striking the postures of the 'Green' while increasingly mouthing the propaganda of the 'Red'.

Today the Official IRA, operating behind and co-operating with a confusing smoke-screen of front organizations and campaigns, aims to achieve a united Irish Socialist Republic. It has clung to a belief in class as against nationalist solidarity and has sought to build contacts across sectarian boundaries. IRA leaders have spelt out these tactics in their own and sympathetic Left Wing publications. 'I think it is terribly important to involve the English working class in our struggle. They have got to understand why we are killing their boys . . .' Thus Malachy McGurran[12] in an interview which is straight Leninist dogma: he talks of the merging of 'the weapon and politics' and the primacy of 'class'. Official IRA leader Cathal Goulding likes to discuss the 'peoples' war situation' obtaining in Northern Ireland and Tomas McGiolla refers to seeking 'contacts with the working class leaders of Protestant organizations' and of 'working towards an awareness of the class nature of the struggle'.

The apparent politicization of the Official IRA should not be allowed to obscure the fact that it remains a fighting organization with a force in being ready to use violence when it judges the moment to be opportune. This capability would be used not merely against 'British imperialism' but also against 'monopoly capitalism'—the aim being to turn Ireland into the 'Cuba of Europe'. In any campaign to achieve those ends the immediate target would be the Republic of Eire.

It was the Official IRA which claimed responsibility for the first major bomb incident in England (Aldershot, see Chapter 10). Despite this miscalculated and bungled operation, a Leninist use of violence remains likely to be better integrated into a programme of political and social activity than does the reflex killing of the Provisionals.

The history of the IRA shows with a remarkable regularity that as each successive leadership came to terms with contemporary realities, so the movement split and extremists carried on the armed struggle. Compromise has been equated with betrayal. In the current troubles the Provisional wing of the IRA has been pushed further in the direction of extremism for its own sake so that it has arrived at a kind of Irish racism, negatively conceived as anti-English, anti-Protestant, anti-colonial and, increasingly, anti-capitalist. It is in the shifting sands of this reactionary extremism that attempts to turn the IRA into a genuinely revolutionary movement have consistently sunk.

Current Russian policy

To the extent that overt support for internal revolution—in Ireland as elsewhere—is politically embarrassing, to that extent will the Russians continue to use the distinction between 'State' and 'Party' which has served them well in the past. The Communist Party of the Soviet Union has frequently found itself honour bound to do that which the USSR finds politically inopportune. Moreover there exist small states eager to prove their revolutionary ardour (or in no position to argue) which can be used as proxies. Just as Czechoslovakia has been the arms supplier, so, improbably, has North Korea become a centre for training in subversive activity. This is partly a matter of convenience and partly due to the desire of the North Korean leader Kim Il Sung to establish himself as a leading theoretician and practitioner of revolution. Mexicans recruited by the KGB were sent via the Patrice Lumumba University in Moscow to be trained in North Korea. Their insurrection, timed for 1971, failed to materialize—due more to the luck than to the judgement of the authorities (a policeman happened on their hideout). A number of Soviet diplomats were subsequently expelled from Mexico. North Korean behaviour has not been consistently subservient to the USSR; indeed on occasion, especially in Chile prior to the military takeover of 1973, it has been competitive. Elsewhere there has however been collaboration; an abortive rising in Sri Lanka (Ceylon) in

1971 led to the disappointed North Korean diplomats being flown away from the scene of their débâcle by the Soviet airline, Aeroflot.

In Western Europe the official Communist Parties have lost ground to the new revolutionary movements of the Left, especially to the Trotskyists. The activities of the USSR in Hungary and Czechoslovakia have presented to the idealistic young the unacceptable face of Big Power Nationalism. Russian ideologues, conscious of this problem, have redoubled the flow of anti-Trotskyist polemic, linking such deviations with the Chinese version of Marxist-Leninism. This interest in the revolutionary situation in Western Europe is not due solely to the need to counter the successes of Trotskyist heretics. Signs of internal decay in the United States of America and the possibility of its consequent abandonment of its commitment to Western Europe make the prospects for political change appear promising. As the moral cohesion of the United States seems fragile the attraction of the USSR to Western Europeans, quite apart from considerations of military and economic prudence, becomes correspondingly more powerful. While local Communist Parties may pursue traditional alliance tactics with 'progressive forces', the Russians, for their part, will continue to exploit and widen the rifts in Western European society.

Separatist tendencies evidenced by the Irish and the Basques, and potentially among other ethnic groups (Bretons, Sicilians, Scots and Welsh) are already being exploited. Smaller states on the Western European periphery such as Cyprus, Malta and Iceland, all display intriguing possibilities for subversion. The Moscow-line Communist Parties in countries such as Cyprus and Ireland are of course in an embarrassing position; their claims to support the working class in general run counter to the ethnic and religious sub-divisions which create the revolutionary situations. Indeed it is among the proletariat that sectional fanatacisms are most evident. Appealing to class solidarity across such barriers is a politically frustrating exercise. On the other hand such doctrinal inhibitions need not frustrate efforts at clandestine infiltration of extremist movements, nor need the KGB allow nice ideological points to hinder arms supply to ethnically or racially extreme organizations. In this process terrorism will continue to play a part for it has been integral to Bolshevism from the start, not an exceptional device to be used only *in extremis*, but a normal political tactic. Paradoxically the most effective utilization of Bolshevik practice after the success of November, 1917, was made, not by Communists, but by those who used the threat from the Left to justify their employment of Leninist techniques in order to destroy it.

NOTES

1 The modern successor of the Cheka, the NKVD and MVD. See Ronald Hingley, *The Russian Secret Service*, Hutchinson, 1970.
2 Prince Kropotkin, *The Terror in Russia*, Methuen, 1909, p. 69.
3 *Daily Herald*, Friday, 23 January, 1914.
4 Rosa Luxemburg, *The Russian Revolution*, New York, 1940, p. 55.
5 A. Neuberg, *Armed Insurrection*, NLB, 1970.
6 Republished as a pamphlet, *Revolutionary Warfare*, Dublin and Belfast, 1968.
7 *Partido Obrero de Unificacion Marxista*.
8 George Orwell, *Homage to Catalonia*, Penguin, 1962, p. 186.
9 14,500 Polish officer POWs disappeared from camps in the Soviet Union in 1940; the bodies of over 4,000 were found in mass graves in the Katyn forest in 1943.
10 *Izvestiya*, 21 December, 1963.
11 Tim Pat Coogan, *The IRA*, Fontana, 1970, p. 305.
12 *7 Days*, March, 1972.

CHAPTER 4

'Sharpen the Long Knives'— Nazi and Fascist Terror

'Sharpen the long knives on the pavements
So that they cut better in the Jewish flesh
And comes the hour of vengeance
We stand ready for any massacre'

S. A. SONG

'A resolute bandit can always prevent an honest man from
carrying out political activity'

HITLER, *Mein Kampf*

Germany in the early nineteen-twenties was vicious and corrupt; the fabric of society had been torn apart—with no new purposes to take their place, old certainties had been utterly destroyed. Inflation reached the point where workers took their wages by the sackful. Wives met their husbands at the factory gate in order to spend the pay before its value declined still further. Middle-class savings were destroyed overnight. A few speculators waxed fat on the chaos, for between contract and completion the purchase money became almost worthless. By 1923 the German mark stood at 4,210,500,000,000 to the dollar. Economically the bourgeoisie became a new proletariat while emotionally still clinging to former attitudes.

Nowhere was the cynicism and despair more evident than in Berlin. The laxity of that capital's society would have made modern permissiveness appear as the starkest Puritanism. Drugs were freely available and widely used. To have walked those Berlin streets where the peddlers of vice rubbed shoulders with the pathetic remnants of war would have given the impression that the country was populated entirely by beggars and whores.

The Government ran the country only because extremists of Right and Left cancelled each other out; each was willing to extend temporary help to the authorities in order to prevent the other gaining a decisive advantage. Rosa Luxemburg and Karl Liebknecht of the revolutionary Communist Spartacus League were killed by men of the Cavalry Guards. In Bavaria the comic opera Government of the poet Kurt Eisner, having sent the erstwhile King into exile, proved totally incapable of anything approaching the efficiency (or the ruthlessness) required to push through an insurrection. After the crushing of the Bavarian attempt at revolution the troops exacted a bloody revenge on the people of Munich, killing foe and frequently friend too—for they attacked a Catholic meeting, slaughtering them like animals and drunkenly dancing on the heaped bodies.

On the Right the Kapp Putsch similarly failed although *Frei Korps* troops, tolerated by the Government as a useful anti-Communist force, had backed the putsch by occupying Berlin. These soldiers, veterans of the war who knew no trade save that of fighting, had formed freelance companies (usually named after their old commanders). They owed allegiance to nobody save themselves but, lacking anyone else, the Government was forced to use them. Their officers felt the bitterness expressed by Goering to a meeting (called to hear the new Republican Minister of War):

'We Officers did our duty for four long years . . . and we risked our bodies for the Fatherland. Now we come home —and how do they treat us? They spit on us and deprive us of what we gloried in wearing . . . I implore you to cherish hatred—a profound abiding hatred of those animals who have outraged the German people.'[1]

These *Frei Korps* soldiers, singing the anthem of the crack Erhardt Brigade, had goose-stepped arrogantly into Berlin, swastikas on their helmets—yet Kapp, for all this apparent military support, failed to see the putsch through. A Prussian Civil Servant to the last, he would not confiscate money from the banks and he shrank from killing his enemies. Regular troops, police and Civil Service stayed loyal to the Republic, while the Left launched a series of massive strikes. After four and a half days the putsch collapsed. An emissary from the South, one Adolf Hitler, arrived in time to witness only the aftermath. Yet the soldiers who marched out of Berlin did so once more singing their anthem; they intended to be back.

In Munich one of the leaders of these troops, Commander Erhardt, founded a terrorist organization called 'Consul' (OC) which sought to revive the rough justice of the medieval 'Vehme' (a tribunal which maintained law and order when the Government was too weak or too pusillanimous to do so). 'OC' assassinated those it judged to have betrayed Germany. Erzberger, who had signed the armistice to end the First World War, was killed and the Jewish Walter Rathenau, Foreign Minister on the Weimar Republic, was gunned down in his car by Consul terrorists Fischer and Kern, who lobbed in a grenade for good measure. The assassins themselves, having shouted a last defiant 'Hoch', died with heavy Gothick symbolism, in a castle.

Amid a welter of street fighting and murder the middle classes sought for reassurance and expiation. Why had this happened to them? What had Germany done to deserve this decadence and misery? Among all the proliferating conspiracies and cabals, new political parties and movements, that of Adolf Hitler provided the most sweeping and emotionally satisfying answer to their deep frustration and bewilderment. The old centre had patently failed to hold; Hitler would create a new national focus and purpose.

The Nazi answer was to offer a global explanation for all evil—the one issue of 'Race'. 'Scientific' theory, evolution seen as the morally necessary survival of the strongest and a medieval suspicion of the 'rootless Jew' combined both to explain economic and social disaster and to excuse the Germans for having failed to deal with their problems. Defeat could be explained—and just as the racial 'Celticist' movement grew out of the French disaster of 1870, so the Nazis were to capitalize on the humiliation of 1918. Ancestral blood, the soil and the mythical glories of the past united a people against a seeming conspiracy of foreigners who sought to exploit, despoil and dilute the purity of German lineage with a bastard effeminacy. Germany's tradition of Jew-baiting supported the theories and actions of Hitler. At the end of the nineteenth century a Wagnerian anti-Semitism was prevalent—and not only in small intellectual coteries; a book on the *Victory of Jewry over Germandom* went through six editions. All genius became Aryan, Christ was held not to have been a Jew and ancient heroes were given suitably Germanic names. Nor did Hitler's adopted Austria lag behind in fervour; no Viennese political party could show favour to Jews and survive.

Jews became the 'counter-Race' in the struggle against which a new Germany might be created. In fighting the Jew moreover one was fighting Bolshevism, 'doing the Lord's work'; the Red Star was, after all, only the Star of David politicized. Yet the Race ideology that was basic to Nazism was not merely anti-Semitic but potentially anti-Slav and anti-Nationalist as well. In the end it envisaged a world organized and stratified on racial lines with a supra-national élite protecting the chalice of pure blood. As Marxist-Leninists called across national boundaries to 'class loyalties' so the Nazis appealed in the name of superior blood to all those with an 'Aryan soul'. Nazis de-humanized opponents who did not possess 'correct' blood just as Marxist-Leninists de-humanized the 'class enemy'; in both cases victims could be eradicated without the intervention of ethical considerations. It was not necessary to hesitate before killing Jews, the bourgeoisie or, in the Russian case, independent peasant farmers (kulaks), since, being categorized as something less than human, they could not legitimately be regarded as being within the sphere of conventional morality.

Tactically too Hitler had much in common with the Leninism which he studied; the experiences of 1923 were to teach him a lesson and reinforce the attraction of a Leninist appreciation of the necessity for political logic to direct the mailed fist. Hitler's minions also observed that under Lenin all the available communications media became the exclusive tools of State propaganda.

By 1923 Hitler felt ready for revolution; his Storm Troopers had paraded in Munich six thousand strong; they appeared as a phalanx of virility and steel amid the weary and feeble decadence of the times. In Bavaria the appointment of the German Nationalist and Monarchist von Kahr as virtual dictator signalled yet more tension with Berlin where Chancellor Stresemann struggled to maintain the equilibrium of the State. In Hamburg and Saxony Communists and Separatists challenged the Government; it seemed that the State must be taken over by the Left or break up. Hitler decided that the time was ripe to seize Bavaria from von Kahr and march on Berlin, as Mussolini had marched on Rome.

On 8 November Hitler arrived at the beer hall where von Kahr was speaking. Storm Troopers ringed the area. Hitler burst into the meeting, firing a shot into the ceiling to command silence and in a few minutes had the crowd on his side. Von Kahr and his aides were less enamoured of the proceedings but they affected to support the putsch, especially when General Ludendorff arrived to back Hitler's appeals. In Berlin the Government moved to suppress the uprising; in the event the army obeyed its Generals—and the Generals were not yet willing to see in Hitler anything other than a vulgar and slightly comic demagogue playing at putsches with the support of some Bavarian yokels and a misguided General. Hitler's support slipped away; von Kahr, having given his support to the putsch, went back on his word.

Faced with the alternatives of flight or defiance Hitler sought Ludendorff's advice. '*Wir marschieren*', declared the General. So they marched; though with little clear idea of where they were going or why—perhaps to rescue some beleaguered comrades, perhaps 'to Berlin'. Hitler and Ludendorff headed the procession, backed by the élite *6th Sturmabteilungen* Company. Initially they met with some success. The marching column engulfed and seized the weapons of the first party of police sent to restrain them. Barring their way further on, however, was a platoon made of sterner stuff and commanded by a young Lieutenant who intended to do his duty. Which side fired the first shot is not known but the police replied to what they took to be an attack with a volley. Hitler's column broke up in disarray; only Ludendorff, followed belatedly by his aide, kept grimly on through the lines of police into the square beyond, where he surrendered, his reputation for physical courage untarnished. Hitler had been pulled to the ground as his companion was hit. The future Führer of Germany fled from the scene of the débâcle in a small Fiat, driven by the SA doctor.

This seeming failure in fact gave Hitler all that his previous years of effort could not—world-wide publicity, an audience of millions, and, in the dead and their bloodied SA banner, a martyrology and a symbol. A farcical trial, easily dominated, gave him a propaganda triumph. Comfortable incarceration lent to the man and his views the mystique which attaches to 'prison writings'.

Subsequent Nazi tactics in the practice of terrorism reflected the experience of the abortive putsch. The *Sturmabteilungen*, originally 'bouncers' at political meetings, then given a uniform of grey with ski-jacket and cap, were reformed under Roehm in 1925. 'Putschism' was rejected in favour of their being used as 'political soldiers'. They were charged, now in their brownshirt uniforms, with what was euphemistically termed 'outdoor propaganda'. An early rehearsal for this role had been the raid on Coburg in 1922. Into this bastion of the Left, Hitler had injected eight hundred SA men to do battle with the locals. Bricks and paving stones flew in profusion but the SA, using rubber truncheons, daggers and alpenstocks, won the day. This type of exercise in provocation and brawling suited Hitler's purposes well; it provided publicity and demonstrated the strength of the SA, the weakness of the Government and the incorrigible obstinacy of the independent Socialists and Communists. Ostentatious SA drill was used as a kind of psychic violence to strike fear and awe into the population. It was an exercise in symbolic menace. SA 'centuries' marched into towns and took them over, regarding such operations as military victories. Their banners, each touched in ritual benediction by the original 'Blutfahne' of the putsch, flew by 1927 at the head of 30,000 men. By 1929 the number had reached 60,000. Horst Wessel, killed by Communists in a vendetta over a prostitute, became the movement's hero—a symbol of Aryan virility and devotion to duty.

Hitler did not believe in sporadic terrorism (in this too he was a Leninist). To use the knife, the revolver or poison was, on the individual level, a mere gesture. Processes of intimidation must be harnessed to a political aim—but that aim was not consistent throughout the years of the movement up to the accession of power. From 1926 to 1928 the Nazis attempted to seize the leadership of the workers from the Left parties. The tactical approach at that time was neither electoral nor putschist; it was an exercise aimed at gaining mass support by dominating the streets and the headlines. Hitler believed that not in secret conclave but in mass demonstrations and the conquest of the streets would Germany be won for the Nazis.

In this operation it was necessary to build up the SA not merely as a demonstration of strength but as a counter to the Left's own para-military organizations—the Communists' *Rotfront Kampferbund* and the Socialists' *Reichsbanner Schwarz—Rot—Gold*. Hitler also made overtures to gain support of the two main veterans' associations, the *Stahlhelm* and *Wehrwolf*.

The Republican Government hesitated to suppress the Nazis for in its eyes it was the uniformed columns of the Left, which marched and counter-marched, demonstrated and brawled as enthusiastically as Hitler's cohorts, which posed the greater threat to the shaky foundations of the State. While underestimating Hitler the Government at the same time saw him as a protection against the Bolshevik revolution which, on the evidence of 1917, they naturally assumed to be the more in accord with the times. The Government's failure either to mount a campaign of ridicule and exposure or to move through legal prohibition played into Hitler's hands. A contemporary observer later commented on the absence of any counter-propaganda—'The only way to guarantee constitutional liberties is to be provided with the apparatus for psychical immunisation.'[2] No attempt was made to do this; on the contrary, liberty of the Press and the freedom of speech and association, guaranteed by the laws of the German Republic, were utilized in order to encompass its downfall. SA men, it was suggested, were needed to protect 'lawful meetings' (at one such 'meeting-hall battle' in November, 1921, 46 'keepers of order' were said to have ejected over 800 opponents). One is reminded of Lenin's remark that bourgeois institutions must be used in order to bring about their own destruction. Indeed Hitler had himself been saved from deportation by the application of those very liberal values which he was out to destroy. In 1922, when all others were agreed, the Left Wing leader, Erich Auer, had successfully argued that, if freedoms were to have any validity, they must also be granted to Hitler. So the future Führer was saved from exile by a Socialist.

Middle-class opinion, even if disgusted or amused by Hitler, tended to regard the Nazis as the lesser of two evils since they were at least 'Germanic'. To some working people the Nazis were also more attractive than their Communist rivals since the former seemed to possess the more efficient machine for the speedy seizure of power.

Throughout the proletarian stage of Nazi activity the SA continued to march and intimidate. The elections, however, surprised the Nazis since it was in the rural rather than in the urban areas that they achieved their greatest successes. It seemed advisable therefore to switch to a more 'National' rather than 'Socialist' line and, in particular, to woo the middle classes. SA usefulness became increasingly propagandist rather than direct. As more middle-class support swung to Hitler (especially after the 1929 economic recession) so the respectability of his origins and the bourgeois nature of the Party was emphasized by the latter's propaganda machine. The SA, now expected to carry out menial tasks of petty organization (such as putting up posters), grew restive. Attempts were made to defy the 'civilian leadership'. Hitler, concentrating on seducing the capitalists and infiltrating rather than destroying the machinery of the State (especially the police and the legal profession), tried to meet the problem of the SA by centralizing and increasing the political content of the training. Ultimate frustration for the SA came in 1932 when they were on stand-by to meet an expected Left Wing coup—which failed to materialize. Increasingly the SA's brawlings and boastings sat ill with the Führer's new-found respectability. In 1934 the SA was effectively destroyed in the interests of German Army support for the Nazi régime. The Party, for its part, could more effectively be represented and protected by an élite force. This new role was assumed by the SS, which was based on the *Stosstrupp Hitler*, a commando bodyguard, originally founded in 1922 by Hermann Goering during his stint as SA leader.

Mussolini had provided Hitler with example and inspiration although success came to the Duce more rapidly than to his Nazi counterpart. Initially racially less rabid—arguing that national pride had no need of the 'delirium of race'—he was at least the equal of Hitler in the symbolic use of violence, although he could never match the latter in ruthlessness. Hitler learned in particular from Mussolini's concept of the 'March' (though the Duce had to be pushed into it by his friends) and in his use of a ritual of salutes and military uniforms. An admirer of the Bolsheviks, Mussolini saw himself as *un apostolato di violenza*, read Sorel[3] and Lebon's *Psychology of the Crowd* and imagined himself as the 'Lenin of Italy'. Mussolini's disappointment, during his Socialist phase, with 'Red Week' in 1914, when the tactics of strike and street barricade proved ineffective, led to a reappraisal of his ideas; perhaps he then realized that only an alliance with capitalists and militarists could in the end guarantee him the power he coveted.

Mussolini formed what he envisaged as his élite force of dedicated revolutionaries from discontented soldiery; on

23 March, 1919, his supporters formed themselves into the *Fascio di Combattiemento*. On the Left there were strikes; rioting over the cost of living was widespread. The Fascists proposed themselves as protectors of the country from the threatened Bolshevik rape; they would, they declared, meet violence with violence, fire with fire. Much of the organization and ritual used by Mussolini was modelled on that employed by d'Annunzio during his occupation of Fuime in September, 1919. After d'Annunzio's withdrawal from that city many of his adherents went to swell the numbers of Mussolini's cohorts. Mussolini's Black Shirt *Squadristi* evoked memories of martial glories by carrying at their head the flag of the Italian commando *Arditi*. Liberals looked the other way as the Fascists rampaged through the streets. In August, 1922, during a General Strike, the *Squadristi* attacked Socialist buildings, ransacked them and burnt them to the ground. They were reputed to have killed over 3,000 people against their own losses of 300.

Mussolini and his henchmen thus succeeded in using an already disturbed situation and escalating it to the point of anarchy; the people were then persuaded of the necessity of turning to the Fascists in order to guarantee peace, law and order and the unity of the State. On 28 October, 1922, the Fascists 'marched on Rome'; the King, fearful of Civil War, refused to sign the law ordering the army to oppose them and Mussolini took over the Government of Italy and began the process of turning his control into an absolute mastery of the State.

During his take-over of power Mussolini continued to use his *Squadristi*, now transformed into militia, to strike terror into the hearts of his opponents. In 1924 some ex-*Squadristi* killed the Socialist leader Matteotti and Mussolini was nearly overthrown in the outcry; by 1925, however, the Duce had consolidated his hold both on the country and on the party and Farinacci was given the task of restructuring the former into a centralized and monolithic party, responsive to the central will.

Both the Nazi and Fascist experience points to the ease with which, in the presence of economic distress and the absence of firm Government, the democratic machinery can be perverted against the State. In such a situation 'Left' and 'Right' provoke and feed on one another; without Lenin, no Hitler; without the 'Red Fronts', no Nazis. Groups created by political parties and used in a role involving violence will first seek autonomy and then, unless swiftly curbed, turn on their creator and destroy him. Once the members of such a group have crossed the psychological divide into direct physical action then the processes of violence—through the 'dictatorship of the proletariat' or the 'will of the nation'—will be self-fuelling and self-justifying.

Thugs of Right and Left, though their numbers are small, still riot and brawl in the streets of Western Europe; there is the danger, especially in Italy, that history may yet repeat itself even more completely than this.

NOTES

1. Manvell and Frankel, *Hermann Goering*, Heinemann, 1962, p. 19.
2. Chakhotin, *The Rape of the Masses*, Routledge, 1940, p. 127.
3. Georges Sorel's work inspired extremists, both Communist and Fascist, see Chapter 7.

CHAPTER 5

Rural or Urban?
The Methodological Debate

In China the failure of the Stalin-directed policy of united front tactics and abortive insurrections in Canton and Shanghai convinced at least one Communist leader at the time of the futility of mechanistic applications of dogma to the local situation. Mao Tse-tung's disenchantment with urban insurrection received confirmation in 1930 when the Communists unsuccessfully attempted to take cities in central China. Mao was later (in 1936) to write:

'We are now engaged in a war; our war is a revolutionary war; and our revolutionary war is being waged in this semi-feudal, semi-colonial country of China. Thus we must not only study the laws of war in general, but also the laws of a particular revolutionary war and, moreover, the laws of the even more particular revolutionary war in China.'[1]

It was Mao's understanding of China, its people and its history, which led to his innovations in the methodology of revolutionary struggle. Clearly the peasantry, so numerous and so brutalized by the burden of debt, were important—as indeed they had been to Lenin and Trotsky—but whereas the latter had seen them as a class to be used, to be seduced away from their feudal loyalties and preoccupations by cries of 'Land and Bread', Mao, in contradistinction, viewed them as capable of revolutionary initiative.

If the peasantry were to be in the vanguard of revolutionary war they must first be indoctrinated; a revolutionary consciousness must be developed. Such a process needed time and patience, especially since many of the soldiers who initially joined Mao, far from being simply peasants, were already professional soldiers from the armies of the War Lords—tough, but more interested in rape and pillage than in politics. It was these considerations which led to Mao's insistence on the need for patience, on his willingness to trade Space for Time; Time with which to create the political Will which alone could sustain his army through the long months of training and perhaps disaster. His Nationalist enemy's loud claims to be the legitimate Government of China meant that, in order to give substance to such boasts, some flag-showing was required. This involved spreading troops thinly on the ground. Mao sought to gain a tactical success and then fade away before the enemy could concentrate his forces. 'Our strategy', he wrote, 'is to pit one against ten and our tactics to pit ten against one.' Such an approach had not occurred only to Mao; his Western contemporary T. E. Lawrence had expressed much the same idea:

'Granted mobility, security (in the sense of denying targets to the enemy), time and doctrine (the idea to convert every subject to friendliness) victory will rest with the insurgents, for the algebraic factors are in the end decisive, and against them perfections of means and spirit struggle quite in vain.'[2]

Lawrence's work was studied by one of Mao's most dedicated and successful disciples, General Giap, who added to it an international dimension, perhaps owing something to Lawrence —with whose work he was familiar—by attempting primarily to influence public opinion in his opponent's homeland and in the world at large. In Lawrence's words:

'We had to arrange [our men's] minds in order of battle just as carefully and as formally as other officer's would arrange their bodies. And not only our own men's minds, though naturally they came first. We must also arrange the minds of the enemy as far as we could reach them; then those other minds of the nation supporting us behind the firing line, since more than half the battle passed there in the back, then the minds of the enemy nation awaiting the verdict; and of the neutrals looking on; circle beyond circle.'[3]

Mao Tse-tung completely reversed the then orthodox way of proceeding; instead of beginning with the urban proletariat and later collectivizing the recalcitrant peasantry, Mao sought instead to cut off the cities from each other by surrounding them with a sea of humanity—physically and ideologically laying siege to them.

Mao's approach has been tried, tested and modified against the French in Indo-China and the Americans in Vietnam and, less successfully, in the Philippines and Malaya. Maoist strategy appears less relevant in today's increasingly urbanized world except in Africa and parts of South America; his disciples, however, do not necessarily accept this argument and do not, in any case, eschew urban activity; Mao himself had his 'urban brigades'.

In Calcutta in 1970 the Communist Party of India (Marxist-Leninist), ideologically a Maoist movement, briefly abandoned its agrarian tactics and embarked on urban terrorism. A poster campaign was followed by student demonstrations and a foray into Calcutta University, where books were burned. By May, 1970, the battle had spread to the streets and pipe guns and bombs were being used against the police. In August and September there were over 1,000 bomb attacks. The terrorists' eventual lack of success was due in part to their expending as much energy in fighting rival Moscow-orientated groups as in harassing the authorities.

A similar attempt to foment an urban uprising had been made in the British Crown Colony of Hong Kong from May, 1967 to January, 1968, as the repercussions of the Cultural Revolution spread throughout China.

Industrial trouble led to demonstrations and demonstrations

to rioting. Strikes were called and, by a combination of intimidation and bribery, workers were persuaded to support them. Eventually, encouraged by incidents on the border with China, the local Communists resorted to urban terrorism.

By July, 1967, matters had become sufficiently serious to warrant joint police/military operations against known Communist organizations. These raids uncovered large quantities of crude weapons, including Kwan Dos—Chinese broad swords. On 4 August helicopters were used to place troops on the roofs of skyscraper buildings. Communist efforts were switched from industrial to terrorist activities. Tactics used included hit-and-run bomb-throwing, the use of time bombs and attacks on individual policemen and known anti-Communists. Two opponents of the Communists were burned to death; their car was petrol-bombed and, as they staggered from the blazing wreckage, they were doused with petrol and set on fire. Types of bombs used varied from the firecracker in a glass bottle to tins packed with explosives and nails, hand grenades and occasionally time bombs and parcel bombs. Police patrols were provoked and led into areas sympathetic to the insurgents where they were stoned and bottled by the local version of 'Rentacrowd' (a particularly appropriate description in this case since the going rate was 40 Hong Kong dollars for planting a hoax bomb, 200 dollars for a real one and lesser sums for demonstrating and stone throwing).

Hong Kong Communists developed some local variations on the terrorist theme. Straw dolls were left hanging or propped up in public places ready to explode when moved, dummy bombs were placed where their 'de-fusing' would cause most public chaos and 'bombs', obligingly marked with flags, were floated in the harbour. Use was also made of 'propaganda bombs'; a pig's head with the inscription 'Slaughter White Pigs' was stuck on railings, a dog with an 'inflammatory poster' tied to its back and an empty tin round its neck was sent wandering through a shopping precinct.

The placing of bombs in the crowded streets of Hong Kong and Kowloon succeeded in causing considerable upheaval but the indifference of the bombers to their victims aroused public revulsion, especially when two small children discovered a bomb and played with it and both were killed.

The disturbances eventually petered out, defeated by a combination of stern police measures, supported by the majority of the community, and by the disillusionment of Peking with the antics of their local supporters. Quite apart from the quixotic spectacle of local Communist businessmen arriving to join demonstrations in their Mercedes-Benz limousines from which they alighted incongruously clutching their copies of *The Thoughts of Chairman Mao*, the campaign also revealed serious political shortcomings in the local Party leadership. A period of self-criticism was called for. Intelligence reports to Peking had been inaccurate and had exaggerated the chances of success and degree of popular support enjoyed by the Party. Money had been wasted. Moreover the local Communists were too prone to capitalist-style junketings to suit the puritans in Canton or Peking. 'Is it revolutionary or counter-revolutionary', demanded posters in Peking, 'to waste people's money from blood and sweat for sumptuous dinner parties as a counter-measure against British Fascism in Hong Kong?' The locals ought to be reminded, said others, about Mao's dictum that the revolution was not a dinner party.

Mao's self-styled adherents in the West can no more be relied upon than those in the East to eschew violent action in urban areas; on the contrary they tend to seek confrontation with hysterical self-dedication. In particular Western Maoist groups seek to infiltrate coloured groups as part of a general strategy of 'the poor encircling the rich'. Leaders of the pro-Peking Communist Party of Great Britain (Marxist-Leninist) have travelled to Tirana, the capital of China's European ally, Albania. This Party has some contacts among Indian workers. There is also the Working People's Party of England, which seeks links with Black Power movements. Its minute Scottish equivalent, the Workers' Party of Scotland, was involved in 'liberating' money from banks and, in 1972, its leader, Matthew Lygate, was jailed for twenty-four years. He claimed that he had guerrilla contacts abroad. The police found arms and ammunition in a bookshop owned by the movement. The small but vociferous Communist Party of England (Marxist-Leninist) grew out of the Internationalists, the English branch of which was originally in Dublin; their activities have included physical attacks on academics of whom they disapproved.

Contemporary debate over guerrilla methodology springs, however, not so much from the contrast between Maoist and Leninist models as from the competing modes of 'Party dominated' versus 'military directed' revolution. Castro's success in Cuba and the myths that have sprung from it, associated in particular with the name of Che Guevara, have led to an attempt to substitute a guerrilla-controlled revolution for the Party's exploitation of existing social and economic grievances. The main theorist of this approach to revolution, Régis Debray —a French philosopher working in the University of Havana— has argued that the small guerrilla band in the jungle, the *foco*, is the 'party in embryo'; it spins the web of revolution from out of its own being. This romantic view emphasizes the 'Guerrilla as Superman' overcoming the inertia of history and forcing events to move in the required direction. Debray's theory celebrates virility and the natural life of the jungle with its return to primitive essentials.

Debray's ideas are mainly contained in *Revolution in the Revolution*, published in Havana in January, 1967, which was seen as providing theoretical underpinning for the export version of the Cuban Revolution. Debray's work was to be added to that of Che Guevara and of the Spanish Alberto Bayo, who had been involved in training the Castro guerrillas in Mexico, to provide a trilogy of guerrilla warfare for Latin America.

In the Debray thesis the rural *foco* is to be a seed, the nucleus of the popular Army:

> 'It is not a front which will create this nucleus but rather the nucleus which, as it develops, will permit the creation of a national revolutionary front. One creates a front around something extant, not only round a programme of

liberation. It is the "small motor" which sets the "big motor" of the masses in motion and precipitates the formation of a front, as the victories won by the small motor increase.'[4]

Worse, from the orthodox Communist point of view, was the insistence that this 'small motor' need not necessarily be Marxist-Leninist, just as Castro had not been at the beginning:

'Fidel Castro says simply that there is no revolution without a vanguard; that this vanguard is not necessarily the Marxist-Leninist Party; and that those who want to make the revolution have the right and duty to constitute themselves a vanguard, independently of those parties.'[5]

Debray is scornful of what he calls 'the descent to the City'; the leadership, he argues, must remain in the rural areas where it is less likely to be tracked down and where it can, in one operation, create the Revolution and the Party. The Peoples' Army will be the beginning of the Party and not the other way round. If the Party hacks try to run the Revolution then they will, he insists, either compromise with the forces of counter-revolution or will prove unable militarily to control their adherents; matters will degenerate into 'uncontrolled terrorism in the city and banditry in the countryside.'[6]

To the orthodox Communist Debray's views are heretical; they fly in the face of established theory and social fact. To emphasize the rural when all over Latin America people are moving into the towns seems merely perverse. Historically too, the Debray—Guevara picture of the Cuban Revolution under-emphasizes the considerable part played by urban organizations —the latter in fact suffered more casualties than did the rural bands.

The role of the urban members of Castro's 26th of July Movement (named after the unsuccessful attack on the Moncada Barracks in Santiago de Cuba on 26 July, 1963) has largely been ignored. Such activities run counter to the myth of the jungle fighter and, perhaps more importantly, many of the urban supporters of Castro were opposed to the takeover of his movement by the Communists after the success of the Revolution. Men who had fought for Castro in the streets found themselves in jail with the supporters of Batista with whom they had recently been locked in battle. Around one hundred and fifty young men, having previously worked in propaganda and sabotage, died for Castro in the abortive urban uprising in Havana of April, 1958.

The record of Castro-based revolutionary exports has not been good. Guevara was killed, a victim of his own myth, in Bolivia. The folly of the naïve version of this approach was dramatized, again in Bolivia, in 1970 and recorded by Alistair Horne;[7] the 'Teoponte Affair' may well have written 'finis' to this type of insurgency for all but the most fanatical.

With no knowledge of jungle survival or combat techniques and with no clear aim, a party of students set out for some of the most inhospitable terrain in the world. 'They went in sheer lyricism for Che.' They wanted to create again Guevara's *Ejercito de Liberacion Nacional*. In July they were fifty strong, by September only twenty were left. They had attacked a US-owned gold mine and kidnapped two German engineers but their discipline soon broke down under the incessant pressure from the army and from the environment. Eventually they gave themselves up—those who were left. Strangely their very inexperience had a political impact; the authorities were accused of taking them too seriously and of needlessly killing captives. The affair was a contributory factor in the Government's downfall and though the succeeding régime was short-lived those young guerrillas, 'who had gone into the worst country in the world with little more than ham sandwiches' had, in spite of themselves, made a small dent in history.

If the rural *foco* no longer makes sense and if conventional political activity (involving the creation of 'fronts', taking part in elections, etc) is regarded, even as a short-term tactic, as likely to suffer the same fate as that which befell Allende's Chilean experiment then, clearly, the revolutionary base must be moved

THE COURSE OF GUERRILLA WARFARE
The Guevara – Debray Model

Guerrilla Warfare first, politicization later: the Guerrilla is the creator of his own politics.

FOREIGN 'CAREER REVOLUTIONARIES'   INDIGENOUS PARTICIPANTS

GUERRILLA 'FOCO' ◄——— SELECTED

PHASE 1

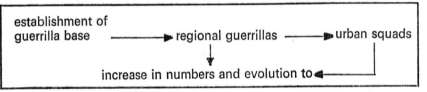

jungle/mountain reconnaissance ——— maximum secrecy ——► adaptation of guerrillas to environment

small training operations ◄——— against régime

OPERATIONAL COLUMNS FORMED

PHASE 2

establishment of guerrilla base ——► regional guerrillas ——► urban squads

increase in numbers and evolution to ◄———

PEOPLE'S ARMY

PHASE 3

OFFENSIVE

Regional/urban groups keep Government Forces tied down; MOBILE FORCE attacks selected targets; General Strike

CONVENTIONAL OFFENSIVE ON CAPITAL

Note: This pattern has only been approximately achieved in the Cuban Revolution. Crisis point comes at the end of Phase 2.

to the cities. Shanty towns on the city's edge will provide the secure base, the city's heart the target. In this model the struggle in the city ties down military and police and either succeeds in precipitating a crisis situation sufficiently acute to cause significant sectors of the population to side with the insurgents, or is a prelude to, and then part of, the main strategic battle in the countryside. It was argued that Debray and Guevara had erred in placing a favourable terrain above securing popular support; the natural focus for insurrection is the city for, as a Uruguayan guerrilla was to put it, 'where the population is, there resides the Revolution'. If a few idealists choose to go into the jungle and call for revolution then, unless they succeed in gaining further recruits, the Government can simply ignore them. Should they gain support then they will find that contemporary Governments have the equipment and military expertise to isolate and destroy them by using surveillance devices and moving specialist anti-guerrilla troops by helicopter. It is better to huddle close to the security forces by operating in the heart of the city.

The best known theorist of this approach is Carlos Marighela, author of the widely quoted and much copied *Mini Manual of the Urban Guerrilla*. Much of Marighela's writing is banal but, as a practical revolutionary who died fighting, his influence has been considerable.

Marighela, while seeing the city as the starting point of the struggle, does not subscribe to any theory of the 'urban foco' creating the revolution. He emphasizes on the contrary that the city is merely the area of the initial tactical struggle; the final confrontation will be country-wide, even continental, in its proportions. Marighela's own experience, which was predominantly in the urban areas, and the weight of his writings, which deal with the latter rather than with rural guerrilla warfare, have led to his influence being entirely and somewhat misleadingly on urban terrorism.

Marighela was a Communist of unswerving loyalty to the Party cause until 1967 when, like so many others at that time, he fell under the spell of the Cuban Revolution. On his return to Brazil from the Conference of the Organization for Latin American Solidarity, held in Havana in that year, he broke away from the Communist Party of Brazil and, as he announced to Fidel Castro in a letter of 18 August, 1967, took up the path of guerrilla war. The pro-Cuban Revolutionary Communist Party, which he founded, achieved some successes—mainly in the robbing of banks. Subsequently the Marighela group brought off two propaganda coups with the kidnapping of the US Ambassador, Charles Elbrick, in September, 1969, and the consequent release of thirteen guerrillas held by the authorities. Marighela was killed in November, 1969, and most of his commando were eradicated by the security forces shortly after.

Marighela's handbook for the urban guerrilla contains a number of exhortations to become the perfect guerrilla fighter, a reading list and a catalogue of desirable qualities—fitness, skill at arms, etc; there are two aspects of the book which, however, provide some insight into urban guerrilla strategy.

Politically the aim is to discredit the Government, to reveal its inability to retain control of the situation and to provoke it into repressive measures which will alienate the population:

'From the moment a large proportion of the population begin to take his activities seriously, his success is assured. The Government can only intensify its repression, thus making the life of its citizens harder than ever: homes will be broken into, police searches organized, innocent people arrested and communications broken; police terror will become the order of the day, and there will be more and more political murders—in short a massive political persecution . . . the political situation of the country will become a military situation.'[8]

The response will, says Marighela, be elections; these must be revealed as a farce and fought against—from the rebellion in the towns, 'we shall soon move on to launch the guerrilla war in the countryside, for which the urban struggle is a necessary preparation'.

THE COURSE OF GUERRILLA WARFARE
The Marighela Model

Immediate inception of guerrilla activity – 'Organizations grow through unleashing revolutionary action and calling for extreme violence'.

URBAN GUERRILLA WARFARE
(Proletariat/Students)

Aims: 1. Expropriation
2. Attacking Government Forces and supporters
3. Attacking U.S finance and capitalism

PSYCHOLOGICAL WARFARE
(Students)
Low level terrorism
Propaganda

GOVERNMENT PROVOKED INTO REPRESSION
(Political situation becomes transformed into a military one)

Polarization of social groups

MOBILE (NOT 'FOCO')
Rural Guerrilla Groups
Attack big estates

P E O P L E'S   A R M Y

Inflicts defeats on Government Forces

General Strike

SEIZURE OF POWER

Note: Crisis point for the guerrilla is reached when the activities reach a scale requiring central co-ordination.

The activities of the urban guerrilla are directed toward two objectives—physical liquidation of their enemies and the expropriation of arms and goods belonging to the government, the big capitalists, the landowners and the imperialists, i.e. murder and bank robbery. Marighela recommends the formation of small, mobile 'firing groups' of two or three; additionally he runs the gamut of other possibilities—kidnappings, executions, sabotage, bomb planting, liberation of prisoners, etc. Under the 'war of nerves' Marighela mentions the importance of fomenting 'baseless rumours' and of keeping the foreign embassies, the UN, the Apostolic Nunciature, the International Commission of Jurists and the Human Rights Commission well informed about 'the violence and terror being used by the agents of the dictatorship'. However, a similar scenario for guerrilla warfare had already failed in Venezuela and Guatemala (as Marighela himself was to fail) and a study of those insurrections would perhaps have revealed the weaknesses in his strategy.

Venezuela
Nowhere in Latin America in the nineteen-sixties promised so well for armed insurrection as Venezuela. The overthrow of the dictator Jimenez in 1958 had aroused expectations which no successor could possibly have fulfilled. In the elections of December, 1958, Romulo Betancourt of *Acion Democratica* emerged as the victor by a large majority. Betancourt was anti-Communist. Nor did he nationalize domestic businesses or expropriate those of foreigners. In the capital, Caracas, which had voted 5 to 1 against him, he was unpopular—an unpopularity dramatized when Fidel Castro visited the city and the crowds, while cheering the Cuban leader, jeered at the name of Betancourt.

By the early nineteen-sixties the country appeared ripe for revolution—a fact recognized by the usually cautious Communist Party which uncharacteristically supported armed action. Early attempts at guerrilla warfare in 1962 were unsuccessful—too many fronts were opened up and too swift a victory anticipated. Lacking co-ordination the guerrilla groups were picked off one by one. Sufficient success was nevertheless obtained to persuade the various anti-Betancourt factions to form a united front. This tactic seemed particularly attractive at that time since there was disaffection in the Armed Forces which had led to mutinies and to the defection of army officers to the guerrilla ranks. In a rare display of unity there was created a political National Liberation Front and, associated with it, the Armed Forces of National Liberation (FALN). The former was dominated by the Communists and the latter contained three main groups: the fighting arm of the Communist Party, the Movement of the Revolutionary Left (MIR) and the military officers who had been involved in anti-Government activity. The FALN was to shift the emphasis away from the rural areas to the cities, especially to Caracas.

Plans envisaged five stages of action leading up to the Revolution. Stage One would see the formation of groups in urban areas, based on those already used in the previous unrest, known as Tactical Combat Units (UTCs). These units, under cover of the urban violence fomented in Stage Two, would proceed to terrorist attacks on the police and army (Stage Three); the Armed Forces, tied down in the cities, would then find it difficult to deal with the rural uprisings of Stage Four and the Revolution would be consummated by an offensive by all elements.

In the pre-FALN campaign the UTCs had been relatively ineffective since their efforts had not been linked to those in the countryside. Guerrilla movements in a country which has extensive rural areas but where the population and administration is concentrated in the cities face a dilemma. Rural activity may provide greater security and may also be psychologically attractive, offering as it does a romantic image as compared with the skulking in alleys and the shot in the back of urban terrorism. Fabricio Ojeda, an MIR guerrilla leader, remarked that the air one breathed was completely different from that of the city. Problems of command and control are, however, increased. Government forces are able to carry out campaigns of encirclement without such actions having much impact on the main concentrations of population. The impact on public opinion, both at home and abroad, of government 'repression and brutality' is considerably less if such actions occur in the peasant village than if they involve large numbers of people in the capital city. The availability of helicopter-borne anti-guerrilla specialists and their generally superior communications network place the rural revolutionaries at a disadvantage.

If, on the other hand, the fight is concentrated in the cities then large numbers of troops may be tied down and the Marighela spiral of 'provocation–repression' may be set in motion. By huddling close to the enemy and the people the former's superior firepower may be negated and the latter's 'revolutionary consciousness' be heightened. Central command and control is achieved and the articulation of political and military action, of strikes and demonstrations with armed attack, is made easier. Yet a city-centred strategy is unlikely by itself to succeed; the effort is difficult to sustain, problems of security and logistics become crucial and the support of the people is likely to be lost if they are asked to hide and succour the terrorist over a long period with no apparent prospect of success against a patient and determined Government. The city is the only place for a sudden putsch; by itself it cannot sustain a long phase of guerrilla war. The ultimately desirable arrangement from the insurgents' point of view is a co-ordinated urban/rural campaign; even in this case destructive arguments about whether the leadership should reside in the urban or the rural areas are likely to break out. Clashes will occur between the more cautious political old guard and the young bloods of the Revolution.

In the event the main effort in Venezuela was in Caracas. The man who faced it was, as the terrorists were to discover, no Batista. Betancourt had been elected. Outside his own country he was regarded as a liberal democrat. Critics who regard any action against armed guerrillas as by definition 'repressive' have of course so accused him; by Latin American standards he appears to others to have been mild.

The FALN Agreement was signed in February, 1963. There ensued for the Government in Caracas a long, hot summer. Together with propaganda exercises—the kidnapping of the footballer, di Stefano, hi-jackings (one ship and two aircraft), the stealing and return of Impressionist paintings in a French exhibition—there was more serious armed action. In the various 'ranchos' of Caracas nightly shoot-outs with the police and army revealed two main tactics—sniper fire and street violence by small 'shock units'. Some areas were briefly 'liberated' from the forces of law and order. The army and police were lured into prepared areas by small incidents and then ambushed. The terrorist organization consisted of five units, each about one hundred strong plus supporting services. Many of the recruits were drawn from the middle classes and student elements as well as from the poor. FALN statements emphasized the desire of the Revolutionaries to co-operate with 'Progressive elements' in the Armed Forces; the FALN would only attack if itself challenged. In the event in Caracas this policy was abandoned. Armed Forces who had been assured that there was a place for them in the post-Revolutionary Venezuela found themselves under nightly attack. Efforts to subvert the Armed Forces from within, rather than to destroy them and start again from scratch after the Revolution, suffered from the terrorism in Caracas. Terrorism's shock effect, if it does not cause the Government to resort to panic repression may, over time, cause such a public revulsion as to produce a flight from the terrorists and a longing for a return to the previous normality. This is less likely to occur where the populace is ethnically or culturally distinct from the troops, but this was not the situation in Caracas.

Army and police units resisted invitations to expose themselves to the guns of the terrorists and concentrated in dominating the city from high buildings and key points such as street intersections. Where they established themselves they took care to do so in such force that attacks on them would be suicidal.

4. The aftermath of the explosion outside an Officers' Mess, Aldershot, 1972, that killed seven civilians

5. Home Secretary Roy Jenkins inspecting the scene of one of the Birmingham pub bomb blasts in 1974. This attack particularly outraged British public opinion and led to the Prevention of Terrorism (Temporary Provisions) Act 1974, which outlawed the IRA in Great Britain

6 and 7. The conquest of the streets. (*Above*) Oswald Mosley and his blackshirts in London; (*below*) Maoists march through Hong Kong brandishing their 'little red books'

The terrorists' policy of assassinating policemen did nothing to endear them to the population. Indeed one commentator[9] sees this policy as perhaps the crucial mistake of the whole urban campaign. Policemen in Caracas, hundreds of whom were attacked, far from being the caricature agents of repression so beloved of Left Wing propaganda, were members of prolific and extended working-class families. Each death thus alienated large numbers of ordinary people from the terrorists' cause. Betancourt stubbornly refused to play the role of Batista; he wasn't going to give way but neither was he about to resort to wholesale counter-terror. Refusing to be hustled into large-scale repressive measures he waited until October, 1963, before withdrawing the personal Congressional immunity of members of the already illegal Communist and MIR Parties. Elections scheduled for December went ahead despite the fact that November, with 252 incidents, produced a major terrorist effort. In late November a large shipment of arms from Cuba was discovered on the Venezuelan coast. This constituted a propaganda victory for the Government which had all along been insisting that the 'Revolution' was not truly a Venezuelan affair but a 'Castro-Communist' import. The insurgents might now quote the hero of Latin-American liberation, Simon Bolivar, as much as they liked; in the face of this arms find the 'Revolution' seemed to have 'Made in Cuba' written all over it.

Polling day duly arrived and, despite a boycott proclaimed by the Liberation Front, a 90% turn-out was recorded. Leoni, the *Acion Democratica* candidate, was elected. All the participants in the National Liberation Front agreed that the election was a major setback; more than that, it called in question the whole philosophy of armed action in Venezuela. MIR split on the issue. The Communists wavered. Leoni had offered to restore their legality if they eschewed violent methods. In April, 1965, the Communists, having been less than enthusiastic for some time, formally decided to concentrate on normal political activities. By November of that year the Party was urging its guerrilla leader, Douglas Bravo, to give up the struggle. The Government granted amnesty to many of its political prisoners; these, once released, urged constitutional activity. Douglas Bravo and the MIR guerrilla leader, Ojeda, found themselves isolated and the objects of the peculiarly virulent vilification which is reserved by Communists for those who leave the fold—though Ojeda of course had never really been in it. In June, 1966, Ojeda was captured and killed. With his death the phase of guerrilla activity which had begun with the proclamation of unity in the FALN was effectively closed.

Both Régis Debray and the orthodox Communists have criticized the Venezuelan guerrillas. Debray concentrated his remarks on the military disadvantages of fighting in the city. The Communists insisted on the primacy of the political aim and the dangers of adventurist militarism. Feeble armed action was, they argued, worse than no action at all since it merely provided an excuse for Government repression. For the remaining guerrillas, stubbornly fighting on in the hills, such comments, coming from those who were either far away or sitting comfortably in their Party Offices, were hard to take. Douglas Bravo made an attempt to salvage something from the ruins of the Liberation Front and FALN. He argued for a protracted Peoples' War based on what he called 'combined insurrection'. This would be based in the countryside but would have a trained urban wing ready to be let loose at a moment made appropriate by political and military conditions. The difficulties and confusion involved in attempting to combine Debrayism and 'urbanism' into a new revolutionary synthesis may be gauged from the language of the following passage of Bravo's:[10]

'The insurrectional elements may be summed up as follows:
1. Politically, militarily and economically, the urban areas form the main centre of enemy potential; more than 70% of the total population lives there.
2. In the urban areas the revolutionary movement has also its greatest potential in political and organizational resources, fighting traditions, mass influence etc.
3. For these reasons the urban area, particularly the capital,

is the most sensitive spot for the confrontation of all the contradictions; firstly the enemy's own internal contradictions, secondly those between them and us. The repercussions of our urban actions are still greater in the short term than those of our actions in the countryside. This is a temporarily true fact that we shall overcome as the guerrilla movement has successes and develops. But we should take advantage of it at the present moment by increasing the technical training of our UTCs and preparing the urban revolutionary movement so that it is always ready to take advantage of insurrectional elements that may result in revolutionary outbreaks or in a heightening of the permanent crises.'

Betancourt's success has been held up as a model of urban anti-terrorist strategy (e.g. by Robert Moss).[11] The articulation of civil and military effort and in particular the holding of elections rather than suspending the constitution in order to fight the terrorists are seen as crucial. However, Betancourt did withdraw the immunity both of Congress and of the universities and such measures may not appear in European eyes especially liberal; compared to other Latin American states, and to what might be expected from a Communist state faced by what it would term 'reactionary terror' his actions do appear to have been restrained. Guatemala in contrast illustrates another, more extreme, mode of response.

Guatemala
The course of events in Guatemala from 1962 to 1967 in many ways parallels that in Venezuela. There was the same involvement of young army officers—to the extent that at one stage insurgents and counter-insurgents had both been taught the techniques of guerrilla warfare by the same US Army instructors. There was a similar initially over-optimistic assessment of the chances of success. Subsequently, as in Venezuela, there was for a time a united front both politically and militarily;

the Communist-dominated Front for United Resistance having the political direction, while the Armed Rebel Forces (FAR) did the fighting.

The insurgency in Guatemala is of special interest in two respects; it was one of the few campaigns in which Trotskyist agents of the Fourth International were for a time involved and it saw the use of self-styled and allegedly spontaneous counter-terror groups.[12]

The Argentine-based Trotskyists arrived in Guatemala to give some political direction to the guerrilla groups and had most success with that led by Yon Sosa, a young army officer who had taken to the hills at the end of 1961. Yon Sosa went through the Socialist hoops convincingly enough; he proclaimed his belief in the simultaneous action of all groups—workers, peasants and guerrillas—in the overthrow of the régime, working through a United Confederation of Workers. Thus he denied the vanguard role of the guerrillas and envisaged mass occupation of factories and land. Such tactics were regarded by his allies as merely invitations for repression. Turcios Lima, the other main leader, was more flexible with regard to the possibility of an alliance with the middle class on the 'road to socialism'. Yet both in the case of Sosa's MR13 (named, in the favourite Latin American style associated with Castro, after the date of an abortive uprising—13 November, 1960) and of Lima's Front, it could still be argued that the commitment was to the people of Guatemala, rather than to any deeply-held ideology; at heart both these leaders remained essentially nationalist soldiers. Their aim was to convert the Army which they had so recently left, not to destroy it. 'Armed propaganda' was their speciality—arriving in a village with guns prominently displayed and then running a series of 'teach-ins' on their political aims.

Yon Sosa soon ejected his Trotskyist advisers from the country. Members of the Trotskyist Fourth International have one inestimable advantage over some other Left Wing groups in that they do not labour under any international inhibitions, i.e. they do not need to consult the national interest of the

Soviet Union or the Peoples' Republic of China. Yon Sosa's advisers succeeded in squandering this advantage by sending some of the money collected from his supporters back to Trotskyist Headquarters in Buenos Aires. His flirtation with Trotskyism—and occasionally with Maoism—was not to the liking of Fidel Castro who roundly attacked such thinking in January, 1966.

Both Sosa and Lima used urban terror tactics directed against North American and 'foreign capitalist' interests as well as against more directly military opponents. The former aim was understandable enough; Guatemala had long been a fief of the American United Fruit Company and the United States had organized the overthrow of the reformist Government of Colonel Arbenz. The American nominee who succeeded Arbenz, Castillo Armas, eventually gave way to a Right Wing Nationalist dictator, Peralta. It was not, however, under Peralta but under the ostensibly more liberal rule of his elected successor, Mendez Montenegro, that US involvement reached its peak. The involvement of US advisers and Special Forces in the anti-guerrilla campaign became more pervasive and more overt. Both economic and military aid was stepped up. Thus on a number of counts the United States became guerrilla 'public enemy number one'.

Yon Sosa is supposed to have been enthusiastic about the efficacy of urban terrorist tactics, holding that the revolution would begin in the city and then spread to the countryside. Plenty of people died, whatever the theory, in the spiral of vendetta and killing in Guatemala City. Two US Heads of Military Mission, in February, 1965, and January, 1968, were killed and in the latter case the US Naval Attaché also died. In May, 1965, the Deputy Minister of Defence was shot dead and in November and December of the same year there were a number of fund-raising kidnappings. In August, 1968, the US Ambassador was shot 'while resisting arrest'.

The elections of 1966 once again proved a turning-point in the guerrilla fortunes, although not for the usual reason. There was general surprise that the military had allowed them to take place at all. The Communists, always lukewarm in their support for armed action, persuaded the FAR to hold their hand and to give at least guarded support to the least objectionable candidate, Mendez Montenegro. The result was disastrous; Communist leaders, returning home from exile to discuss electoral tactics, were captured and shot. Nor did things change once Montenegro had been elected (March, 1966). Turcios Lima, regarded as the best leader the FAR possessed, was killed (not in action but by crashing a Mini Cooper in which he was giving a girl-friend a ride). Cesar Montes assumed the leadership of the FAR. United States' involvement and support for the Government led to extreme pressure on the guerrillas and, while Montes and Yon Sosa sought to close ranks, the Communists began to withdraw their support, eventually forming their own token Revolutionary Armed Forces. The generation gap had opened again. All the bitterness and disillusionment of betrayed youth is to be found in the following statement by FAR leaders (early 1968):[18]

'After four years of fighting this is the balance sheet: 300 revolutionaries fallen in combat, 3,000 men of the people murdered by Julius Mendez Montenegro's régime. The ruling clique of the Guatemalan Communist Party supplied the ideas and the FAR the dead '

The 'radical vision', as Cesar Montes called it, 'revolutionary, young, audacious, dynamic', had gone down once more before the apparatchiks. Yet the apparatchiks had a point. Montes might be scathing about the Guatemalan Army's Green Beret US advisers—but they and the freelance anti-Communist squads had kept him very much on the move, 'foot-slogging' from place to place from dawn to dusk. The revolution had, for the time being at least, lost its impetus. ·

In Uruguay, however, affairs appeared to be better organized; there the Tupamaros, full of youth, audacity and dynamism, seemed likely to become the first contemporary continental Latin-American movement to create a revolution by choosing its tactics carefully, applying them boldly and adapting them to the particular circumstances of their homeland. Perhaps in Uruguay a new urban model for revolutionary change might be created?

NOTES

1 Stuart Shram, *The Political Thought of Mao Tse-tung*, Pelican, 1969, p. 275.
2 T. E. Lawrence, article in *Army Quarterly*, October, 1920, in *The Essential T. E. Lawrence*, Garnett, Cape, 1951, p. 220.
3 Lawrence, *Seven Pillars of Wisdom*, Cape, 1935, p. 195.
4 Régis Debray, *Revolution in the Revolution*, MR Press, 1967, pp. 83–4.
5 op cit, p. 98.
6 op cit, p. 75.
7 Alistair Horne, *The Guerrillas of Teoponte*, Encounter, December, 1971.
8 Carlos Marighela, *For the Liberation of Brazil*, Penguin, 1971, p. 95.
9 John Gerassi, *Latin America—the Next Vietnam*, Viet Report, 1967.
10 Quoted in Richard Gott, *Guerrilla Movements in Latin America*, Nelson, p. 141.
11 Robert Moss, *Urban Guerrillas*, Maurice Temple-Smith. 1972.
12 See Chapter 12.
13 Quoted Gott, op cit, p. 83.

CHAPTER 6

The Tupamaros—New Model for Revolutionary Change?

'Where the population is, there resides the Revolution'
                                              TUPAMAROS LEADER

Some have argued that the Tupamaros of Uruguay constitute a new approach to the problem of revolutionary violence.[1] Rejecting both the doctrinaire assumptions of traditional ideologies and the theoretical debates about methods to which Leninists, Maoists and Guevarists are destructively prone, the Tupamaros, it is suggested, evolved a new pattern which might be emulated by embryo terrorists in all places. This approach is characterized by flexibility in methods and by a determination to tailor activities to the objective demands of a particular environment.

Officially called the Movement for National Liberation (MLN) the Tupamaros contained socialists, anarchists, Marxists and some who might best be described as 'Left Wing Nationalists'. Their name derives from that of an Indian chief, Tupac Amaru, who led a revolt against the Spaniards in 1780 and was executed by quartering in May, 1781.

The Uruguayan situation in the early 'sixties contained, from a revolutionary point of view, a number of 'exploitable contradictions'. Unusually for Latin America, the régime was liberal reformist and committed to a programme of increasing expenditure on welfare. At that time Uruguay had experienced neither a military dictator nor a military coup this century. The standard of living was comparatively high. Uruguayans, and especially the middle class, planned their lives on the

94

expectation that these standards would continue to rise. The country was heavily urbanized—some one and a half million people (about fifty per cent of the total population) lived in the capital, Montevideo; thus to disrupt that city was to paralyse the country as a whole. By the mid-'sixties these expectations of continuing prosperity, already disappointed, were rudely shattered. World prices of meat and wool, Uruguay's main exports, fell drastically. Budget deficits grew ever larger and, combined with swingeing devaluations, (22 pesos to the dollar in 1965, 600 by 1971!) led, by the end of the decade, to Uruguay's being top of the Latin American league for inflation and bottom of that for growth rates. Sociological analysis indicates that revolution is most likely to occur when a long period of prosperity is succeeded by a sudden and extreme reversal; this was certainly the case in Uruguay. The welfare state had run to seed. The middle class in particular was psychologically vulnerable to such a process and tended, not unnaturally, to turn on the politicians, 'the system' or 'foreign exploitation' for an emotionally satisfactory scapegoat. Processes of economic disruption alienated the very class on whose support the Government could normally rely. Systemic breakdowns in Latin America are always likely to result in a reversion to deeper traditions of political violence which are never far away from such societies—either geographically or historically. Even liberal Uruguay had possessed a Nazi-type extremist movement, the *Alianza Nacional*, during the Second World War. Thus there existed a suitable climate in the early nineteensixties for a reassertion of patterns of violence to which Uruguay had constituted an apparent exception. Street fighting and factional strife would not perhaps have excited much comment had it not been for the fact that the Tupamaros' tactics were unusually imaginative and that they succeeded, for the first few years of their operations, in creating a 'Robin Hood' image, sedulously fostered by sympathetic journalism,[2] which served to contrast their youthful exuberance with the apparently dull and repressive stupidity of the Government.

The Tupamaros first came into prominence in July, 1963,

with a raid on a rifle club. One Raul Sendic was the instigator of this incident. Sendic had previously been active as a Trade Union organizer of sugar-cane workers in the north of Uruguay and had in 1962 led a 'workers' march' on Montevideo. Sendic fled the country after the rifle club affair, returning to take charge of the movement in 1969. He is thought to have spent some of the intervening years in Peking. The remainder of the movement, boosted by some refugee terrorists from Argentina, spent 1964 mainly in training and in creating an organization based on 5–7 man 'cells'. Tupamaro leaders have claimed that during this preparatory period they studied the French Resistance movements during the Second World War, the Irgun campaign against the British and the Algerian insurrection; clearly they intended to approach their task with proper professionalism. Their theorist was allegedly a Spanish political exile called Abraham Guillen (variously described as an anarchist and a 'neo-Trotskyist') who provided an alternative to the Guevarist–Debrayist rural guerrilla thesis by emphasizing the importance, for armed insurrection, of a favourable population rather than a favourable terrain.

The Tupamaros' philosophy of urban warfare was stated in a document captured in 1967:

'If capitalism concentrates the population, the wealth, the industries, the communications in the large cities a revolutionary movement cannot ignore this tendency in the development of capitalist production. The law of the concentration of capital is at the same time the law of population and it would be a strategic error to isolate ourselves in the rural area abandoning the poor and hungry masses of Montevideo. In countries having a greater than 50% urban population (Uruguay has 84%) the revolutionary struggle should not be in mountains and fields but rather urban warfare, because where the population is, there resides the revolution.'

The rural areas were to be the scene of armed commando

raids to keep the security forces stretched and allow more freedom of action in the main strategic area—the city of Montevideo. In order to compensate for their lack of the traditional guerrilla 'firm base' the Tupamaros constructed an elaborate system of hideouts in the city itself. Additionally they dug sophisticated underground bunkers in nearby rural areas; one, on a hacienda they called 'Spartacus', was concrete-lined and large enough to serve as a miniature range for small arms training.

The Tupamaros hoped to discredit the Government and to isolate the Armed Forces as 'agents of oppression'. They aimed to use the issue of foreign investment and 'exploitation' in Uruguay as a means of increasing the public hostility towards capitalist interests and the Government in general. By forcing the authorities to adopt security measures which would alienate a sensitively liberal public opinion, they hoped to foster a climate of collapse which would lead either to a direct takeover by a Tupamaros-backed alternative Government or to an election whose result they could at best dictate or at worst seriously influence. They seem to have hoped to spark off a revolution of continental proportions encompassing the whole of Latin America and to that end they maintained some contact with Argentinian and Brazilian groups in particular; as a result the activities of subsequent Argentinian groups have been strongly reminiscent of Tupamaros' tactics.

From 1965 to 1967 the Tupamaros concentrated on gaining publicity and funds (including 'expropriations' from banks) and on infiltrating the university and some public service corporations. Membership became predominantly middle class, including civil servants, students and members of the professional classes as well as a number of 'career revolutionaries', as Sir Geoffrey Jackson was later to call them. Some 'hunger commando' operations (seizing foodstuffs and distributing them) were also carried out at this time.

The Tupamaros' main effort dates from 1968 when they kidnapped the Director of the State Power Company, Ulysses Reverbel, who was released unharmed some five days later—

the Government having in the meantime mobilized some 5,000 troops and police in an unsuccessful attempt to find him. This incident was a huge propaganda victory, especially as the Tupamaros had not injured their captive (Reverbel was kidnapped again later and spent a record $13\frac{1}{2}$ months in a 'People's Prison'). Robberies of two casinos further enhanced their public image—particularly when an offer was made to return that portion of the haul representing staff 'tips'. At the same time, however, they resorted to more orthodox terror tactics, directed mainly at the Police.

The most celebrated enterprise of the whole Tupamaros' campaign occurred on 8 October, 1969—the second anniversary of the death of Che Guevara—and has now entered, partly by this association with his memory, into the mythology of the revolutionary Left. On that day the guerrillas took over the small town of Pando (population 10,000) which is situated some twenty-five kilometres north-east of Montevideo. They drove in, disguised as a funeral party, complete with hearse, mourners, black cars, etc, and proceeded to cut communication links and rob all the banks. Despite their precautions, however, the alarm was raised, somewhat improbably, by a long distance bus. The Army arrived in armoured cars and helicopters and chased the Tupamaros' funereal transport into the countryside. Twenty-five Tupamaros were captured. The remainder dispersed to their hideouts, 240,000 dollars the richer.

The Pando incident galvanized the police and army into more energetic action and arms caches, field hospitals and bomb factories were discovered. (The Tupamaros were apparently actually exporting Viet Cong-type booby-traps to Argentina and Brazil.) The guerrillas struck back with further kidnappings (e.g. Pelligrini, September, 1969—200,000 dollars), gold bullion robberies, assassination (the head of the police 'anti-terrorist' squad) and an attack on a naval barracks. It was at this time that the public attitude to the Tupamaros began to show signs of change—in particular, murders of policemen proved counter-productive from a propaganda point of view. There followed the kidnapping of the American police adviser,

Dan Mitrione, and his subsequent killing when President Pacheco refused to negotiate. On 8 January, 1971, Geoffrey Jackson was kidnapped and held for eight months. That year was, however, to witness the beginning of the end for the Tupamaros, despite a spectacular tunnelling operation at one jail when all 106 Tupamaro prisoners escaped. A vigorous 1971/2 election campaign showed that the democratic processes had not lost their appeal and the poll resulted in the *Frente Amplio*, to which the Tupamaros had given some qualified support, being decisively defeated by the traditional Uruguayan political parties.[3]

Early in 1972 the new President, Bordaberry, with the mandate of the recent election to confer the necessary legitimacy, declared a state of internal war and the Armed Forces, already placed in charge of the counter-insurgency operation by the former President Pacheco (9 September, 1971), were finally given their head. The results were dramatic. Large numbers of terrorist leaders were captured and much of the support organization destroyed.

> 'According to the Uruguayan Army's critics, the reason is simple enough; the Army has not scrupled to use very rugged interrogation methods designed to make up for its initial lack of intelligence (which was compounded by the fact that the guerrillas had infiltrated the police) and to make mass arrests that pulled in liberal intellectuals along with Marxist extremists.'[4]

By October, 1972, over 2,400 suspects were in prison, Sendic was wounded and captured and more than 300 hideouts, including a number of 'People's Prisons', had been discovered. In addition to Sendic several other founding members of the Tupamaros were also arrested in mid-1972 including Saenz, a former Professor of Art History.

The prestige of the Armed Forces was correspondingly high and they were not about to retire gracefully from the scene and allow the politicians the opportunity to create further chaos.

Moreover, interrogation of the Tupamaros and seizure of compromising documents which the latter had stolen, revealed chicanery in high places and gave the Armed Forces a correspondingly useful degree of political leverage. The Army, for example, found evidence that information about impending devaluation had been leaked in 1968 so as to enable speculative profits to be made. Proof of illegal insurance and exchange operations was also unearthed. Some of the Generals were known to be interested in the reformist military régime of Peru and the involvement of the Armed Forces in the political life of Uruguay, given their defeat of the Tupamaros, now appeared inevitable.

Under these pressures the Armed Forces had split politically by August, 1972, into a number of factions—constitutionalists, nationalists who were prepared to negotiate with the Tupamaros and rightists impressed by the military régime in Brazil. Continued economic decline accompanied by further inflation exposed to military eyes the apparent inefficiency of Congressional government. The Navy alone of the three Services clung to constitutionalism.

In order that the insurgents might be defeated, the traditional liberal freedoms previously enjoyed in Uruguay were abandoned. Press censorship to deny publicity (the lifeblood of the urban guerrilla), detention without trial and military interference in the normal processes of government succeeded where a benevolent but irresolute administration had failed. By late 1972 the Government was running the country only with the permission of the Armed Forces. In the 1972 5-year Budget projection the Army was scheduled to expand from 9,000 to 18,000 men. In February, 1973, the President and the Military Commanders reached an 'agreement' by which most of some nineteen demands submitted by the military were conceded. Significantly the Left Wing coalition, hoping presumably for some Peruvian-style reforms, was at that time receptive to the Army's virtual takeover, apparently preferring it to the 'cattle oligarchy' allegedly represented by the President. Some of the Army's demands were indeed mildly Socialist, including workers' participation in industry and tax reforms. The shape of things to come was clear, however, in the formation of a National Security Council and the Services' veto over the appointments to the Ministries of Defence and the Interior. The Armed Forces also undertook to defend the country from 'Marxist-Leninist doctrines'.

On 27 June, 1973, in what amounted to a Presidential *coup d'état* Bordaberry dissolved Congress and announced that he would henceforth govern through a Council of State. Matters between the Armed Forces and Congress had been brought to a head over the question of the Congressional immunity of Senator Erro, leader of the Leftist *Union Popular*, who was suspected of collaboration with the Tupamaros. Erro eventually sought political asylum in Argentina. After the takeover there was a general strike and denunciation of Bordaberry as 'the enemy of the people'. The Armed Forces had foreseen such eventualities and had taken the precaution of imposing restrictions on the Press, taking power to run public services and closing all schools and colleges. They were helped in their activities by a degree of recovery in the economy and were able to meet the unrest by a round of pay rises while at the same time threatening to draft strikers into the Armed Forces. After clashes between security forces and demonstrators on 9 July the trade unions called off the strike on the 11th.

The Tupamaros thus succeeded in bringing about the destruction of 'the system' in their country, though through the manner of their defeat rather than by any victory. In its stead has been set up, not a 'People's Democracy' but a 'General's Uruguay'.

What conclusions can be drawn from the Tupamaros' campaign? Their defeat, from a technical point of view, was partly due to their switching their attack to the military at a comparatively late stage of their campaign (thus directly challenging a force which, as subsequent events have shown, was not necessarily totally antipathetic to some of their arguments) and partly to the over-recruitment to the Tupamaros ranks that occurred at the height of their success. Many of these new

101

BRUCE B. MASON

members cracked once pressure was applied by the authorities and, to make matters worse, Tupamaro security procedures had become lax during the period of euphoria surrounding their more spectacular successes. The result was that Army Intelligence was able very quickly to break up the organization once an initial penetration had been achieved. Public tolerance of the Tupamaros was put under strain by their increasing resort to terror tactics and they swiftly lost their 'Robin Hood' image. A public opinion poll in September, 1972, showed that only 4% of the population thought that the Tupamaros were motivated by a sense of social justice—compared with 59% a year before.

In more general terms the Tupamaros failed to become the first exception to the general rule that an urban guerrilla movement cannot stimulate a revolutionary war unless it is supported by a credible rural equivalent—an objective that the Tupamaros, despite some effort, failed to attain; their plan for the countryside (code-named 'Tatu' after a small burrowing animal) was never a success. Moreover, even limited change in the desired direction is unlikely to be forthcoming unless such a movement has a persuasive political programme beyond the discrediting of the government in power. Thus the failure of the Tupamaros (judged on their own aims) reinforces the view of most commentators—both radical and conservative—that a determined government can crush an urban guerrilla movement, particularly if that government takes care to give at least an appearance of adverting to popular grievances and legitimises its stand through traditional devices such as elections.

There appears to have been an over-estimation of the 'armed struggle' while political leadership was undervalued. The image of the 'urban guerrilla' held by the Tupamaros seems to have been that of a calculatingly committed intellectual who can outsmart the opposition by the superior mastery of technique. As one Tupamaro leader put it, 'The armed struggle is a technical phenomenon.' He goes on to speak of 'combat psychology' and is dismissive of any reliance on 'the masses'.[5] The guerrillas failed to convince the Uruguayan people that they represented a viable political alternative and they were singularly unsuccessful in stimulating that 'revolutionary upsurge' of the people of which Lenin spoke. The very middle-class background which aided them in infiltrating government services proved a handicap when it came to political mobilization, particularly in the countryside.

The extent of the Tupamaros' influence is difficult to gauge. Some other movements have adopted the same name, for example in West Germany and Persia. Similarities may be traced between the methods of the Tupamaros and those of other urban terrorists, particularly the FLQ in Canada and the various movements, especially the Trotskyists, in Argentina. The aims and styles of kidnapping adopted by the Basque ETA and the Italian *Brigate Rosse* have also been modelled on those of the Tupamaros. On the other hand the more orthodox Left parties, whether Peking or Moscow-orientated, are likely to point to the failure of the Tupamaros as further vindication of their respective doctrinaire positions on the proper way to wage a guerrilla war.

Although the urban terrorist even in such a situation as that of Uruguay is unlikely to succeed there is equally no doubt that unless his campaign is halted at a very early stage indeed he will so disrupt the structure of his host society as radically to change its organization and ethos. But he cannot foresee the direction of that change, a consideration which the 'post-Communist Revolutionaries' of the New Left might ponder.

NOTES

1 e.g. (from opposite standpoints) Robert Moss, *Urban Guerrillas*, Temple Smith, 1972, and Hodges and Shanab, *National Liberation Fronts 1960–1970*, Morrow, 1972.
2 See, for romanticized accounts, Maria Esther Gilio, *The Tupamaros*, and the film *State of Siege*.
3 The *Frente Amplio* (*Wide Front*) was a coalition of Left

Wing groups, one of which, the *26th of March Independence Movement* was a Tupamaro front organization. Frente Amplio won 19% of the votes.

4   *The Economist*, 29 July, 1972.
5   Interview in Carlos Nunez, *The Tupamaros*, Times Change Press, New York, 1970.

CHAPTER 7

Post-Communist Revolutionaries— The New Left

'Ask not what you can do for your country? Destroy it.'

The cynicism of Russian action in Hungary and Czechoslovakia removed any moral appeal that the Muscovite version of Communism may have had for the idealistic young—were any left who had not been already disillusioned by the Spanish Civil War or the satellization of Eastern Europe. A new moral dynamic was required. The 'New Left' provided it.

The movement which came to be known as the 'New Left' is usually held to have begun as an attempt to infuse a new intellectual radicalism into the generally Social Democratic traditions of the parliamentary Left. Thereafter its adherents became involved in the tactics of direct action, especially in 'Ban the Bomb' marches and demonstrations. It was not until the mid-'sixties that a more violent dimension was added. Not only the Vietnam issue but the apparent failure of technology to solve its own problems and a disenchantment with traditional gradualist politics contributed to an espousal of violence as a means of speeding the processes of change. In the United States of America the frustration of the candidature of Senator Eugene McCarthy by the Party *apparat* and the Kennedy and Martin Luther King assassinations led to a disillusioned youth which sought escape in drugs, religious cults or drop-out sub-cultures or, for those of a different psychological make-up, a determination to strike back at the 'violence of the system'.

Europe produced, in the May, 1968 student/worker revolt in Paris, an incident which, gaining in dramatic intensity by the historical traditions of its venue, served to heighten expectations even as its almost immediate failure disappointed them. The shooting of student leader Rudi Dutschke gave European students a wounded hero of their own, while those already predisposed to violence found in it an encouragement and rationale for their own retaliation.

New Left extremists tended to see themselves as 'post-Communist revolutionaries'—Marxist-Leninists who had successfully sluiced off the 'muck of history' (Stalinism) in the pure waters of a new baptism. Clean-limbed and young, they had as their model the myth figure of Che Guevara while others such as Herbert Marcuse confirmed them in their good opinion of themselves. Youth was the focus—the young Marx, the early Bolsheviks, and before them the populists and anarchists, especially Bakhunin. New ideological foundations were to be found already available in the early work of Marx; the identification of the capitalist system as above all alienating the worker-victim from his own individuality seemed psychologically as well as economically relevant. New Marxist primitivism received further expression in the writings of Marcuse in which the system inherent in industrialization is seen as oppressing the individual and programming him so that not only is he unable to become truly human but indeed has no realization that he is being victimized. Man in capitalist industrial society is, on this view, merely a human receptacle, into which is decanted the values and attitudes that are needed by that society for its own protection and propagation. Add to such a view the arguments of Fanon[1] to the effect that violence has a positive value both for personal catharsis and for the realization of social identities and the implications become alarming.

To attack a policeman, or indeed any representative of 'Authority' is, on this kind of reasoning, socially desirable and a matter of moral indifference—for such people are regarded as less than fully human; in place of anti-Semitism the young revolutionary is to substitute class membership as the badge of evil. The intellectual arrogance of this process is directly comparable to the racial arguments of the Nazis; not in the name of Aryan purity but in support of 'progressive' ideas versus the 'reactionary' is the contemporary terrorist to kill. Marcuse reifies the situation so that the soldier/policeman/official is seen as the embodiment of a social role, as 'Fascist beast', 'pig', 'human receptacle'. This de-personalization of the opposition has always been the aim of the terrorists' masters; the Russian Social Revolutionary terrorist, Savinkov, records the effect as his comrade waited to carry out an attack, 'In Ilinka Street, people came and went, hurrying past us. *How far away they all seemed to us* . . .'[2] The few who have been granted the vision are 'saved'; having grasped the extent of their own alienation they may now proceed to purge themselves (and punish their fathers who betrayed them into that state) by killing those whom they deem to have obscured the vision and imposed the alienation. The need to absolve oneself grows in proportion to the amount of guilt of which one is conscious; hence the involvement of middle-class youth, like the Weathermen, is required to be more dramatic than that of the working classes—the latter, since their social distance from responsibility for the evils of the system is greater, are not to the same degree tainted. Faith in the prophetic aspects of Marxism adds to the motivation; the violent act is seen as inevitable and the actor is not merely impelled by historic forces over which he has no control but is actually the agent of an inexorable Fate. The terrorist of the New Left believes therefore that he attacks not men, but puppets; the presentation of violence in stylized dramatic form in contemporary youth culture removes him still further from the real world. Nazis created a new Gehenna in ritual slaughter of Jews, the Soviets in the eradication of minorities; the 'Final Solution' of the terrorist 'New Left' would be no different, for intellectually (if unconsciously) the line of argument of the extremist fringe leads via Fanon, to the writings of Georges Sorel (1847–1922).[3] In Sorel the two genealogies, of Fascism and of the totalitarian New Left, find a common patrimony so that the similarity of the latter's youth organizations and Hitler Youth seems more than coincidental.

Sorel believed in the necessity and inevitability of violence for social change which accords well with the apocalyptic mood of young revolutionaries. Two elements, in his thesis, are locked in struggle—the 'incumbent élite' representing 'decadence' and clinging to its privileges, and the opposing revolutionary élite, standing for 'renascence', new life and hope. Between them lies the uncomprehending multitude. There remains the possibility of that multitude itself becoming a renascent society—for such a role it needs the unifying and motivating force of a 'myth'. It hardly matters whether this myth has any correspondence with reality, it is enough that it is believed. Sects of revolution, if they are imbued with sufficient faith in their own charisma, can become 'revolutionary brotherhoods' with each member being prepared to sacrifice his whole being to revolution. Fanon was able to extend the vision by emphasizing that self-discovery stemmed from the act of dedication to, and the moments of, violent action. So in the moral re-creation of society the heroic brotherhood would find its corporate identity and the individual member his own very self.

Yet Sorel hated 'thinkers', intellectuals who had broken the sanctity of ancient tribal bonds. In his emphasis on each part of the social complex playing an autonomous role according to its own nature he prefigures Fascism ('I owe most to Georges Sorel,' said Mussolini). It is in their attempt to inject some ardour into the tired categories of Marxism without being sensitive to the individual horrors of unrestricted violence that the accusation of 'Sorelianism' can be levelled against the 'revolutionaries of the "New Left"'.

Sorel's emphasis on strikes as 'phenomena of war' leading to the culminating battle of the General Strike is shared by the only already existing political grouping to take significant advantage of New Left sentiments. Trotskyists, however split and however minute their organizations, were at least not tainted either with 'social democratic compromise' nor subservience to Russian national interest. They could be seen, with a little imagination, as a primitive sect who had kept the pure flame of revolution burning through the dark night of Stalinism, unsullied by time-serving or chauvinism. A vigorous youth policy both in schools and universities has succeeded in turning these advantages to some practical account. Just as Stalinist vices threw the virtues of Lenin into sharper relief so too was the reputation of Stalin's *bête juif*, Trotsky, enhanced. The three groups in the United Kingdom which principally benefited were the Socialist Labour League (transformed into the Revolutionary Party in November, 1973), the International Socialists and the International Marxist Group.

Trotsky's leadership of the Red Army after 1917 to crush the reaction which then set in, his defeat at the hands of Stalin and his odyssey from Europe to the Americas have lent to his memory an association with the pristine days of Revolution. Others remember him as the 'Butcher of Kronstadt', crushing the sailors who dared oppose the Bolshevik new order on the grounds that the commissars lived in the palaces; this is the 'bloody Field-Marshal Trotsky who stands up to the waist in the fraternal blood of the workers'. Trotsky believed that the only way to Socialism was the road of revolution and that the only way to break the 'class will' of the enemy was by the 'systematic and energetic use of violence'.[4] To him terrorism was an accompaniment to, and succeeded, armed insurrection; it killed individuals and intimidated thousands.

Both historically and on the contemporary evidence Trotskyist groups are likely to use or support those who use terrorist tactics.

Trotsky's theory of 'permanent revolution' emphasizes, in its international aspects, the global nature of the phenomenon, the necessary links between revolution in one country with that elsewhere. Ethnic, cultural and national distinctions will on this thesis be unable to withstand the revolutionary tide; pausing to create 'socialism in one country' is both to lose the impetus of revolution and to sacrifice the world proletariat on the altar of sectional interest. Trotskyists point to the internal violence of the twentieth century as evidence that the 'age of permanent revolution' is upon us. Such an approach has even less in common with separatist movements than has

Communism; any alliance must necessarily be short-term. Trotskyists will argue, however, that anything which weakens the capitalist system anywhere is a contribution to world revolution. A terrorist sub-culture with trans-national contacts attacks the foundation of the nation-state and so constitutes a coincidental ally of Trotskyism. Trotskyist organizations, having contacts across and owing no allegiance to national entities, can provide channels of communication for terrorists and offer them logistic support. Should such terrorists need or appear ripe for a more sophisticated political direction, then Trotskyists will be only too willing to supply it. Trotskyist organizations constitute a potential source of recruitment for propaganda, passive resistance and occasionally active service roles in or on the fringe of terrorist groups.

The tactics of the New Left 'revolutionaries' range from 'psyche-ing the system' by refusing to play by its rules, through various attempts to copy or adapt Leninist, Trotskyist or even Maoist models, to the compulsive violence of the Weathermen.

Some argue for 'Psychic guerrilla warfare', 'psychic blitz' and de-sanctifying the system by, for example, obscene language and exhibitionism, ridiculing authority—and especially its more vulnerable servants—by asserting that 'Revolutions are *fun*' and chanting Mickey Mouse jingles in committee meetings to prove it. Others more seriously attempt to produce an analysis of the contemporary European or North American situation from which to derive a new revolutionary strategy. Yet the New Left, especially in America, is above all so verbose and quarrelsome that those who deem themselves serious about revolution are likely swiftly to lose patience with its frequently self-indulgent posturing and take up direct action. At the extreme those who cry 'Do it!' and proclaim 'revolutionary happenings' are merely substituting action for thought, a tactic also used by the Nazis with their slogan of 'No programme but action!'

Some efforts were made to subvert the US Armed Forces via the American Servicemen's Union and the Movement for a Democratic Military. Attempts, generally markedly unsuccessful, were mounted to form revolutionary coalitions with the aims of 'Revolution in the White Mother Country and Liberation in the Black Colony'. Not only in Black communities[5] but also in the Chicano (Mexican-American) and Puerto Rican minorities, New Left as well as more directly nationalist elements were involved.

The Puerto Rican Young Lords represented an alliance of street life and college students; the movement has been active since 1969. With their purple berets and cries of 'Viva Che' they proclaimed themselves initially as Revolutionary Nationalists; by 1972, however, they were professing Maoist sympathies and had become the Puerto Rican Revolutionary Workers' Organization.

Attempts to adapt a Maoist approach to the West have been less than convincing in theory and unsuccessful in practice. *Venceremos*, a self-proclaimed 'diversified multi-national organization' with its Young Partisans youth wing (motto: STP—'Save the People, Stomp the Pigs') has urged the importance of experiencing revolution rather than theorizing about it, of establishing bases on 'the outer limits of society'. These 'limits' are psychological and social rather than physical and comprise social and ethnic 'out groups', especially in the cities. Even in so small a group as Venceremos solidarity has not proved possible; the contradictions between national and proletarian, direct action and 'saving the people' have not been resolved.

A consideration of New Left 'revolutionary movements' to date leads Lasch to conclude that they exhibit 'a mindless revolutionary militancy based on irrelevant models'.[6]

The Weathermen
The group known as the Weathermen arose out of a split in the Students for a Democratic Society (SDS) which, after a rancorous factional argument during 1968 and early the following year, finally divided the movement at the June Convention of 1969. One group, the Maoist Worker Student Alliance moved

to Boston, coming under the aegis of the tiny Progressive Labour Party while the rump left in Chicago split yet again. Revolutionary Youth Movement II, dedicated to working for and among the community, soon disappeared; Revolutionary Youth Movement I, known as the Weathermen after a conference motion which they had sponsored,[7] turned to terrorism.

Ritual violence was deified; the Weathermen found the Sharon Tate murder[8] and other exploits of the Manson Gang fascinating, praised Sirhan Sirhan for the Robert Kennedy killing and announced that they were applying themselves to 'urban guerrilla warfare'. After what they called a 'wargasm' in Chicago (smashing things up) the movement 'went underground' (February, 1970). In March an apartment building in Greenwich village was blown apart; three bodies and the remains of an explosives workshop were found in the rubble. In May came an announcement from the group's leader, Bernadette Dohrn, likening the Weathermen to the Tupamaros and the Viet Cong and promising an urban terror campaign. Weathermen bombings continued in 1970 but by December they had apparently decided to call a halt. The death of their friends had, they said, halted the military approach to their task; self-critically they admitted that conspiratorial activity had lost them the essential contact with the people. Some would-be 'urban guerrillas' have gone on using the name; in October, 1973, charges against fifteen Weathermen were dropped since the prosecution's case would have revealed methods of surveillance.

The Baader-Meinhof Gang

Those who are alarmed at political extremism among youth in the United Kingdom might care to ponder the situation in West Germany; the 1972 Report of the Office for the Protection of the Constitution lists 123 New Right organizations—held responsible for 428 'outrages'—and, on the extreme Left no less than 390 groups (total membership 89,000) which were held to have committed 515 acts of terrorism.

The most notorious of these groups was the so-called Red Army Faction (recalling the Japanese Red Army) or Baader-Meinhof Gang. This group was one of several which splintered off from the extreme Left Extra Parliamentary Opposition after 1968. A Department Store was the organization's first target. Baader was eventually arrested for his part in this affair. There followed an extraordinary sequence of events when he jumped bail, was rearrested and finally, when visiting Berlin under escort in connection with studies he claimed to be making, was freed by members of the Gang. One of those in the party which set him free was a girl called Ulricke Meinhof. The Gang then committed a series of bank robberies and thefts which netted over £50,000; these raids were usually followed by shoot-outs with the police. Meinhof and Baader began to look more like Bonnie and Clyde than revolutionaries.

In May, 1971, one of the gang was arrested and another shot dead. By early 1972 the police were beginning to have some success and in March they discovered arms, ammunition and equipment for forging identity papers in a flat in Hamburg; one of the Gang received fatal injuries. Reaction followed swiftly; the Gang master-minded a series of bombings in German cities. In Frankfurt a US officer was killed and on 19 May the Axel Springer publishing building in Hamburg was attacked; Springer was—and still is—a particularly unpopular figure with the Left in West Germany. The Red Army Faction, influenced by urban guerrilla activity in Latin America, were going for 'capitalism and US Imperialism'. Two more US soldiers were killed by a car bomb in Heidelberg (24 May). Time was running out for the Gang, however, and they were tracked down in June. On the 1st Baader was arrested after a gun battle and Ulricke Meinhof was apprehended on the 16th. This formidable lady was in possession at the time of her arrest of a number of pistols, a sub-machine-gun, two grenades and a bomb.

This group of terrorists is usually described as 'anarchist' and certainly their activities were gestures devoid of any possible immediate political significance. On the other hand the fact that they had received training at Al Fatah Arab guerrilla camps in mid-1970 suggests that this label is a little naïve. It would be more accurate to place them as New Left terrorists. The failure of student revolution in 1968 and the lack of any electoral support for the extreme Left drove them to seek a polarization of social forces via a terror which would provoke 'repression'. They affected to see the shooting of student leader Rudi Dutschke in 1968 as forcing them to take the road of violence—'the bullets which struck Rudi ended the dream of peace and non-violence'. Herr Brandt refused to oblige them with a repression, however—to the extent that he was accused of going 'soft' on Left extremists. On the other hand his critics from the other side considered that police action was, if any-thing, too vigorous. The police were accused of being 'trigger-happy'—as for example when a British subject was shot dead during a police search. In the event no sweeping legislation or suspension of civil rights was found necessary. The Red Army Faction was West Germany's Weathermen; both sprung from the conflicts of the student-based extreme Left.

A macabre aside on the activities of urban terror is provided by the Patients' Collective, another West German group. Since psychiatric disorders may be traced to the pressures of the urban environment and the demands of the capitalist system (cf Fanon) it would seem logical, in the fight against disease, to destroy that system. So ran the reasoning of Heidelberg psychia-trist Wolfgang Huber and his wife, Ursula. Terrorist activity might also prove incidentally therapeutic for the participants. Establishing a cell in the university the Collective planned to blow up a train carrying West Germany's President Heinemann and were implicated in planning to murder a policeman. The Hubers were sentenced to four and a half years each in Decem-ber, 1972; an accomplice was given a three-year sentence.

Others, such as Ingrid Siepmann, have taken up the trail of bank robbery where the Red Army Faction left off; while loudly proclaiming their revolutionary intent, the £60,000 or so stolen seems to have been used on fast cars and fast living rather than for the relief of poverty or the arming of the revolution.

NOTES

1 See Chapter 8.
2 Quoted Gaucher, *Les Terroristes*, Editions Albin Michel, Paris.
3 Georges Sorel, *Reflections on Violence*, trans Hulme, Collier-Macmillan, 1961.
4 Leon Trotsky, *Terrorism and Communism*, Ann Arbor, 1961, p. 55.
5 See Chapter 8.
6 Christopher Lasch, *The Agony of the American Left*, Pelican, 1973.
7 The motion read, 'You don't need a weatherman to know which way the wind blows'.
8 'Dig it,' cried the Weathermen. 'First they killed the pigs, then they ate dinner in the same room with them, they even shoved a fork in the victim's stomach. Wild.'

Black and White Racism

'This is revolutionary art—pigs lying in the alleyways of the colony, dead with their eyes gouged out.'

The Black Panther, 1969

'I don't make no difference between big rattlesnakes and little rattlesnakes because I know it's in the nature of all rattlesnakes to be my enemies and poison me if they can. So, I kill 'em all, and if there's four less little Niggers tonight then I say, good for whoever planted the bomb. We're all better off.'

Member of the Ku Klux Klan

It is possible when considering violent movements from a political viewpoint to identify two types of racism; there is what might be termed 'genuine' racism when a deep sense of racial identity is felt not to be accorded a sufficient degree of cultural and political recognition and, conversely, there exists an almost 'artificial' version which is either a defensive reaction to the former or involves an attempt to stimulate a presently dormant emotion. When colour has apparently labelled a minority group for poverty or when a similar misfortune has been visited on a section of the dominant population, for no reason that they can comprehend, then the subsequent emotion and violence is understandable enough. Beyond such groups lies the 'silent majority' which feels neither fear or frustration until reasons are provided by political activists.

Newly achieved independence from colonial rule in Africa, and especially in Ghana, led to a resurgence of racial pride among Black Americans. Consciousness of past slavery and exploitation together with the contemporary condition of many

Blacks in America combined to produce both peaceful reformist and violent revolutionary moods. 'Pan African' ideas of the 'fifties emphasized a unity of colour and obscured other deeply divisive issues which have since been bloodily reasserted in the Congo, Nigeria, the Sudan and Ruanda Urundi. The fate of the 'Pan Black' movements was no more successful than 'Pan White' Slavism or Aryanism.

The movement which was to spawn 'Black Power' was begun in the 1930s, allegedly by one W. D. Fard who passed on the leadership to Elijah Poole, later known as Elijah Muhammed. Thus was born the Black Muslim movement (originally known as the Nation of Islaam). Its teachings were a mirror image of those which were held to have enslaved the Black—the doctrines of an institutionalized Christianity, enthroning White Supremacy under a White God. Christian pacifism had been, it was argued, the opium of the Black people—it had taught them to endure and to forgive. Elijah Muhammed, on the contrary, asserted that God was Black, it was the Whites who were the brood of Satan. The Black Muslim aim became the establishment of a Black Homeland in America; about ten states would, it was calculated, be sufficient. The original movement was, and is, puritan in its insistence on sobriety and honesty. It believed in black apartheid, physically and politically. The family must not, as Elijah Muhammed put it, be 'spottied up'.

The evolution of an armed and aggressive wing of such a movement was natural in the violent environment of American society and politics. Emphasis was originally on defence and the early armed force, the Fruit of Islaam, was assigned such a role. A more aggressive attitude became associated with Malcolm X, for many years Elijah Muhammed's Chief of Staff.

Malcolm X broke away from Elijah Muhammed and formed his own Organization of Afro-American Unity. To the religious separateness of the Black consciousness was added the idea of emancipation from quasi-colonial rule; thus the concept of 'Afro-America' came into vogue in which 'Black America' is seen as an oppressed nation and black rebellion is equated with the global struggle for 'liberation'.[1]

Travelling extensively in the Middle East and Africa Malcolm X visited Mecca and had talks with Kwame Nkrumah of Ghana, then attempting to become the 'Redeemer' of all Africa. Malcom X was suspended from the Black Muslim movement in 1963 over a remark he made about the assassination of President Kennedy to the effect that the chickens were coming home to roost. In 1965 Malcom X himself was murdered; his widow Betty Shabaz has kept his particular tradition alive through the *Republic of New Africa* (1968) in association with a lawyer, Richard Henry.

Black Power's specific association with guerrilla warfare grew out of the originally mis-named Student Non-Violent Co-Ordinating Committee (SNCC) (the 'non-violent' was dropped in 1969) and the work of Stokeley Carmichael.

Carmichael came from Trinidad. He had been brought up in the United States in a middle-class area among Whites, which served only to heighten his sense of racial identity. He is said to have inaugurated the phrase 'Black Power' during a Civil Rights march on 17 June, 1966:

'The only way we gonna stop them white men from whuppin' us is to take over. We been saying freedom for six years and we ain't got nothing. What we gonna start saying now is *black power*.'

Thus the non-militant, peaceful 'social engineering' approach of Martin Luther King was rejected and, over the years, his eloquent Biblical phrases have been replaced by the emotive slogans of hate and destruction; 'Burn, Baby, Burn'; 'From Molotov Cocktails to Dynamite!'

Subsequent failures of educational crash programmes to break down the effects of Black disadvantage have reinforced the importance of political activity for Black emancipation.

Activists in SNCC, said Carmichael in Havana (1967), knew that the struggle would end in violence. They envisaged guerrilla warfare in the Deep South of the United States. Operations at that time might take the form of classes for young Blacks in the making of fire and acid bombs—with an immediate increase in arson, as occurred after 'Field-Marshal' Donald Lee Cox had been around Mobile, Alabama for a few weeks in 1966. Carmichael has pointed out that the cities are the hubs of a highly industrialized nation. 'Aim for the eye of the octopus', he urges. Carmichael became swiftly disillusioned with the prospects of success in America and lost out in the struggle for dominance to the more extreme Black Panthers and Revolutionary Action Movement (RAM). In particular he disagreed with the Panthers' united front tactics with white Left Wing students; Carmichael despised the latter as being mainly interested in loose living and drugs. SNCC under his leadership had expelled white liberal sympathizers. His opponents felt that Carmichael was adopting a kind of romantic Utopianism—'going back to the culture of eleventh-century Africa'; they were for revolutionary action.

The Black Panther Party (BPP), although started in Alabama, became notorious in Oakland, California, in 1966. The main early leaders were Bobby Seale and Huey Newton. Soon armed Panthers were on the streets of Oakland, trailing the police. Newton himself, armed with an M1 rifle, would harangue and outface the 'pigs'. In October, 1967, in a 'shoot out' a policeman was killed and Newton wounded. Newton, jailed for a total of thirty-three months, stood trial three times before being released on a 'hung jury' in August, 1970. Since his release the Panthers have increasingly 'gone constitutional'. In 1973 Newton was living in some style in a closely guarded luxury apartment overlooking San Francisco Bay.

Evolution to the present position has involved violence and a damaging split with the BPP's erstwhile 'Minister of Culture', the confident and eloquent self-confessed rapist and Presidential candidate, Eldridge Cleaver. Cleaver, from his exile in Algeria, continued to urge bloody revolution and guerrilla war as the only road for the American Blacks.

Another leading activist group was the Revolutionary Action

119

Movement (1964). Its most notorious leader was Robert Williams, who spent the 1960s in Cuba and Peking, making provocative broadcasts to the United States over 'Radio Free Dixie'. Williams, an ex-Marine, had initially been involved in organizing Negro self-defence groups against the Ku Klux Klan in North Carolina.

The ideologue from whom Black Power leaders have derived attitudes to guerrilla warfare and revolution is most obviously Frantz Fanon—although Cleaver also read Bakhunin and Nechayev. Fanon's writings influenced Newton, together with those of Mao, Che and Malcolm X. Fanon's *The Wretched of the Earth* was regarded by Cleaver as the 'Bible of Black Revolutionaries'. Like Che, Fanon has been mythologized so that only those parts of his writing which deal with violence have become well-known and much-quoted. In Fanon's case it is this reincarnation rather than the original which provides the motivation for extremists.

Fanon came from Martinique and worked as a psychiatrist in Algeria during the FLN uprising. This experience forced him to choose between his Frenchness and his '*négritude*'; he chose the latter.

Fanon insists that racism and exploitation are necessary concomitants of colonialism and that the attitudes of the subjugated race can only be changed by violently accomplished political emancipation. The colonized 'object' becomes a person through violence, which creates him as a man at the same time as it creates a new society. Violence then becomes in itself necessary for the realization of the oppressed individual's personality. Cleaver found catharsis in rape:

'It delighted me that I was defiling and trampling on the white man's laws, upon his system of values, and that I was defiling his women . . . I felt I was getting revenge.'[2]

Fanon writes that catharsis can also be found in violence:

'Violence alone, violence committed by the people, violence educated and organized by its leaders makes it possible for the masses to understand social truths and gives the key to them ... at the level of individuals violence is a cleansing force ... (it) frees the native from his inferiority complex and from his despair and inaction; it makes him fearless and restores his self respect.'[3]

So the violence of the exploited, turned inwards and repressed by the coercive power of the imperialists, has to escape by a reciprocal violence—escapist substitutes such as orgiastic religion or cultural expression cannot achieve it; only a blunt instrument can smash down the walls of the prison and bring release. As Sartre wrote in the preface to Fanon's book:

'To shoot down a European is to kill two birds with one stone, to destroy an oppressor and the man he oppresses at the same time.'

To Fanon the revolutionary classes are the peasantry and, in the cities, the marginal elements of the *lumpenproletariat*. Only these groups have the necessary desperation, having nothing to lose, to hurl themselves at the existing order of things. In Fanon the intellectual Black could find an ideology and a psychologically persuasive support for his actions. Cleaver felt, in reviewing *The Wretched of the Earth*, that the book gave justification to the revolutionaries' mood of violence and assured them of the normality of their hatred and the cathartic utility of killing their 'Slavemasters'.

Urban violence could therefore, in the eyes of Black leaders, serve a racially cohesive and creative purpose, both for those present and for the millions watching on TV. Demonstrations of armed Black Power could also hustle the Whites into some recognition of the strength and new found manhood of the Black population. Carmichael argued that for real negotiation there was needed some perceived threat from both sides—the American logic that spoke of 'bombing Hanoi to the negotiating table' could also be applied internally.

Urban warfare, said the Congress House Committee on Un-

American Activities in a Report (1968), would never be a serious threat because of the isolation of the ghettoes from supplies and the overwhelming power available to the authorities. Only if large numbers of American troops were abroad might there be a problem. These comments show a misunderstanding of the nature of the threat; the aim is not a 'six-day war' or a 'victory' which not even the crassest terrorist would foresee. The process is essentially one of erosion of confidence and gradual escalation of incidents.

The leading theorist of urban terror tactics produced by Black Power movements was Robert Williams of RAM. Williams' sojourns in Cuba and Peking brought him into contact with leading contemporary exponents of rural guerrilla warfare; he made the necessary adjustments to such doctrines in his *Black America* (1968) and in the RAM journal, *Crusader*. He advocated the use of 'gasoline fire bombs' and was in general strong on arson: 'America is a house on fire. Freedom now, or let it burn, let it burn.' This reflects a similar preoccupation on the White side of the revolutionary fence, for Jerry Rubin had the same advice, 'When in doubt, burn; fire is instant theater.' Williams grandiosely asserted that his concept of revolution defied military science and tactics.

> 'The new concept', he asserts, 'is of lightning campaigns conducted in a highly sensitive urban community, with the paralysis reaching the small communities and spreading to the farm areas. The old method of guerrilla, as carried out from the hills and the countryside, would be ineffective in a country like the USA. Any such force would be wiped out within an hour; the new concept is to huddle as close to the enemy as possible so as to neutralize his modern and fierce weapons. The new concept creates conditions that involve the whole community, whether they want to be involved or not. It sustains a state of confusion and destruction of property. It dislocates the organs of harmony and order and reduces central power to the level of a helpless, sprawling octopus.'⁴

Organizationally, Williams favoured three types of armed squad; one of these would be overt and prepared for self-defence in Black areas. The other two would be clandestine, anti-police riot squads and 'fire teams'. (Williams again mentioned his favourite simile when he envisaged violence and terror spreading 'like fire storms'.)

The credibility of urban activity by such groups was enhanced by the penetration of the American Armed Forces achieved by Black Power movements. Young American Blacks, trained to fight in Vietnam, might provide the 'young bloods' of whom Carmichael spoke with approval. In the United States' forces the Black Power clenched fist has been used as a mutually given and returned salutation by enlisted men. It has been sanctioned by authority provided it is used as a mark of recognition and not as a military salute or 'a gesture of defiance'. The BPP worked hard at the propaganda of the word, aiming especially at the young; language became 'revolutionized'. Panther cartoons showed obese and jackbooted police 'pigs' being confronted by virile young Panthers.

Seeing itself as a kind of Black urban *foco* the BPP aimed to be the fuse to explode the powder keg on the American Revolution. On other occasions a situation of more general guerrilla war was envisaged, especially by the exiled Eldridge Cleaver:

'Another front . . . needs to be created . . . the North American Liberation Front. I think it's very timely, because many people see the situation that we are confronted with as one in which politics have been transformed into war, and there is no point in kidding ourselves anymore; what we have to do is fight. We have the terrain there to fight. Many people think that armed struggle carried out in the mountains in Cuba or Vietnam is one thing, and that it could not happen in the United States. But the United States has more mountains than all of these other areas, it has the advantage of mountainous areas, and a highly organized situation and it has rural areas. It's so large that the Government forces would be forced to spread out very thinly, at the same time that dissatisfaction in the United States Army is at an all-time peak. The stockades and military prisons are overflowing with people who have deserted and don't want to fight in Vietnam. And I think that the contradictions that have arisen in the ranks of the United States Army will continue to increase, more so when they are finally turned against the American people.'[5]

Despite Cleaver's protestations of Marxism and those of other leaders such as Bobby Seale and David Hilyard (Cleaver described himself as a 'universal Marxist-Leninist') one has the impression that their violent rhetoric disguised an uncertainty of purpose; they knew what they wanted freedom *from* without being clear what they wanted it *for*. They talked of turning 'the white suburbs into shooting galleries' (Cleaver), 'smashing the system' (Carmichael); yet while the 'Look out Whitey, Black Power's gonna get your Momma' approach was dramatic it was hardly constructive. While Black Power leaders were sometimes eager to assert the defensive nature of their activities their attitude was in fact ambivalent; they were against war as Mao was against it—'in order to get rid of the gun it is necessary to take up the gun'. Moreover some Black Panthers (and members of smaller groups) mixed a little crime with their politics. Proceeds were of course divided, as the nineteenth-century anarchists had split theirs, between the individual and the movement—but these proceeds by no means always came from the 'exploiting Whites'.

Whither Black Power now? Newton and Seale are apparently following the path of 'community organization'—medical centres, electoral programmes with a reserve defensive armed capability.

Cleaver resigned as the head of the Panther's 'International Section' in January, 1972, and left the Panther Headquarters in Algeria. He has been attacked by Newton as 'Hidden Traitor, Renegade Scab', which makes the latter's attitude reasonably clear. Two of Cleaver's lieutenants also left the movement shortly afterwards. Thereafter seven hi-jackers took up residence in the Panther's villa; Holder and Katherine Karkow (Western Airlines Boeing in June, 1972) and five others (Delta Airlines Boeing in July). In both cases the aircraft and the ransom money were returned by the Algerian Government to the United States. The Panthers did not endear themselves to the Algerians and were asked to take their 'international headquarters' to Syria; the militant wing of the movement is in disarray. Cuban interest in Black Power, at its height in the mid-sixties when, apart from Williams' broadcasts, revolutionary leaflets were printed in Cuba for distribution in the United States, appears to have declined. Withdrawal from Vietnam has taken some of the heat out of the internal American situation—the endemic divisions of the American Left will continue to enervate and, unless another unifying issue is discovered, subvert its effectiveness.

The burgeoning Black Power of the nineteen-sixties seems already old-fashioned; violence in the ghettoes will find other leaders to urge bloody revolution but hopefully the politically experienced generation of the earlier years will be able to turn that activism into community construction and renewal rather than rioting and death. Depending on the treatment they receive Black veterans of Vietnam will make their choice between these paths. Sporadic shoot-outs will continue to occur, internecine as much as against the authorities, on the lines of that in Brooklyn where four young Black Muslims held thirteen hostages in a store after originally attacking it to obtain guns in order to 'unify the fragmented Muslims'. Any unified 'revolutionary' movement, however, seems at the moment a distant prospect.

Black Power in Britain was modelled directly on that of the United States. Malcolm X was in Britain in 1965 and there met Michael de Freitas, who took the name 'Michael X'. This ex-seaman had a criminal record and had been involved with the slum landlord Peter Rachman. In 1966, on his conversion to the Black Muslim Islaam, de Freitas changed his name again, this time to Abdul Malik.

Malik was able to expand his organization through the financial support he received from rich Whites. (Similar support had been given to the Panthers in the United States by white liberals who imagined that by giving money to extremists they were honouring the memory of Martin Luther King.) Malik's RAAS (Racial Action Adjustment Society) concentrated on propaganda and assistance to Blacks, achieving some notoriety by its activities during a strike at Courtauld's plant in Lancashire. RAAS became a recognized part of the progressive scene both in Britain and abroad. Malik cultivated a 'front' approach with hippies and drop-outs as being similarly deprived and oppressed and thus natural allies for Blacks. RAAS emissaries travelled extensively, especially in the West Indies, and, as a result of these trips (so Malik claimed), emphasis was shifted to grass roots activity among the immigrant population on the individual level.

Malik also came into contact with the Internationalists, a Maoist organization and forerunner of the Communist Party of England (Marxist-Leninist). In a speech at Reading (1967) Malik apparently urged the murder of Whites and was imprisoned for a year. His movement, already selling works on guerrilla warfare, began to make yet more aggressive noises. In 1968 Malik's replacement, Frankie Y, mentioned that the movement was also dealing in the manufacture of weapons and training in the handling of explosives.

On Malik's release he began to dabble in finance and property speculation; in 1970 he was arrested on charges of burglary and blackmail. In 1971 he fled to Trinidad before being brought to trial. In the following year he was convicted of the murder of Joseph Skerritt, a Trinidad barber.

If Michael X's organization was the British equivalent of the Black Muslims then Ogi Egbuna was its Stokeley Carmichael—or at least attempted to be. Egbuna founded UCPA (Universal Coloured People's Association) in 1967. This body aimed, as its name suggests, to forge links between the various coloured groups in Britain. Egbuna openly advocated violent revolution, even to the Institute of Race Relations as the only way to achieve coloured emancipation. In 1968 he founded the British Black Panthers and the exiled Ghanaian leader Kwame Nkrumah agreed to become its patron. Nkrumah sent a message to his British devotees; the black people of Britain, he said, must wake to the full realization of their revolutionary potential, situated as they were in the very heart of capitalism and colonialism. Egbuna was convicted of planning the murder of police officers (November, 1968) and given a suspended sentence.

Black People's Alliance (1968) was started in order to 'combat racialism'; it confined itself to demonstrations and, like the London-based Black Radical Action Movement, was more interested in community organization and specific social problems, such as housing, than in 'revolution'. Another group, the Black Eagles, were active in patrolling Notting Hill.

Black Power movements in the United States have extended their influence both directly and via the West Indies. The fortunes of Blacks in the United States, in the ghettoes, on the streets and in constitutional political activity, have instant repercussions in Britain. These links have been maintained by regular lecture tours in Britain by Black militants.

Efforts have been made by Maoists and Trotskyists to infiltrate Black Power movements and turn them from the path of Black cultural nationalism towards proletarian solidarity. Communists have insisted that the way to Black emancipation is via a change in the living standards of the whole 'working class' but they have been less enthusiastic in taking over Black groups than have the International Marxist Group. The IMG has given consistent support through its speakers and in its publications to 'Black Power' and has urged the need for an alliance of 'progressive' elements in combating capitalism, US imperialism, etc.

The Times investigated Black Power in 1968 and heard rumours of arms caches. Pamphlets enumerating the tactics and weaponry needed for urban terrorism have been circulated.

Generally, however, Black Power movements in the United Kingdom have to date not gone over to terror tactics; the law still runs, though beset by problems, in Black areas. Threats have been uttered but the most rabid and blood-curdling of them have come from visiting American Blacks rather than from domestic militants. Here, for example, is a Mr Kingsley Tweed of New York:

> 'Every black man better get himself a gun, a sub-machine gun, a hand grenade, and shoot everyone that is white. He must do it now. We'd better start now right here in bloody old England.' (*Daily Telegraph*, 7 October, 1967.)

Whether British Blacks turn to urban violence and terrorism will depend crucially on the employment prospects for Black youth and on relationships with the police.[6]

Black extremism breeds White extremism; in the racial as in the political context prejudices feed on one another. So in the United States both the moderate demands of the Civil Rights movement and the struttings of Black militants led to a revival of White extremism, and especially that associated with the name of Ku Klux Klan. The Klan, though historically very much a rural phenomenon, is psychologically the archetypal poor White movement, likely to appear in any context where underprivileged members of the dominant group feel threatened by the emancipation, actual or impending, of a hitherto despised minority

Set up originally after the American Civil War the Klan sought to preserve the political and economic hegemony of the Southern White man, which it saw as weakened by an unholy alliance of Northern carpet-baggers, renegade 'scalawags' —locals gone over to the Republicans—and Negro freedmen. In its pristine form it represented a genuine fear and conviction, even among its leaders; in its later manifestations organizations have used its name in order to exploit fear commercially and politically. Twice dissolved, for tactical rather than substantive reasons, the Klan has each time re-emerged in a new guise.

While the motivation of Black movements is commonly held to be frustration, that of the White extremist is fear—fear, literally, of the 'dark unknown'. A poor White has only his colour to sustain his self-respect. If he lacks education, knowledge and skills the only factor, or so he thinks, that stands between him and unemployment is his heritage as a White. So it is that the Klan has always emphasized the White, Anglo-Saxon, Protestant (WASP) and native-born American virtues and attacked Jews, Catholics and immigrants as 'Un-American'. The Klan imbibed in full measure the 'scientific' racial theories prevalent at the turn of the century. A pamphlet published in 1921 (and reissued in 1941) gives the flavour:

'The Anglo-Saxon is the typeman of history. To him must yield the self-centred Hebrew, the cultured Greek, the virile Roman, the mystic Oriental. The Psalmist must have had him in mind when he struck his soundless harp and sang, "O Lord thou hast made him a little lower than the Angels, and hast crowned him with glory and honour. Thou hast made him to have dominion over the works of thy hands; thou hast put all things under his feet". The Ku Klux Klan desires that its ruling members shall be of this all-conquering blood . . . The Ku Klux Klan was planned for the white American.'[7]

After the Second World War the Klan splintered into a number of floridly-named new organizations; the rise of the Civil Rights movement and Black Power revived the fortunes of such as The Association of Georgia Klans and the Original Southern Klans Inc. Once again Kyclops and Klaliff met in Konklave.

Ku Klux Klans and similar extreme White racist groups trade on the bewilderment of a changing world. You will be given someone to hate—and blame—Jews, Catholics, Communists, Blacks, Liberals, etc. At the same time your own pride will be reinforced by your membership of the Knights of the White Camelia, the National Christian Church, the National Association for the Preservation of the White Race, the

129

Southern Gentlemen or the Knights of the Ku Klux Klan of America, one of whose Imperial Emperors was the splendidly named Dr Lycurgus Spinks.

Historically the Klan and their allies have sought to set up a subversive political system which controls votes, hence the elections and, ultimately, the elected. Through intimidation and the exploitation of fear White extremist organizations seek to nullify the effect of laws which they do not like and, while paying ceremonial respect to the trappings of democracy, in fact to run affairs through secret cabals.

NOTES

1 Allen, *A Guide to Black Power in America*, Gollancz, 1970, p. 1.
2 Eldridge Cleaver, *Post Prison Writings and Speeches*, Cape, p. 143.
3 Frantz Fanon, *The Wretched of the Earth*, trans. Farrington, Penguin, 1967, p. 74.
4 *Revolution*, March 1964 quoted Grieg, *Today's Revolutionaries*, Foreign Affairs Publishing House, 1970, p. 20.
5 In Lutz and Brent, *On Revolution*, Winthrop, 1971, *Eldridge Cleaver discusses Revolution: An Interview from Exile*.
6 See Chapter 13.
7 William Pierce Randel, *The Ku Klux Klan*, Hamish Hamilton, 1965, p. 170.

CHAPTER 9

Separatist Terror

The terrorist in a colonial or separatist situation undertakes a campaign which requires as much technical but less political sophistication than making a social and political revolution. In separatist environments the aim is to force the patron State to relinquish its grasp on the territory concerned. The question of what is to happen after the moment of 'freedom' can be left until it is achieved. Terrorism's objective is to raise the penalties of a continued presence to the point where that presence ceases to be cost-effective. Initially there is a greater chance of success in the strictly colonial context since world opinion and aid is more likely to be on the side of the insurgent. Elsewhere the separatist is faced with a greater problem of establishing the legitimacy of his claim to self-determination since, whatever that claim's cultural and linguistic merits, there rarely appears much likelihood of an economically viable unit being created.

The terrorist target in both situations—colonial and separatist—is public opinion, firstly in the patron country and subsequently in the world at large. The battle, therefore, is essentially one of publicity. An action's effect must be measured in terms of its propaganda value. Liberal democracies with a relatively free Press are better propositions from the terrorist viewpoint than more closed societies. On these grounds alone terrorism in Cyprus or Algeria was more likely to succeed than similar movements in the Ukraine or the Basque country of Spain.

Governments must be convinced that the costs of continued control are insupportable in human and economic terms. In particular the expense of maintaining a military presence must be escalated. This can be achieved by making it necessary to guard all public installations and large commercial undertakings. Attacks on individual members of the Security Forces and their families increase the human cost of the situation and tie down numbers of troops in protecting one another. Further strains may be imposed by attacking or infiltrating locally recruited forces and civilian organizations to the point where they become more of a liability than an asset to the authorities. Allies of the country in question will become alarmed at the signs of decay and disruption exhibited and apply pressure for concessions to be made; hence, in the case of the United Kingdom, public opinion in the USA and Western Europe becomes a target.

Simultaneously, emphasis is laid on the possibility of future good relations with the occupying Power in the event of withdrawal. In this respect separatist insurgents frequently make politically tactical errors, usually brought about by a rigid adherence to ideology. In order to gain the support of the population they spend too much energy in threatening 'nationalization' and blaming the 'occupying Power' for every imaginable economic and social problem; since they are aiming primarily at public opinion in the patron country and in the world at large they achieve more when they promise to respect foreign property and investments. Granting their demands might in that case look, from a capitalist perspective, a better proposition than continued opposition. Intransigent cupidity openly expressed by the insurgents will lead on the other hand to pressure from business interests for a continued military presence in order to 'protect the investments'.

Security Forces, if they are those of a relatively open society, will be goaded into an indiscriminate response, especially against women and children. Passive resistance techniques may also be used. Simple disobedience by large numbers of people places the authorities almost automatically in the role of oppressors should they take action. If enough people can be mobilized in this activity against a liberal democracy then terrorism becomes unnecessary.

Provocative tactics contribute to the attainment of three separate but interrelated objectives. In the first place the inevitable inconveniences and injustices involved in security operations may tend to harden neutral local opinion against the authorities. 'Atrocities', whether real, exaggerated or fictitious, can be revealed or alleged; liberal public opinion in the patron country, never especially well-disposed towards soldiers, will be inclined to believe such stories and will demand a softening of procedures or accession to the insurgents' demands.

Sympathizers can be relied upon to give reports of military violence the widest possible circulation. Such sympathizers may be bound to the insurgents by ties of blood, ideology or history but, should the terrorism appear likely to succeed, a host of artificial friends will come out of the woodwork eager for pickings from the triumph of the cause.

Meanwhile collaborators with the authorities are terrorized and if necessary, shot dead. In this respect the separatist faces greater problems than the obviously colonized. Attempts to persuade a government to give autonomy to a region, especially if that region has been part of the patron country for several generations or more, are likely to come up against deeply entrenched individual and commercial interests. Personal and economic integration may be such that the prospect of the population reflecting a self-consciously ethnic identity is insufficient to support a programme of violence. Moreover it is easier for the patron state to meet separatist demands by granting some degree of control in specifically local matters, while making a show of respecting the regional language and customs; in the colonial context the issue is much more clearly 'all or nothing'. Therefore the more closely a separatist movement can identify itself with the 'colonial struggle' the greater the chance of its succeeding. Geographical isolation from the patron country is thus important.

Such tactics were utilized at the turn of the century by the Internal Macedonian Revolutionary Organization (IMRO); IMRO adopted a counter-State technique, setting up its own courts and police force. Urban terrorism, with the aim of persuading the West to pressure the Ottoman Empire into conceding separatist demands, was most spectacularly undertaken in Salonika in 1903. Modelling themselves on the Russian populists, IMRO members blew up a French ship, attacked banks and the local security forces; one terrorist, finding himself surrounded by policemen, activated his bomb and stoically sat on it. IMRO, however, lacked the logistic and technical stamina to mount a sustained campaign of urban terrorism. The organization lingered on into the 1930s when it had contacts with the Croat Ustashe (q.v. below).

In contemporary terms the principles of separatist terror have been tried and tested by the Irgun Zvei Leumi and Stern Gang, the Algerian FLN and, in Cyprus, EOKA; such movements have been studied and emulated by the Uruguayan Tupamaros and the Provisional IRA.[1]

The FLN

The Algerian insurgents opened their military campaign for independence on 31 October, 1954, with a mere five hundred men. They were faced, as had been the Irgun, with a weakened Imperial power. France had been defeated in Indo-China. Independence had been granted to Tunisia and Morocco, territories bordering on Algeria. Unlike the Irgun, however, the FLN had to contend with one million Europeans who regarded the operational territory as their home. The insurgents possessed at the outset little political credibility. Their first task was to gain control of the Moslem population. Control implied the setting-up of a counter-State and the imposition of its authority through threat and, if necessary, physical liquidation. This task was to be undertaken by the terrorist groups; when they had brow-beaten the population into submission then the Political and Administrative Organization (PAO) would move in. In the cities both pro-French and rival nationalist groups were to be attacked or, in the latter case, betrayed.

At the beginning of the campaign little sense of Algerian national identity existed; it had to be created. Pan-Arabists who saw the discarding of the colonial yoke as a necessary preliminary to wider dreams of Moslem unity and, more practically,

Colonel Nasser and his supporters, were prepared to help. Processes of re-education towards such a new ideology involved first terror, then persuasion and organization, followed, if the population showed signs of a 'correct attitude', by a switching of attention to the Algerian European community.

Nor were the FLN up against amateurs; the French Army was a formidable enemy. The French doctrine of '*la guerre revolutionnaire*', the product of much study by French Generals as well as the experiences of combat against the Viet Minh in Indo-China, suggested that anti-colonial movements were part of a global conspiracy against the West. To defeat the guerrilla the West must use the guerrilla's tactics against him; the aim was to 'out-Mao the Maoists'. Such a course involved an articulation of military, ideological and psychological measures. The doctrine's weakness lay in the danger of the Army becoming so enmeshed in local affairs and techniques that the overall political realities were ignored. Such a danger was at that time increased by the inconsistencies and vagaries of the political direction under which the Army had suffered. In practical terms the doctrine resulted in the military direction of population, counter-organization and a militarily dominated psychological offensive.

For their part the FLN possessed a precious ideological counter-weapon, the principle of self-determination, a slogan of emotional effectiveness in both the Communist and Liberal democratic vocabulary and one which may be used even if there is as yet no 'self' to be 'determined'. Not merely Algeria, therefore, but first Metropolitan France and then the world constituted the battlefield. For the FLN there were three battle fronts—in Algeria, in Metropolitan France and before the world, and especially the 'Third World'. In order to achieve maximum impact in these areas it was necessary to switch the point of attack from the countryside to the towns, and especially to Algiers.

'Which is better for our cause? To kill ten enemies in some gulch . . . or one in Algiers, which will be written up in the

American Press the next day? If we are going to risk our lives we must make our struggle known. We could kill hundreds of colonialist soldiers without ever making news. Let us reflect on the consequences of our acts and be sure that they will be profitable, that they will unfailingly draw attention to the noble struggle of our people and its army.'[2]

Thus Abane Ramdane, a guerrilla leader. The tactic was to be put into operation by a former bakery worker, Yacef Saadi. Just as the countryside was divided into districts in which the rebels set up a parallel administration, so in Algiers there were three sectors.

From 1956 until July, 1957, a few hundred terrorists succeeded in focusing world attention on the Algerian situation. They held the city in a grip of terror. Bombs exploded daily; they were placed where they would kill and maim the maximum possible number, in 'bus stations, coffee shops and waiting-rooms. They were not all planted by Moslems; 'liberal' Europeans sympathized, gave shelter and in some cases planted bombs. The FLN also made extensive use of women couriers and operatives; from their point of view the most effective bomb-carrier was a European woman, since such a terrorist was doubly unlikely to arouse suspicion. It was a European, Danielle Milne, who placed a bomb in a milk bar on the opening day of the terror, 30 September, 1956.

Hidden in the intricate windings of the Casbah the FLN created what amounted to an 'autonomous zone' ruled by terror. Governmental response was to place the Army, and in particular the 'paras' under General Massu, in charge of the counter-terrorist operations (February, 1957). As the FLN had imposed its will and broken the Police Intelligence network in the Casbah by terror so in its turn it was smashed by similar methods. Military use of preventive detention, quick reaction to intelligence (and if necessary torture to acquire it) proved effective. Massu was prepared to flood the streets with troops and to allow the terrorists no respite and no targets. The FLN took to placing explosives in the bottom of lamp standards, the keys being supplied by a sympathizer, and in September, 1957, they bombed a dance hall; these proved their dying kicks in Algiers. They had no further targets. Finding no place unguarded, no street unwatched and few hiding places, some were blown up by their own bombs while others flung them down in the streets and took to their heels, only to be shot down. In October, 1957, Ali la Pointe, the last of the hard-core terrorists at large in Algiers, was tracked down; he used his remaining *plastique* to destroy his refuge and himself with it. The paras had broken the FLN in Algiers; they had killed, captured or forced into exile all the top leadership. The 'no go' area of the Casbah had ceased to exist. Intelligence, however gathered, had been excellent; Colonel Godard, then head of the Algiers Police Intelligence, later in the OAS, remarked of this period that he knew more about the FLN than Yacef Saadi. Massu had made effective use of counter-terror squads composed of informers who hunted down their erstwhile friends. Individual responsibility was secured by the *ilot* system, down to family level; for each family, street and area there was one man responsible who thus had a very real interest in preventing incidents or, if that failed, knowing who was responsible.

The FLN was not active in Algeria alone. Like the IRA of the nineteen-thirties it carried the fight to the homeland. Although the police were fired on and there was some sabotage the main thrust of the FLN effort in France was directed at their fellow Moslem Algerians. Determined to be the only effective Algerian movement in Metropolitan France, the FLN set about achieving that position by using the same tactic which had proved successful in similar operations in Algeria. Both pro-French Moslems and the leaders of the rival National Algerian Movement and their families were systematically assassinated while criminal elements stepped in and used the confusion for their own purposes. Control of the Algerian workers in France represented a weapon of some potential; it gave access to sympathetic movements of the Left and constituted a power base from which industrial or terrorist operations might be launched. The network of sympathizers provided intelligence and maintained a complex and highly detailed dossier on any Algerian of potential usefulness. In Algeria, too, internecine fighting occupied much of the FLN's earlier efforts. In Algeria itself the FLN campaign was, in strictly military terms, a failure. The Challe Plan of 1959 led to a disintegration of the logistic support apparatus behind the insurrection. Challe went for the PAO, the brain of the insurgency, at the same time stepping up the psychological war. His plan, with its accompanying emphasis on mobility in the countryside, forced the FLN's military arm back to the 'survival' stage of guerrilla operations. The French Army mounted a co-ordinated civil and military campaign aimed at combining efficient administration with the counter-organization of the population. Lessons learned from Ho Chi-minh and Giap were applied. In effect the Army became the Government; it ran courses for administrators while locally enlisted troops were given instruction in hygiene and civics. By 1957 the Army was running over twenty-five 'professional centres' with twenty-six thousand, mainly teenage, pupils. Concurrently with such efforts the Army's Psychological Action and Information Services (*SAPI*) created their own 'parallel hierarchies' based on what were felt to be natural social groupings, concentrating particularly on ex-servicemen, women and the young. Giving themselves to programmes of civic action with enthusiasm, some in the Army saw the creation of a 'new consciousness' based on an *Algerie fraternelle* rather than an *Algerie Française* as their goal. The Army fought on all fronts; operational, psychological and propagandistic; it ran the gamut of the then available techniques. Counter-guerrillas, sometimes led by reformed ex-terrorists, were set up. In sensitive areas 'regroupment' was used; villages were moved to more easily administered and defensible areas where Special Administrative Sections (*SAS*) moved in to reorganize the civil life of the community. Less successful were the involuntary regroupments caused by the establishment of 'forbidden zones' (where anything moving could be shot), for people ejected in this way tended to migrate to the fringes of the towns where their shanty areas made for good terrorist recruiting. In the cities Urban Administrative Sections (*SAU*) were set up. These organizations were the off-spring of the Army's Fifth Bureau which, though originally a mainly civilian undertaking, fell under Army control. Captured insurgents were subject to intensive psychological pressures and then, reformed, let loose to hunt their former comrades.

SAS and SAUs aimed to regain the allegiance of the Moslem population. They attempted both to bring real economic and social benefits to their areas and also to keep some tabs on the shifting population by issuing identification papers. They were the military equivalent of the PAO.

While the French effort lasted the SAS and SAUs were generally successful; they seemed an earnest of France's inten-tion to stay and win. At the first signs of French prevarication, however, the population deserted back to the FLN.

In military terms one of the Army's most important successes lay in their sealing off the borders with Morocco and Tunisia in order to prevent guerrilla infiltration. The 'Morice Line' along the Tunisian frontier was over 300 kms long, much of it was electrified and a system of computer-like efficiency enabled any contacts to be swiftly pinpointed. Motorized columns would then move out on roads parallel to the defences. Search-lights illuminated the Tunisian side while the Army operated in darkness. It was expensive and it tied down tens of thousands of men, but it was effective.

The French Government also enjoyed some notable successes in cutting off external arms supplies to the insurgents. Ships were intercepted and a 'black list' of illegal arms suppliers was published—forcing their governments into action.

Inside Algeria the unremitting pressure of the Army slowly suffocated the insurgents; one of the costs was the politicization of the Army. In such a campaign identification with the people is an operational necessity. Officers became mayors, adminis-trators and judges. Orders cannot be carried out in a mechanis-tic manner. Forced to improvise and initiate the officer finds, whether he wills it or not, that he becomes a politician. The people become 'his' people and their destiny becomes part of his concern—emotional as well as intellectual. Thus the fate of those Moslems, soldiers and civilians, who had been persuaded to co-operate with the Army was a matter of personal honour. How could they in conscience be abandoned to the tenderness of their revolutionary brothers? SAPI's rising politicization led to its disbandment by de Gaulle in 1960.

Against this background the realization by the European Algerians and those who identified with them that de Gaulle, for whose return to power they felt themselves responsible, was about to concede that which the Army had apparently prevented was, not unnaturally, traumatic. De Gaulle's sense of *realpolitik* (and of the war-weariness of the French people) led to a switch of FLN tactics and from the beginning of 1960 they concentrated on political rather than military methods.

To some elements in the Army it appeared that de Gaulle was about to deliver the southern shores of the Mediterranean into the hands of international Communism—betrayal was heaped on betrayal. The Army had taken an oath to defend Algeria; now they were to be ordered to deliver it up. Larger questions of world power, the projections of a future changing pattern of global relationships and France's part in them were to the Army either incomprehensible or, if understood, were regarded as wrong in honour if not in expediency.

For de Gaulle, wrote Charles Kelly in *Lost Soldiers*, 'France's position in the world depended on dozens of factors; for much of the Army, all of France's honour, esteem and success centred on a single issue—Algeria.'

It was in this atmosphere of frustration and anger that the Generals' attempted putsch of April, 1961, took place and that the OAS, the secret Army of white resistance, struck its roots.[3]

The original objectives of the FLN had been to dominate the Moslem population and set them and the Europeans in mutual hostility. At the same time the insurgents sought to remove rival movements and pre-empt a similar attempt begun rather tardily by the Algerian Communist Party which, having eschewed independence previously, sought to jump on the bandwagon when it showed signs of rolling. Independence lay beyond these objectives as the ultimate strategic aim. That the FLN's success was so complete and so comparatively swift was due to its finding a powerful patron in Colonel Nasser and in becoming a *cause célèbre* in the Third World, which seemed to be riding on the tide of the future; to alienate it in the interests of a million Europeans and a victory for the French Army was, in de Gaulle's view, a bad bargain.

The affair was one more lesson for soldiers in the primacy of the political will. The uncomfortable difficulty in being the agents of the 'diplomacy of force' is that the diplomacy keeps being altered. The Army thought it had found the answer to the Algerian question; unfortunately de Gaulle changed the question.

Ustashe (The 'Rebels')

Between 1970 and 1972 the fragile cohesion of Yugoslavia came close to breakdown. In April, 1971, Tito warned, 'Our existence, our State, our community are at stake'. By the middle of 1972 over five hundred people had been arrested for 'nationalist excesses'. The Croatian Communist leadership, accused of complacency, 'rotten liberalism' and lack of vigilance, together with the Croatian cultural association with which it had been associated had, said Tito, attached to itself, 'members of the lumpen proletariat, counter-revolutionists, various nationalists, chauvinists, dogmatists and the devil knows who else'. A sweeping purge of the Croatian League of Communists resulted.

Tensions between centralism—control from Belgrade—and regionalism—the granting of some degree of autonomy to the federal republics which made up the state of Yugoslavia—had reached crisis proportions. The largest ethnic group after the Serbs (just under 40%) are the Croats who constitute some 22% of the population and it was in Croatia that the most serious disintegrative pressures showed themselves. Ethnic divisions were highlighted by inequalities of job opportunity and economic imbalance. Croats pointed out that in Yugoslav institutions, allegedly representative of the universalism of the State, they were grossly underrepresented—in the Army, the Security Services and in Public Administration. What particularly rankled was the Serbian influence in top jobs in Croatia itself where, although in a minority, the former dominated the Army and the public services. Croats felt, moreover, that while they earned the foreign currency through tourism and working abroad (mainly as *gastarbeiter* in West Germany—some 37% of all Yugoslavs in jobs abroad are Croat) the rest of the country, especially the backward south, spent it. The vexed question of language was also involved; the Croat Communist leadership used cultural organizations to propagate a nationalist message. Tito was caught in a dilemma; the Yugoslav form of socialism deliberately gave play to market forces, regional planning and local initiative, but these were now leading to a desire for political autonomy. Journalists, film producers and students were all enthusiastic supporters of what they saw as the progressive elements in the Croatian leadership. Politically, however, if Yugoslavia was to remain united, the centre of decision had to remain in Belgrade. Such a dual system—decentralized economically while centralized politically—might work where the Yugoslav League of Communists formed a strongly cohesive bond overriding ethnic loyalties. Yet the League was not proving able to meet the aspirations of students. In Croatia the loyalty of the young was demonstrably to the nationalist sentiments expressed at the 10th Plenum of the Croatian Communist League (late 1969).

Given the bitter background of the years of the Second World War when the Fascist Powers set up a puppet state for the Croats, resulting in bloody clashes between them and the Serbs, it may seem surprising that Yugoslavia had held together for the subsequent nearly thirty years without more strain. Fear, after the break with Stalin in 1948, of a Russian invasion engendered the most powerful unifying factor of all—the instinct of self-preservation. Russian ambitions in Yugoslavia have not changed; indeed Soviet interest in the Mediterranean has increased. If it now appears that a post-Tito Yugoslavia will be weak and quarrelsome then the Russian tactic is clearly to await that eventuality while giving centrifugal pressures such clandestine encouragement as may from time to time appear expedient. For the present Yugoslav leadership the disappearance of the overt Russian bogey is to be regretted and occasionally they attempt to revive it—over, for example, the activities of pro-Russian emigrés in Moscow—for purposes of internal solidarity.

In all these circumstances it is not surprising that the rump of the wartime Nazi-backed Croatian Ustashe should attempt to seize the chance apparently being offered it by the internal malaise of the Yugoslav state. Ustashe has been strengthened by fresh adherents recruited from among Croat *gastarbeiter* in West Germany and emigrés in Australia. Ustashe has been seen by sections of the Western Press as descendants of 'resistance freedom fighters' or Croat 'liberal nationalists' fighting 'Serb hegemony'. It may be conceded that they are Croatian separatists but, in view of their history, they can in no sense be described as 'liberals'.

Ustashe can be traced back to the Croat opposition to the creation of the Yugoslav state after the First World War and, in particular, to the attempt in 1929 by King Alexander to hold his crumbling State together by taking authoritarian powers. Croatian nationalist opposition to Alexander's concept of an integrated Yugoslavia received support from the Nazis and in particular from Mussolini's Italy.

In 1934 the King visited Marseilles; as the entourage drove away from the docks a terrorist ran forward shouting '*Vive le Roi*', jumped on to the running board of the King's car and emptied his revolver into Alexander and his companion, the French Foreign Minister, Berthou. The chauffeur, turning, pulled the assassin back by his hair while the mounted escort attacked with his sabre; their actions were to no avail. Alexander I, King of the Yugoslavs, of the Karageorgevic dynasty, lay dying. Berthou staggered from the car and died in hospital that afternoon. Knocked to the ground and kicked unconscious by the crowd the assassin died at Police Head-quarters.

The attack had been organized by the Ustashe, at that time headed from Vienna by Ante Pavelić, a Croatian lawyer. It was expected both by Ustashe and their paymasters in the Italian Secret Service[4] that the assassination would be followed by an uprising in Croatia; this failed to materialize, but the terrorists continued their activity.

Ustashe had contacts with other Balkan separatist movements such as the Internal Macedonian Revolutionary Organization (with whom it had an agreement) and the *Kosovari*, who sought the union with Albania of the southern Yugoslav region of Kosovo. Operatives were trained in camps in Italy, Hungary and Bulgaria. Both then and now Ustashe has specialized in bombing—in particular trains and railway stations.

During the Second World War Pavelić became for three years *Poglavnik* (leader) of the Axis Independent State of Croatia. At the end of the war he escaped to South America although many of his *apparat* were caught and executed by Tito's partisans.

Since 1945 a number of terrorist groups have existed under the umbrella of Ustashe. Pavelić directed his organization from Buenos Aires until his death in 1959. In 1956 a break-away group under General Luburić was set up in Madrid known as Croatian National Resistance. Australia with 140,000 Yugoslav immigrants, mainly Croat, became a centre of activity involving in particular the Croatian Revolutionary Brotherhood, whose members took part in incursions into Yugoslavia in 1963 and 1972. Other small groups include the Croatian Illegal Revolutionary Organization and the United Croats of West Germany.

Another factor encouraging Ustashe terrorists in their campaign apart from the evidence of internal unrest in Yugoslavia was the possibility of Russian assistance. It is not to be supposed that because of the nationalistic or fascist nature of Ustashe that the KGB would for that reason hesitate to use it (They had been involved in dealings with Ustashe in the 1930s and, during the Second World War, had supported a faction opposed to Pavelić). Ideological niceties have rarely stood in the way of Russian national interest, and certainly not where the prospect of Mediterranean ports accessible overland from the Soviet Union is in view.

In 1970 in West Germany the Croatian National Committee abruptly became pro-Russian. Jelić, the head of this body, after meeting one of the Australian emigré leaders, did a sudden and spectacular volte-face from being anti-Russian and offered military facilities to the Soviets in an independent Croatia. Mysterious circumstances surround Jelić's death in Berlin in May, 1972.

Ustashe terrorists have continued to pursue their campaign against the Yugoslav Government. Apart from the 'mini-invasion'[5] there was the murder of the Yugoslav Ambassador to Sweden, Vladimir Rolović (7 April, 1971) and the destruction of an airliner over Czechoslovakia by a bomb. In January, 1973, seven Croats were detained in Gothenburg, Sweden on suspicion of terrorist activity.

Tito has weathered the storms of separatism by reverting to a tighter ideological and party control. He has been able to do so because the reins of power remained in the hands of the Army and of Serbs loyal to the centralist concept, although some who thought otherwise were forced to resign. Croatian Generals were not prepared to risk Civil War and thus refused invitations to meet Croatian political leaders. For their part those leaders, despite appeals for moderation, lost control of their supporters—possibly due to the activities of *agents provocateurs*—especially in the universities. Student riots thus changed nothing but merely played into the hands of the hard-liners.[6]

Ustashe's future role will be to keep the issue in the public eye. Bombs in Belgrade may help further to polarize Serb opinion against the Croats (an attitude which will be reciprocated with interest) and, since nothing breeds separatism in a federal state more quickly than somebody else's separatism, Croat extremism will lead to the Slovene and Albanian minorities asserting their claims even more strongly. Should the Yugoslav centre fail to hold and the State fall apart there will be rejoicing only in the Kremlin; at the moment no one else gains. Ustashe must therefore look to the USSR for external support. Ustashe terrorists must also know, however, that Russia, once having divided Yugoslavia, will seek to rule, just as everybody has in the past, ultimately through the Serb majority.

Logic would seem to point to autonomy within a federal state as still the best practicable alternative open to the Croats; in such matters, however, logic is the first and most enduring casualty.

Front de Libération Québecois (FLQ)

Pierre Laporte, Minister of Labour and Immigration in the Quebec Government, was abducted on 10 October, 1970; one week later he was strangled by one of his captors. James Cross, British Trade Commissioner in Montreal, kidnapped on 5 October was released on 4 December; his abductors were allowed to leave Canada for Cuba. These two incidents guaranteed the notoriety of the FLQ.

The FLQ numbered among its many antecedent influences the wartime French and Belgian Resistance to German occupation, the writings of Fanon and Marcuse and the biographies of Lenin, Trotsky and (incongruously) Goering. The motivating example was most clearly that of Cuba. Identification was sought, especially by the young middle-class students who made up the bulk of the movement, with the oppressed minorities of the world; the sense of historical injustice and the stereotyping of the French Canadian as the 'serf of North American capitalism' lent a certain justification to such attitudes. The history of the FLQ does not reflect these idealistic ambitions; it is a story of the deterioration of personnel and methods into a bloodily unproductive terrorism. The movement went through a period of some middle-class support but ended by alienating all but the most rabid of those whose involvement was essential for its survival, the French Canadians themselves.

The first period of FLQ activity dates from 1963 when it was formed as an extremist breakaway from the Resistance Network. Its early militancy was associated with a Belgian, Schoeters, who had observed the Resistance movements of the Second World War and sought also to emulate the FLN of Algeria. The FLQ announced itself by planting bombs at a radio station and on railway lines; most spectacular, both in physical and historical terms, was the blowing up of the monument to Wolfe, the English General who had defeated Montcalm on the Heights of Abraham in 1759.

Propaganda was disseminated through posters headed, as during the Second World War in Belgium, '*Avis à la population*'. They were signed for good measure with the phrase 'Independence or Death' (probably modelled on Castro's '*Revolucion o Muerte*'). Bombs were also planted in letter boxes, which were regarded as symbols of Anglo-Saxon domination. Inevitably there was a death and, as is usual, it was an innocent bystander who was killed, in this case a night watchman. In June, 1963, the first groups of terrorists were apprehended. There was at this time some liberal sympathy with and romanticization of the movement. Books were published defending and excusing the terrorists (*La véritable histoire du FLQ* and *Les Résistants du FLQ*).

Late 1963 and early 1964 saw the revived FLQ (now calling itself the Army of Liberation of Quebec) switch tactics to holdups and arms thefts. In six months the group stole 40,000 dollars in cash plus equipment worth some 15,000 dollars. Although this section was broken up in April, 1964, the terrorism continued. An ex-Foreign Legion sergeant, Schirm, led a raid on a gunsmiths which resulted in the death of the manager. The group was swiftly apprehended and Schirm sentenced to life-imprisonment.

These incidents, though extreme and terrifying enough for the victims, were only a prelude to the main effort which followed. The subsequent course of events is associated with the only ideologue of note produced by the FLQ, Pierre Vallières. Vallières' ideas are contained in articles written for the underground Press and in his autobiography, *White Negroes of America* (1968), written in prison.

Vallières by his own account passed a rootless and restless adolescence; he drifted from one job to another, flirted with the religious life (leaving the Franciscans shouting '*Masturbez-vous, Monsieur*') and tried to write; he had an article published in 1957. He went to France for a while, returning to Quebec in 1963. In 1965 a 'new' FLQ under Vallières and a Left Wing political dabbler and journalist, Charles Gagnon, was founded.

The new movement began to publish advice to the budding terrorist and advocated the creation of a 'striking force'. Dynamite was stolen, then guns. A 64-year-old woman died after a strike-bound factory was bombed. More was to follow; two of the victims were terrorists killed by their own bombs— one in the Parliament buildings in Ottawa, one close to a factory. In the latter case the bomber was sixteen years old. Arrests followed and Vallières was imprisoned in the United States whither he had fled.

In Vallières' theory the small, violent movement is seen in Debrayist terms as the 'motor' of revolution. He repeats the familiar assertions of the rottenness of the system together with Utopian assurances that its destruction will bring about something better. Beyond Quebec, beyond Canada, Vallières envisages a global revolution which is to be achieved through the young; like Marcuse, Vallières sees the old as crass or evil or both.

How is this revolution to be carried out? The translation of the apocalyptic vision involves a certain vulgarization from revolutionary semantics to common slaughter, from fine words to dead bodies.

Bodies were not long in arriving; terrorism began anew in late 1969. An underground pamphlet, *La Victoire* gave instructions in bomb making, as well as in such matters as using an M1 carbine and manufacturing petrol bombs. *La Victoire* gave its version of the position:

'We live under a régime of violence created by the English

and the Federalists. In order to preserve their interests, and to continue to exploit us, they have installed, on our Quebec soil, their federal police dogs, as well as their federal armed forces.'

The conclusion was obvious: 'One must combat violence with violence.'

The pattern envisaged may be discovered by considering a manifesto of the *Front de Libération Populaire*, another fringe Québecois movement.

Phase 1 in their revolutionary model consists of demonstrations and some small-scale terrorism in order to polarize the situation. In Phase 2 the unions become 'revolutionary' which results in the final phase of armed activity and the 'destruction of the bourgeois order'. Bombs, suggests the manifesto, are designed to increase class-consciousness and 'radicalize the conflicts produced by the inner contradictions of the system itself'.

A programme of bombing began in September, 1969, directed at 'Anglo-Saxon' factories where there was industrial unrest but also against banks and 'symbols of repression' such as Canadian Army establishments. In February the Montreal Stock Exchange was bombed; the arrest of a single middle-class youth, Pierre Paul Geoffrey, on 5 March brought these attacks to an end. No more dramatic example of the sensitivity of the technological society could be imagined; Geoffrey admitted to over thirty bombings, his support cell seems to have been minute and he acted almost entirely alone.

The stage was thus set for the final act; the bacillae of hate and jealousy had been injected into the society and had infected some of the young; elsewhere in the world 'revolutionary example' abounded; in Latin America the wave of diplomatic killings and kidnappings was mounting. Dynamic youth was everywhere in arms—in Cuba, in South America, in protests against Vietnam and against racism. Guilt feelings among the affluent young at their own lack of a properly proletarian background and at their comfortable inaction sought release. Fanon and Vallières assured the young both that they were repressed and that self-liberation could be found through violence. 'Do it now,' urged Gagnon. 'We must put fire everywhere in Quebec. We must speak words of fire, do acts of fire, and escalate them.' The young French Canadian could persuade himself that he could fight for a global revolution against colonialism, racism, capitalism and the United States simply by blowing things (and people) up. If such idealists found themselves mixed up with criminals and psychopaths, they could comfort themselves with the thought that these were after all the very people in whom anarchist writers, and now Fanon, had seen revolutionary potential. Violence was the key—'Violence' which, Vallières asserted, 'attracts and fascinates the masses, as the ritual dances fascinate certain societies which are called primitive'.

Late in 1969 new action groups were formed; there followed a series of robberies, splits in the ranks of the FLQ, demonstrations and bombings culminating in the death of a woman in the Ministry of Defence in Ottawa. In June, 1970, attempts at kidnappings failed; the targets were Israeli and US consuls. The communiqué intended for issue in the latter case was found by the Police. It ended:

'Long Live the Cuban People! Long Live Fidel! Long Live the Cuban Revolution!'

It demanded that all 'political prisoners' (terrorists) were to be released.

On 5 October James Cross was taken. There followed seven communiqués containing various demands. Another FLQ cell took Laporte. Two thousand students rallied in support of the FLQ. Laporte was murdered and his body found in the boot of the car used to seize him. At 0230 hours on 4 December James Cross was released and the terrorists granted safe conduct to Cuba.

The Canadian public seem to have been ambivalent in their attitude to terrorism; in particular they disliked the use of troops in the streets. The Central Committee of National Trade

Unions in Montreal and some politicians tried to score debating points over the issue.

From 15 October, 1970, there was declared to be a state of insurrection; detailed arrangements for dealing with it were given in the Public Order Regulations, 1970. Ten thousand police, supported by troops, arrested two hundred and fifty suspects in one hundred and seventy separate raids throughout Quebec. There were complaints at the draconian measures adopted by the Government. Prime Minister Trudeau replied:

'There are a lot of bleeding hearts around who just don't like to see people with helmets and guns. All I can say is, go on and bleed, but it is more important to keep law and order in the society than to be worried about weak-kneed people . . . I think society must take every means at its disposal to defend itself against the emergence of a parallel power which defies the elected power in this country.'[7]

Trudeau made this comment when under pressure. In a more studied statement in the House of Commons he said:

'I recognize that this extreme position into which governments have been forced is in some respects a trap. It is a well-known technique of revolutionary groups who attempt to destroy society by unjustified violence to goad the authorities into inflexible attitudes. The revolutionaries then employ this evidence of alleged authoritarianism as justification for the need to use violence in their renewed attacks on the social structure. I appeal to all Canadians not to become so obsessed by what the Government has done today in response to terrorism that they forget the opening play in this vicious game. That play was taken by the revolutionaries; they chose to use bombing, murder and kidnapping.'

Separatism in Quebec is still alive but is generally now being pursued in a constitutional manner. The Quebec Party is now the main opposition party in the province.

151

The ETA, seeking 'Freedom for the Basque Homeland', has grafted a Left Wing terrorism on to traditional Basque Nationalism. The 'Basque Homeland' consists of four Spanish north-eastern provinces and the French areas of Labourd, Basse Navarre and Soule. ETA is an offshoot of the less extreme Basque National Party. The movement has been characterized both by clerical involvement and by the degree of support given by intellectuals in Spain and elsewhere. 'Basque separatism' has become a convenient stick with which to beat General Franco and his Falange Party, especially among older European liberals who remember the Spanish Civil War.

Unrest during 1968 led to the assassination of the head of political security in Guipozcoa Province, Señor Manzanas, in August of that year; the Government reacted strongly, immediately taking Emergency Powers and making over two hundred arrests. Four Basques were jailed in December for acts of a 'separatist, Communist and terrorist nature'. The arrests and trial of a number of priests in 1969 resulted in five of them being sentenced in Burgos; two were imprisoned for twelve years and three for ten. Strong protests were made by the Church authorities at the manner of their arrest—they had been forcibly removed from the Bishop's Palace in Bilbao. Four more priests were imprisoned in October for having been accessories after the fact in the shooting of a taxi driver.

In December, 1970, there opened the 'Burgos trial' which received widespread international attention and resulted in strikes and demonstrations throughout the Basque country. The Government's insistence on holding a military rather than a civilian trial led to protests by lawyers and students in Madrid in addition to the disturbances in the north of Spain. At the trial the defendants admitted belonging to the ETA but denied having shot Manzanas. Unlike terrorists elsewhere they defended themselves vigorously, to the point where they had to be removed from the court after one of their number had tried to attack the Judge. They were led away to shouts of 'Long Live Basque Freedom' and the strains of a Basque marching song from the Civil War. Eventually the Tribunal concluded that the accuseds' aim was the setting up of an independent Basque Marxist-Leninist State. More demonstrations followed (December, 1971) and the Government granted the police power to hold suspects for up to six months without trial. In Catalonia artists and intellectuals staged a sympathy 'sit in' at the Abbey of Montserrat.

Internationally the Burgos trial aroused great interest. Pronouncement of the death sentence on some of the accused resulted in diplomatic comment and organized protest. Left Wing groups attacked Spanish diplomatic premises in Paris, Brussels, Frankfurt, Rome and Naples while demonstrations were held in London, Copenhagen and Stockholm. In Spain the West German Consul in Saragossa was kidnapped by a splinter group of the ETA calling itself *Among Brothers*. This move was apparently intended to produce a bargaining counter for the lives of those in custody. The Consul was, however, released before the verdicts in the Burgos trial were given.

Franco's followers organized counter-demonstrations; the General, in a nationwide broadcast, agreed, in view of the support he had received, to commute the death sentences to thirty years' imprisonment. He waited until the day fixed for the firing squad to do its work before making the announcement.

In 1971 the Spanish authorities pursued the ETA vigorously and on both sides the battle was intensified. ETA itself split into two factions; the nationalist wing did most of the fighting while the Marxists (themselves divided as to whether to remain specifically Basque or to co-operate with the Spanish Communist Party in a nationwide proletarian-based movement) did most of the talking. There was also a small Maoist clique called *Kommunistak*. The ETA thus displayed similar alignments to those of the IRA and is reported to have had some contact with the Provisionals.

Tactics used by ETA have included bomb attacks, bank raids and kidnappings. In December, 1971, they stole £60,000 from a Bank and bombed a yacht club (Yacht clubs, bastions of bourgeois influence, appear to be a favourite target. Another was burned down in 1973). January, 1972, saw the kidnapping of a well-known businessman, Señor Zabala. ETA's demands were industrial—wage rises and reinstatement of dismissed workers. Eventually the workers themselves asked for the release of their boss; he was dumped on a road, hooded and tied, but alive.

During the rest of 1972 ETA kept up the pressure though with heavy losses. While several policemen were killed and bombings continued ETA lost a number of its leaders; a handful were killed and over sixty arrested. The announcement by the French Government (8 October, 1972) that it was banning ETA constituted a serious blow to the organization which was now deprived of a relatively safe base from which to operate. In Saragossa the French Consul died of burns received when terrorists tied him up and then, as they left, detonated an incendiary bomb. ETA disclaimed responsibility which was claimed by a breakaway group, the Hammer and Sickle Co-Operative. Five students at Saragossa University were subsequently arrested and sentenced to thirty years' imprisonment each. Further attacks were mounted against the offices of Government-backed Trade Unions and in January, 1973, in a carbon copy of the Zabala affair, Señor Huarte, a member of one of the richest families in Spain, was seized. After negotiations over wages and reinstatements (and possibly a ransom) Huarte was released. In their search for the kidnappers the police made twenty arrests. In April the 28-year-old leader of the military wing of the ETA, Señor Mendizabal, died in hospital as a result of injuries received in a shoot-out with the police. Further disturbances occurred on May Day. ETA activity has continued; in a gun battle in the middle of Bilbao in September two ETA members were wounded and arrested. In December, 1973, at a meeting held in France, the ETA factions agreed to paper over the doctrinal cracks once more and attempt a unified strategy.

The chances of success for ETA appear very slight. They are facing a Government which has no need to observe democratic processes; ETA has no secure base and no substantial inter-national support. Internecine feuds have weakened the organi-zation and the claim to the southern French provinces as part of an eventual Basque state is both unrealistic and counter-productive in terms of fighting the Spanish Government. Despite the involvement of Left Wing priests, (The area of Burgos is gaining a reputation in this respect.) and intellectuals there is little evidence of mass insurrectionary support. A con-fused situation arising in a post-Franco Spain might afford some opportunities but it is unlikely that any Government in Madrid would be prepared to grant anything further than a greater degree of autonomy and cultural recognition to an area so economically important to the whole country. The present Spanish Government has given every indication that in any confrontation with the ETA it intends to be ruthless and has backed this with a massive police presence and by re-equipping its security forces with more sophisticated weaponry. Nor does international pressure hold out any promise for the ETA; such pressure is anti-Franco rather than pro-Basque. The 'Basque dimension' would swiftly be forgotten by any central Spanish Marxist-Leninist régime, which on all the historical and con-temporary evidence, would be equally as rigorous as Franco in dealing with nationalist and 'anti-State' elements. Franco has dismissed international pressures as 'Communist-orchestrated'; to bow to them would be construed in Spain, both by his sup-porters and enemies, as a sign of weakness. The Catalans would, in their turn, increase the pressure for further de-centralization, should any concessions be made to the Basques.

In almost every respect where the Provisional IRA, which some members of the ETA affect to admire, is strong, the Basques labour under severe disadvantages.

NOTES

1. Movements which have operated against the British are considered in the following Chapter.
2. Quoted Gaucher, *The Terrorists*, Secker and Warburg, 1968, Chapter 11.
3. See Chapter 11.
4. Some evidence also suggests Russian involvement.
5. See Chapter 1.
6. See P. Lendvai, *National Tensions in Yugoslavia*, Institute for the Study of Conflict, 1972, p. 15.
7. Trudeau, interviewed about the introduction of War Measures, October, 1970.

CHAPTER 10

The British Experience of Urban Terror

No Army has had greater experience of combating contemporary urban terrorism than that of the United Kingdom and no country has been so consistently outmanoeuvred in the psychological and political aspects of the matter. The post-First World War Irish insurrection (seen by one expert as a 'milestone in military history')[1] exploited the war-weariness of the British and their unwillingness to employ mass terror. Significant sections of liberal opinion in Britain sympathized with the Irish and the employment of the auxiliary police, the 'Black and Tans', handed a propaganda victory to the Irish which is still paying dividends. Publicity matters were excellently handled by the insurgents even to the extent of laying on special trains for foreign correspondents known as 'Irish Scenic Railway trips'. Insurgent intelligence, the key in all such operations, was superior and British attempts to repair this defect met with the killing of thirteen out of sixteen newly introduced agents. Retaliation at Croke Park on 21 November, 1920, led to a second 'Bloody Sunday'.

Settlement of the affair was a political victory for the insurgents (though seen by some of them as a betrayal), who were almost exhausted militarily by mid-1921. Violence had been used in a politically calculated manner, taking due account of the existing mood of British and world opinion. It was an example of the application of Lawrence's dictum.[2]

The lessons of these events were applied against the British in Palestine, in Cyprus and, less skilfully, in Aden; they are currently being used again in the homeland with far greater technical resources. The most proficient and politically effective campaign was that waged by Jewish military and terrorist organizations in Palestine.

The Irgun Zvei Leumi and the Stern Gang
Jewish emigration began in earnest when the assassination of the Tsar in 1881 produced one of the characteristic Russian reflexes to internal tension, an anti-Semitic pogrom. Thus begun, the graph of movement to Palestine continued steadily upwards thereafter with steep surges in 1904, 1925 and 1930. Nazi persecution added further impetus; the Arabs, already alarmed, stepped up terrorist activities. Jews organized self-defence units but for some these were not enough; fire, they argued, must be answered with fire. Biblical quotation has been used by terrorists from Guatemala to Algeria and in Palestine the *Irgun Zvei Leumi* (National Military Organization), formed in 1937, began to exact an 'eye for an eye, a tooth for a tooth'.

Irgun aimed not only to take reprisals against Arab terrorists but to strengthen the will and sense of national identity of the Jewish people. The heroic myth of the Jews was one of suffering, not of doing. Irgun's ritual militarism with its secrecy and ceremony were designed to give the Jews a virile self-respect, a collective *machismo*. The Irgun leader felt that the new generation must supplement the traditional Jewish intellectual subtleties with a new physical resolution:

'We fight therefore we are.'

(This myth of socially and racially creative violence came from and was to be used by other very different groups.)

In 1917 the British had conceded the principle of a Jewish Homeland—though not a Jewish State; immigration had been far greater than they had envisaged and, with another world war apparently imminent, they set about mending their fences with the Arabs. Immigration into Palestine was virtually suspended, the new policy being contained in a White Paper of 7 May, 1939. It appeared to the Jews that Arab terrorism had

158

played some part in stimulating this decision. Irgun drew their own conclusions; they would out-terrorize the terrorists. If violence influenced the British then Irgun would undertake to be more persuasive than the Arabs. The logic of such a policy was, however, called in question by the outbreak of the Second World War. Most Jewish activists, including the Irgun, agreed to suspend operations in favour of the common anti-Fascist cause.

Irgun now suffered the defection of its own extremists. To one of the most dedicated activists, Abraham Stern, postponement of the struggle was unthinkable. War was an opportunity rather than an impediment. Britain remained the main enemy. Thus was born the Stern Gang, a small (under two hundred) and fanatically single-minded terrorist sect. They were of the same mind as the Russian populists *Narodnaya Volya*. Avigad, a leading Sternist, studied the techniques of terrorism (even Al Capone was included in his researches). Libraries are the intellectual terrorists' arsenal (Sternist code reflected this— 'books' meant 'guns' and 'library', 'warehouse'). Stern was killed in February, 1942. Terrorism continued, now under the name of Fighters for the Freedom of Israel. It was the terrorism of the weak.The organization lacked numbers and resources. Compromise was rejected, even with death. If challenged the terrorist was to fight—'no surrender'. Unable to undertake mass action or mount large scale operations at logistic targets such as fuel dumps and the communications system they turned to one of the few remaining alternatives—assassination. Assassinations were designed to dramatize and publicize and, in the case of British pro-consuls, *pour encourager les autres*. Unsuccessful attempts (at least six) were made on the life of the High Commissioner. Eventually a less well-guarded target was chosen—Lord Moyne, Minister of State for the Near East, resident in Egypt. In November, 1944, he was shot dead outside his villa in the suburbs of Cairo. His attackers, attempting to escape by bicycle, were captured. They used their trial as a propaganda exercise, professing themselves willing to die. In March, 1945, they were duly hung; one was twenty-three years' old, the other seventeen.

Their deed achieved publicity but little else. Most Jews denounced the killing. Quite apart from any moral considerations such actions were at that time and place technically counter-productive. Irgun's campaign, which returned to the offensive in 1944, was politically more effective, although no less ruthless.

Irgun's superior political logic led them to concentrate on propaganda, both internally and internationally. In Palestine the target was British prestige which was to be shaken by attacks on public buildings and by quasi-judicial retaliatory executions and humiliations of British Officers and NCOs. Internationally the object was to capitalize on an already favourable world opinion which, horrified at the revelations of Jewish concentration camp sufferings, was not likely to favour further 'oppression'.

The Zionists won the propaganda war against the British completely and almost conclusively. (They have continued to do so; the film *Exodus* was an excellent demonstration of what Marxist-Leninists call the 'creative function of history'.) Every incident was given the full treatment before the World's Press; the body of a child, who had died at sea in one of the miserable craft in which the Jews attempted to sail to Palestine, was held up, 'gassed by the Nazi-British'. 'Boat propaganda' achieved its greatest success with the sinking of the refugee ship *Patria* (almost certainly the work of Irgun); two hundred and forty refugees and some policemen were killed. This, coming after earlier disasters, was presented as an act of desperate self-destruction by the passengers. The authorities played into the hands of the terrorists' propaganda on a number of occasions, notably when General Barker, commanding in Palestine, issued a non-fraternization order designed partly to 'punish the Jews in a way the race dislikes—in their pockets'. This kind of action was manna indeed to Jewish publicists; they succeeded in equating anti-Zionism with anti-Semitism—once that had been accomplished the British were branded as no better than the Nazis.

Army and police in Palestine were hampered by being unable to identify their enemy—not merely because he merged with the civilian population but because the status of the various groups involved was so nebulous. *Haganah*, the most moderate group, at times made common cause with Irgun and the Sternists—thus in October, 1945, they produced a co-ordinated example of their joint power; Haganah hit the railways, Irgun the stations and the Sternists the Haifa oil refinery. At other times Irgun operated independently as when, on 25 April, 1946, they murdered seven British soldiers in their tents.

Politically the position was absurdly complicated; if someone was caught breaking the law and arrested it depended whether he was Haganah, Irgun or Stern as to whether he would be charged or released.

Attempts at counter-terrorism under the aegis of Major Roy Farran were of doubtful value. Farran organized a special squad of the Palestine Police (March, 1947) which operated in plain clothes. Eventually he was accused of murder on flimsy evidence and, after two escapes from custody, stood trial and was acquitted. The whole exercise, however viewed militarily, was politically ill-conceived and delivered yet another propaganda bonus to the Zionist cause.

Internationally the Irgun sought to influence particularly the United States, with its powerful Jewish minority and its historic commitment to a vague principle of 'self-determination'. In the event the United States Jewry through the Hebrew Committee of National Liberation provided considerable financial and pressure group support for Irgun.

Irgun accomplished its publicity aims, both internally and internationally, by providing a detailed news service via a secret radio station and a press and poster campaign. The British were to be persuaded that the game was not worth the candle. Irgun appreciation of the situation included an appraisal of the post-war weakness and weariness of Britain, both economically and psychologically. Militarily the British lines of communication were extremely vulnerable; half the Army, observed Farran, were engaged in guarding the other half.

In July, 1946, Irgun blew up a wing of the King David Hotel in Jerusalem. Its leader, Menachem Begin, claimed that a warning was given but casualties were high, over two hundred people being killed or wounded. *Haganah* disassociated itself from the affair, which was of doubtful political value since non-combatants were killed and the nature of the attack tended to divide the Jewish community. More effective was the rescue of a number of prisoners from the ancient fortress of Acre (May, 1947); this attack, at once spectacular and sacrificial, achieved its impact despite—or because of—the losses sustained by Irgun during the withdrawal.

Jewish terrorism has been closely studied and attempts made at emulation by groups as disparate as the Uruguayan Tupamaros and the Algerian OAS. In Northern Ireland the splinter group, Ulster Freedom Fighters (UFF) made reference, during their initial Press briefing, to the 'Star of David' and claimed common ground with the 'Jewish people'. Their model was probably the Stern Gang, also known as Fighters for the Freedom of Israel; it too operated in small three-man sections.

Copiers of the Irgun's tactics have been less politically aware than their original. Irgun showed a degree of imagination in raising the environmental pressures on the occupying forces— including such ruses as the placing of dummy bombs and the creation of false alarms, in contradistinction to the Sternists who, kamikaze-like, aimed to take as many as possible of the enemy with them should they be challenged, Irgun were prepared to prevaricate and deceive. Hiding among the flora and fauna of the human jungle Irgun would strike and then disappear into the faceless city hordes. While the use of crowds as cover is part of the common heritage of the terrorist, other Irgun ideas have largely been ignored. Irgun always attempted to present Jewish solidarity against Arab and British alike. Generally the temptation to attack fellow Jews who adopted a more peaceful line was resisted. Later terrorist groups have not always grasped the importance of maintaining ethnic solidarity. To terrorize those on your side who are seeking a peaceful solution may imperil the attainment of the overall political objective. Such people, especially when members of lower income groups, constitute the base for terrorist operations. Blurring the ethnic divisions in a colonial or separatist campaign enables the 'occupying power' to appear as protector rather than exploiter. Unselective terror leaves scores to be settled and tears asunder the unity of the ethnic minority which in turn tends to lead to internecine warfare subversive of the main aim. Divisions among the terrorists also facilitate the operation of counter-terror groups by the authorities.

Irgun was also careful to be clear in its reportage. While the propaganda of allegation should for maximum effectiveness be as vague and exaggerated as possible the underlying facts must be accurately presented. If material is in principle open to refutation it must not be tampered with.

Irgun's precise and ruthless retaliation methods involved the flogging of a Brigade Major of the British Airborne Division when Jewish terrorists were beaten and, when the Jewish terrorist Gruner was hanged, two British sergeants were executed by Irgun, the bodies being booby-trapped.

Jewish activists were tough and efficient. Hardened in the bitter school of a strife-torn Europe where they had to be clever and unscrupulous in order to survive they became, in Palestine, a formidable enemy.

EOKA—Cyprus

On the 10 November, 1954, George Grivas arrived back on the island of his birth. His career up to that time had been compounded of disappointments and frustrations. Now at the age of 54 he could put behind him the defeats of 1922 at the hands of the Turks and the German victory of 1941. The years of study which, instead of bringing him the General's rank which he coveted, had resulted in his being pensioned off and in the rejection of his ideas by the Greek voters after the Second World War could now be fulfilled in a new campaign. All that he had observed of the Turkish irregulars, the tactics of the

Greek dictator Metaxas, of the Gestapo and of the Greek Communist terrorists could now be put into bloody practice. Three passions dominated his life—anti-Communism, loyalty to the Orthodox Church and a self-conscious Hellenism which led him to seek to create a Greater Greece through the incorporation of Cyprus. His military experience and his knowledge of his native Cyprus and the Cypriot psychology could at last fuse to give him a final triumph. *Enosis* (union with Greece) had been a main concern since his days at the Royal Hellenic Academy and, as a practical possibility rather than a romantic hope, since 1929. Now he might realize his ambition.

When he left the island of Cyprus some four and a half years after that dusk landing in 1954 he would leave behind five hundred and eight dead, among them more than one hundred and forty British and two hundred and eighteen Greek. He would also leave a legend which has waxed more exaggerated and more complex with the passing years . . . but he would not have achieved Enosis.

Political exploitation of the campaign was to be in the hands of Archbishop Makarios, whom Grivas had first met in Athens in 1946. Makarios could provide the assurance of divine assistance as well as the more practical co-operation of his monks; churches and monasteries could provide sanctuary for men—and arms. To the outside world the Greek Government would be Grivas' propagandist and patron.

Much has been made, especially by Grivas and his supporters, of the difficulty of fighting a terrorist campaign in a comparatively small island (140 miles long, 60 miles wide) but the chances of success were in truth limited more by political than by geographical factors. Cyprus was strategically important both as a listening post and 'aircraft carrier' in the Eastern Mediterranean and negatively in that denial of it to the West might open up possibilities of subsequent infiltration by the Russians. The presence of a Turkish minority—almost 20% of the population—and the proximity of Turkey (40 miles away) further confused the political position. Turkey regarded Cyprus, both on historical (she had once possessed it, Greece never had) and geographical grounds as at least as much her concern as that of the Greeks. Kutchuk, the Turkish leader in Cyprus, expressed this attitude in his newspaper in 1954:

> 'From a legal as well as a moral point of view, Turkey as the initial owner of the island just before the British occupation has a first option to Cyprus. From a world-wide political point of view as well as from geographical and strategic points of view Cyprus must be handed to Turkey if Great Britain is going to quit.'[3]

Grivas' history as a Right Wing activist in Greece was not to the liking of that section of the Cypriot population represented by the Communist Party (AKEL). Grivas had been on the Communists' death list before and some members of AKEL might have been willing to finish the job. The attitude of the Greek Government had to be ambivalent; on the one hand they were bound to support Grivas since public opinion at home was strongly on his side. Yet to have the Cyprus problem landed in their laps would have involved a conflict with Turkey and would have split the North Atlantic Treaty Organization on its most sensitive flank. Greece had to take a longer view than Grivas. While arguing before the world for 'self determination' and giving (sometimes virulent) propaganda support and arms to Grivas the Greek Government did so in the sure knowledge that Britain would have in any case to remain in Cyprus for some years.

Grivas, who liked to affect the pose of the 'simple soldier' while pursuing the most outrageously political initiatives, claimed to see himself as the strong right arm of Makarios; he, Grivas, would supply the diplomacy of force, Makarios that of words.

The aims of the EOKA campaign were articulated with precision; international public opinion must be roused and the British discomfited until, under United Nations' pressure, they were forced to give way 'in accordance with the desires of the Cypriot people and the whole Greek nation'.[4] Three main tactics were to be adopted—sabotage, attacks on British forces and the organization of the population in a policy of non-co-operation and hindrance.

Grivas eventually organized a number of different types of 'fighting groups'; mountain guerrillas, chiefly concerned with ambushes and sabotage, village groups armed with shotguns (mainly of nuisance and morale value) and finally town groups aiming at attacks on installations, barracks, police stations and terrorism against police, troops and 'informers'. According to Grivas (February, 1956) the strength of these units was some 53 men in the mountains, 220 in the towns and 750 in the villages. Town groups also organized special 'execution squads' (like those of Opla, the Communist killers Grivas had observed at work in 1944-5).

It was the urban activities of EOKA which made most impact on public opinion, especially in the United Kingdom and the organization in the towns was essential to the campaign, particularly in Nicosia which is the hub of the island's communication system.

Grivas prefaced his campaign by invoking the shades of Marathon, Salamis and Thermopylae; he hoped, it would seem, to fight an heroic battle which would shame the British in the eyes of the world.

The reality was different:

'. . . at 6.00 pm they saw a Briton watering his garden with a hose. Pavlou walked up to the garden wall and shot him at close range; then, as he screamed and fell, fired three more shots into him at close range . . . I sent my congratulations on this attack.'[5]

Personnel for these execution squads was drawn from the young who might graduate to them via faithful service as couriers or demonstrators and by the efficient carrying out of orders to harass and beat up fellow Greeks who did not share their views. Grivas placed great emphasis on the recruitment and indoctrination of the very young and reports his successes in this respect with pride. Loyalty to the 'Leader' was to take precedence over friend and family. Total subjection of the individual to the cause, that was the ideal: 'Discipline to the voice of duty to the struggling Fatherland. Cyprus commands us not the family. The Fatherland is more honest, decent and more sacred than the father, the mother and all the other ancestors.'[6]

Two main support organizations were set up, PEKA (Political Committee of the Cyprus Struggle) and, on the pattern already created by Makarios' PEON (Pan Cyprian Organization of Youth) the young people's movement ANE (Young Stalwarts). ANE undertook the organization of schoolchildren and denounced those of all ages who were suspected of anti-EOKA sentiments. This group also constituted an instant juvenile 'rentacrowd' and a reserve pool of manpower so that shot or captured terrorists might be instantly replaced. ANE activities ranged from beating up opponents to the flying of Greek flags over schools so that the troops, obliged to take them down, might be the object of harassment and provocation. The difficulty facing troops carrying out political orders given without careful thought as to their military practicability is well illustrated by the business of hauling down flags or erasing slogans. In the event of a population refusing to carry out instructions in these matters the soldiers had to do the job themselves. They were then provoked and, even if they succeeded in keeping their tempers, their activities would be described as insulting (in the case of flags) or as desecration if, as was often the case, the offending slogans were painted on the walls of a Church. ANE could also be used to back up assassination squads whose members might find it useful to have children at hand to whom guns might be handed immediately after a job.

EOKA also used women mainly as couriers and as decoys to divert the attention of the Security Forces at roadblocks and during search operations. The inexperience of the large numbers of National Servicemen involved in Cyprus gave such tactics a greater chance of success. Occasionally EOKA girls undertook a more active role. Attempts were made to lure servicemen to flats where they might be taken hostage against the life of a captured terrorist; an RAF sergeant met his death in this way when he resisted capture.

EOKA's campaign was confined to Cyprus. Makarios vetoed Grivas' plan to carry the fight to England; large scale and indiscriminate bombing was also avoided, the preferred method of operation in urban areas being the individual 'execution'.

The procedure involved in these operations was that the squad would nominate potential victims to Grivas, who would examine the plan, suggest amendments and give the go-ahead. Alternatively groups might be sent out to look for targets of opportunity—military patrols or off-duty soldiers or policemen. The tactic was then to shadow them and to shoot the victims in the back in as crowded a place as possible in order to use the pedestrians as cover and an impediment to any pursuers. Urban groups were so organized that links between sector chiefs and individual sections were direct, with no lateral contact allowed. Sabotage, Execution and Shotgun groups were later (1957) supplemented by anti-Turkish groups. Sector chiefs could also utilize PEKA and ANE.

In addition to assassination EOKA used bombs, both thrown by hand into army vehicles and time bombs. In the latter case they had difficulty in mastering the techniques of manufacture. Their lack of expertise was just as well for Field-Marshal Sir John Harding who slept with a bomb under his mattress (the bomb was discovered in the morning) and for the passengers in an RAF Comet, the bomb in that case going off too early. Pressure or wire-detonated mines were also used, often in conjunction with an ambush; hairpin bends were favourite spots. Only once, as far as is known, did EOKA use a parcel bomb; disguised as a book, it killed a British Civil Servant.

EOKA's record is, much more than in the case of most similar movements, the reflection of the personality of one man—Grivas. Some EOKA fighters made the self-sacrifice which their leader demanded, refusing to surrender Afxentiou, one of the earliest recruits to EOKA, was burnt to death in his hide. Kyriakos Matsis, having ordered his men to give themselves up, was killed by a grenade thrown into his refuge. Yet the shooting of off-duty soldiers, especially of one doing his Christmas shopping in 1955 and the brutal murder of the wife of an army sergeant on 3 October, 1958 (the former on the infamous 'murder mile'—Ledra Street, Nicosia, the latter in Famagusta) did the cause of Enosis no good. Such acts did result in a predictably violent reaction by the Army with consequent bad publicity. Yet they failed to stimulate a significant public demand in the United Kingdom to get out at any price. From the EOKA viewpoint they must be regarded as counter-productive and the same judgement must be applied to the teen-age campaign of intimidation especially during the boycott of British goods and firms ordered by Grivas from 6 March, 1958.

Sabotage of British installations, especially those of a military nature, was effective both tactically and politically. Attacks on water and electricity supplies were less sensible; in the first place such targets were softer and thus produced less propaganda effect and secondly they hurt the Greek population more than the British, who were better able to make alternative emergency arrangements.

Despite Grivas' efforts the movement suffered from internal dissensions; in particular the defection of Ashiotis in October, 1957, revealed the extent to which EOKA was holding the countryside in a grip of terror. Ashiotis spoke of the amount of anti-British propaganda, atrocity accusations, etc, which the public were forced to produce; as Grivas remarks in his memoirs, 'the gentlemen of the Press are easily deluded'. EOKA occasionally overplayed its hand, however, as when numbers of 'wounded and beaten' villagers were asked to remove their bandages—to reveal that the whole affair was a charade since there were no marks to be seen. Neither Irgun nor the FLN would have made such an error; they would have called for volunteers and beaten them themselves before sending them before the doctors.

To a remarkable degree Grivas saw the battle as a personal affair between himself and the British Commanders in Cyprus

—especially Harding. The latter was given the full propaganda treatment by Grivas and Athens: he was a 'butcher', 'anthropoid Harding', 'a blood-stained ogre', etc. Grivas' memoirs are peppered with insults directed at British Generals, together with references to the divinely guided infallibility of Dighenis.

Yet, despite some successes, the British failed to catch Grivas or destroy EOKA. In the urban context the 'Q' patrols, with an innocent civilian car looking out for incidents or wanted individuals but in instant communication with troops and police, achieved some impact. But with the local police infiltrated or terrorized, the lack of accurate and reliable intelligence critically hampered the Security Forces, a disadvantage which the introduction of Special Branch experts from the United Kingdom never fully overcame.

In the last analysis there is only one criterion on which a terrorist movement may be judged and that is in terms of its political effectiveness; not on heroism, nor on the amount of blood spilt or the legends inspired. On that count Grivas failed. There was no union with Greece. Cyprus became independent. The British retained two sovereign base areas on the island. Grivas' draft of the EOKA ceasefire was edited by Makarios who cut out references to the lack of achievement of 'untrammelled freedom' and the fact that the compromise 'does not satisfy our desires'. Divisions between the two men, latent during the campaign, were ready to come into the open.

From 1964 to 1967 Grivas commanded the Cypriot National Guard in which role he continued to provoke the Turks, worry the United Nations Peacekeeping Force and embarrass the Makarios Government. In November, 1967, after a particularly serious period of inter-communal strife Grivas was recalled to Athens. Still obsessed by *enosis*, however, he returned secretly to Cyprus in August, 1971 and resumed his campaign of terrorism. His fighters were reconstituted as EOKA 'B'. Makarios survived assassination attempts and finally outlived his rival; a heart attack killed 'Dighenis' on 27 January, 1974. At the funeral 70,000 mourners followed his coffin.

Grivas was dead but his presence continued to haunt the

island. Makarios offered amnesty but fighting continued and in April, 1974, EOKA 'B' was formally outlawed. The Archbishop's counter-terrorist organization, the Police Tactical Reserve, met EOKA with its own weapons of terror and assassination. *Enosis* by terrorism had failed; the National Guard therefore tried *enosis* by *coup d'état*. In the event all the previous fears of anti-Grivas Cypriots were proved to have been justified. The Turks invaded Cyprus. In Athens the Government of the Colonels collapsed.

Thus Grivas' supporters failed even as he had failed—yet his earlier campaign against the British had considerable influence on the Irish Republican Army. Over thirty Greek Cypriots were jailed in Britain where they made contact with fellow prisoners from Ireland. In particular the leader of the Nicosia execution team, Nicos Sampson, was personally known to IRA men. Sampson's squad were instrumental in some twenty murders in Nicosia in late 1956 and early 1957 before his arrest in February, 1957. In July, 1974, Sampson surfaced briefly as the National Guard's 'President of Cyprus'.

It is instructive to compare the story of terrorism in Cyprus with the contemporary situation in Northern Ireland.

Eire has proved unwilling to play the part of Greece but in other respects there are striking parallels. Like EOKA the Provisional IRA seeks through violence to cauterize the wounds of history, it too looks to dead heroes to provide motivation rather than to contemporary social realities. Elements of the Church have proved ready to provide succour to terrorists. As the Greeks had the Turks with their Volkan underground movement so the Provisionals have the Protestants and the UFF. Inter-communal rioting and the need for defence of 'their' areas provides a justification for the IRA even as it did for EOKA. There are certain tactical similarities although the Provisionals' campaign has been far more bloody and indiscriminate. The Provisionals too are unlikely to achieve their 'enosis'.

Before facing the IRA, however, the British Army had to fight another anti-terrorist campaign—in Aden.

NLF and FLOSY—Aden 1964-7

The British Army fought two separate campaigns in South Arabia from 1964 to 1967; a war in the desert and on the streets in Aden State. The latter area was well suited to urban violence; the shanty towns of Sheikh Othman and Dar Saad, straddling the route to the Yemen, provided cover for supply movements while the mountain-ringed bowl of Crater proved a hot bed of terrorism.

Two main terrorist organizations were involved: the National Liberation Front (NLF) and the rival Front for the Liberation of the South Yemen (FLOSY). Both used violence against the British and each other, and both received weapons, training and financial support from Egypt's Colonel Nasser. FLOSY was the more politically sophisticated and was closely aligned to Egypt. NLF, while prepared to use Egyptian aid, tended to maintain a more independent line and regarded FLOSY as over-theoretical for the business in hand. FLOSY created its own terrorist arm (PORF—Popular Organization of Revolutionary Forces) but it was used mainly to fight the NLF rather than the British. During 1966 NLF was for a time incorporated into FLOSY but broke away in December of that year.

The Aden situation was analogous to that in Cyprus—even down to having its own 'Murder Mile'—the Maalla Straight. In propaganda terms the Arabs were better placed than had been Grivas. From the Yemen, which provided a training and logistics base, came a steady stream of anti-British virulence, backed by a similar barrage from Cairo. Arms were smuggled from the Yemen in a variety of improbable containers, including the insides of camels. The most potent product coming out of the Yemen was, however, the radio broadcast; the terrorists most insidious weapon was the transistor radio, which in Aden was in cheap and plentiful supply.

The Security Forces had not only to contend with a terrorist organization which enjoyed a safe haven and supply base in the Yemen, outside help and encouragement from the then Saviour of the Arab World, Gamal Abdel Nasser, but, on top of all that, a complicated and unsteady political direction from their own side. The original British aim (as contained in a White Paper of 1964) was to establish an independent Federation of South Arabia while retaining a base in Aden itself. Adeni politicians were obstructive; they had a (fully reciprocated) dislike of the feudal Sheikhs who were to be their political bedfellows. Failure to obtain agreement among the various parties led to the imposition of 'direct rule' in Aden in September, 1965. Originally the changeover from British to local control was scheduled for 1968; in February, 1966, however, this was changed—there was to be a complete withdrawal. Notice was thus given of the decision to quit. The time remaining was in fact to be taken up with competitive terrorism between the NLF and FLOSY each of which wanted to be able to say that it was *they* who had 'kicked the British out'. The 'timetable for withdrawal' exacerbated rather than quietened the situation.

Once it became clear that the British were indeed pulling out the security situation rapidly worsened. Those who had previously relied on British assurances, notably the Federal Government, swiftly lost heart; the Adenis, for their part, were clearly not going to allow themselves to be seen, come the day of 'freedom' (and judgement) to be anything other than rabidly anti-British.

Since 1964 the terrorists' aim had been to destroy the authorities' sources of intelligence by intimidating the population and physically eliminating members of the Police Special Branch. Anybody co-operating with the British, either politically or by giving evidence in court, was threatened and, if he persisted, killed. While in the early years the terrorists had been in general inept—instances occurred, for example, of bomb throwers (paid about 50p a time) hurling the pin and hanging on to the grenade—the announcement of withdrawal gave them new encouragement. The Egyptians, who had been having some doubts about the cost-effectiveness of their investment in terrorism, now saw political dividends ahead and hastened to support the cause more fervently than ever.

Terrorism increased by 50% and continued to escalate up until the time the British left. Profiting from Egyptian instruction the terrorists became technically more proficient. They began to use mortars and parcel bombs, their murder squads became more aggressive and more successful—not merely in seeking targets of opportunity but also in selecting the time and place for the assassination of leading political figures. Infiltration of the police ensured good intelligence. Allegations of brutality, principally at the Al Mansoura detention centre, brought investigators to Aden—the International Red Cross, Amnesty and a further enquiry by Mr Roderick Bowen QC. Little evidence was found to support the charges. The result was that the deterrent effect of rumour was lost. It seemed obvious to the citizenry that, since the British were 'paper tigers', the only people they had to fear were the terrorists—and they acted accordingly. Egypt's defeat in the 1967 Arab-Israeli War, while it momentarily dented morale, in the end sent the NLF back into the fight with renewed energy. Stories of British collusion with Israel meant that the local terrorist could regard the British soldier as a substitute Israeli, with a corresponding rise in motivation.

Strikes and demonstrations were used both as an illustration of control over the population and as a cover for their attacks on the Army; schoolchildren, as in Cyprus, played a prominent part in these activities. NLF also urged its supporters to sabotage British installations and property—one of the more imaginative suggestions was that air conditioning systems be destroyed. More seriously, bombs were thrown into Army Messes, in one case killing a schoolgirl on holiday, and private homes were booby-trapped.

In fact the British Army faced a problem which, because of the time factor, could not be solved in normal counter-insurgency terms. There was in fact no 'security' situation at all, only a military one. The logic of 'minimum force', co-operation with the Civil Power and winning the 'hearts and minds' of the people is to avoid alienating the population and enlist their support against terrorism. In post-1966 Aden the

174

terrorists could not be divided from the people nor the people moved away from the terrorist. All the variables of Time, Space and Will were against the Security Forces—and especially Time. Only the comparative inefficiency of the local terrorist and the resolution of the Security Forces prevented the situation getting entirely out of control.

In such circumstances there is no point in attempting to woo the population by being nice to it, or by trying to bribe it. Attempts to buy information were rarely successful in Aden; one unfortunate who collected a reward also collected a lump of concrete around his feet and a trip to the bottom of the harbour. It is perfectly sensible to argue that if politically speaking there is 'money in the bank' it can only be protected by 'minimum force'; if on the other hand the position is one of bankruptcy then the logic of the matter is lost; *sauve qui peut*. In attempting to preserve the pretence of a politically meaningful programme the military initiative is allowed to pass to the terrorist.

In Aden amid an atmosphere of distrust, betrayal and apprehension the NLF and FLOSY fought out their quarrel before the startled eyes of the British Army. Tribal tensions in the South Arabian Army erupted into mutiny. Rumours of fighting and British reprisals reached elements of the Armed Police in Aden. The outcome was tragic. A truck of the Royal Corps of Transport was attacked; eight soldiers were killed. In Crater the Armed Police opened fire on a Land Rover, instantly killing all but one of its occupants. On that day, 20 June, 1967, the Army lost twenty-two killed; over thirty were wounded. Crater became a 'no go' area. The NLF were in charge. Correspondents reckoned that the British Flag would never again fly there. The Argylls, who had taken over from the Royal Northumberland Fusiliers (both units had lost men in the Crater ambush) thought otherwise. The story of the move back into Crater is well known. Lt-Col Mitchell, commanding the Argylls, was determined to dominate the area, physically and psychologically. This he did. Geographically Crater was a better proposition for control than Sheikh Othman; it formed a natural enclave and could be cut off from the rest of the area. The Argylls were able to concentrate their efforts.

As the British abandoned the 'barren rocks of Aden' the NLF and FLOSY went for one another's throats; the new State was born in a welter of assassination and only the eventual intervention of the South Arabian Army, which finally declared for the NLF, stabilized the situation.

Today the port of Aden is heavily used by the Soviet Navy. Further up the coast Communist rebels, supported by the Government in Aden (and by both the USSR and China) are fighting in the Dhofar to overthrow the Sultan of Muscat and Oman. The prize of victory for the Dhofari rebels would be control of the southern shores of the narrow neck of the Persian Gulf; they have spelt out their views in the 'Gulf Liberation Manifesto':

> 'We are one with the heroic peoples of Vietnam and with the people of Palestine and we stand with the people of Rhodesia and Northern Ireland who like us are fighting disguised forms of British colonial rule.'[7]

Withdrawal from Empire had been an inevitable result of economic weakness; in the eyes of others the British record in Palestine, in Cyprus and in the precipitate evacuation of Aden betokened a lack of resolution and a weary inability to bear the costs of violence. They too could kill British soldiers, plant bombs and terrorize civilians.

Northern Ireland—the Provisional IRA
There are plenty of books, pamphlets and orators to tell when it all started; in the myths of history with the protagonists frozen for ever in attitudes of tribal heroism, in the scruffy streets with their high unemployment rates, in the relationship of master and subject groups, in rival religions.

Whatever one's judgement as to the exact constituents of the mixture it has always been volatile—and the bottle has been regularly uncorked; it was in the 1870s and 1930s, but the latest and most violent explosion grew out of the Civil Rights movement of 1968. From marches and demonstrations, through communal rioting of a savagely committed intensity, there has finally arrived the bloody reality of urban terrorism, sectarian murder and reprisal. There have been three administrations (O'Neill, Chichester-Clarke and Faulkner), internment, direct rule, one referendum, six 'Enquiries' (Cameron, Scarman, Diplock, Hunt, Compton and Widgery) and finally two elections—followed by power sharing and its collapse. To date over 200 soldiers have been killed, more than in Cyprus, Aden or during the confrontation with Indonesia. Few among those original demonstrators foresaw such bloodshed but, in crying 'Havoc' they 'let slip the dogs of war'.

On 5 October, 1968, the Northern Ireland Civil Rights Association (NICRA) marched in Londonderry. They were demanding 'one man, one vote', equality in housing and job opportunity, an end to gerrymandering and strong action on unemployment. Scuffles broke out, followed by police use of water cannon and baton charges. There were allegations of police brutality, made both in Northern Ireland and in the House of Commons. William Craig, the Minister for Home Affairs in the Northern Ireland Government and bête noire of the NICRA, called the latter a 'Republican front'. From the beginning there was strong Left Wing student representation in the NICRA and later the organization was to fall firmly into the hands of extremists. Trotskyist students with contacts in England and Dublin were particularly prominent.[8] The Irish Republican Army, the split between the 'Official' Marxist wing and the 'Provisionals' as yet latent (though it was inevitable from 1967 when a Marxist programme was put to the IRA conference), acted as stewards; at this juncture they constituted a restraining influence.

Extremist Protestant groups fed on the fears aroused by Republican militancy and waxed more aggressive with every sit down and march held by NICRA.

The Northern Ireland Government, under Captain Terence

O'Neill, attempted to stem the tide with reform proposals published on 22 November. Suggested measures included sections on housing, the abolition of the company vote, the appointment of an 'Ombudsman' and a development commission for Londonderry. Blood was up on both sides however; the one with hope, the other with fear. The turn of the year brought one of those incidents which serve to dramatize situations and reinforce myths.

Protestant extremists set out to 'hinder and harass' a Civil Rights march. On 4 January, 1969, the marchers were ambushed, stoned, dispersed and beaten up at Burntollet Bridge. The record of the scenes of confusion and the inability of the police to afford protection made a powerful impression. Both sides retired to their entrenched positions and NICRA swung further to the Left.

Later the same month the Cameron Commission, to enquire into the disturbances of 1968, was set up.

Violence escalated from demonstration and confrontation to communal rioting in April; on the 19th and 20th the police battled with Bogside Catholics in Londonderry. On the 21st, in view of attacks on public utilities—electricity, water supplies and the Post Office—the British Home Secretary announced that troops would be used to guard key installations. Their role would be 'passive' only.

In April the new MP for Mid Ulster, the then Miss Bernadette Devlin, made her maiden speech in the House of Commons; it was couched in the language of the New Left rather than that of the old Republicanism. The division between those who wished for the Six Counties of the North simply to join Eire and those who envisaged a Workers' Republic of Ireland —a 'Cuba of Europe'—was becoming clearer.

By August, 1969, the switch to communal rioting was complete and both Belfast and Londonderry erupted into bloody confrontations with the police; attempts were made to spread the violence to other towns—especially Armagh—in order to take the pressure from Belfast. In Londonderry the march of the Apprentice Boys of Derry, traditionally parading their insignia past the Catholic Bogside on 12 August, had drawn a large proportion of the Royal Ulster Constabulary and also the world's Press and TV to the city. The stage was perfectly set for battle and the heady thought that the eyes not just of Ireland but of the world were upon them served to make the two sides even more bloody-minded than usual.

The result was that the police and Bogsiders battled to the point of exhaustion. At 5.15 pm on 14 August the British Army, in the shape of the Prince of Wales' Own Regiment of Yorkshire, assumed riot duties in Londonderry. On the following day other units did the same in Belfast.

In the wake of these riots a Royal Commission under Lord Hunt recommended the disbandment of the part-time policemen of the 'B' Specials. The Royal Ulster Constabulary was to be disarmed and integrated into the normal structure of the British Police Force.

The General Officer Commanding in Northern Ireland, having been appointed Director of Security Operations, ordered the construction of a 'peace line' in Belfast (10–15 September). Barricades in Catholic areas were removed. The disbandment of the 'B' Specials provoked savage Protestant riots during which the troops came under fire. By now the Army's strength in Northern Ireland was up to 7,500 men.

During the lull that followed, the IRA, the split between the Provisionals and the Officials now becoming clear,[9] co-operated in peace-keeping.

During the British elections in June, 1970, the Provisionals opened fire on Protestants threatening a Catholic area and killed five. There was further rioting in the Bogside over the imprisonment of Bernadette Devlin for her part in the August, 1969, incidents. More troop reinforcements were brought in. In July Army searches for arms and ammunition were followed by a hardening of working-class Catholic opinion behind the IRA. Allegations of looting and wanton destruction of property were levelled at the soldiers in newspapers, especially in Dublin. The stage was now set for Phase 3—urban terrorism. The

179

Provisional IRA considered that they were now sufficiently identified as the defenders of the Catholic areas against both Protestants and the British Army to rely on the support of their people in a campaign of urban warfare.

That campaign opened in 1971, the first British soldier being killed on 6 February. Initially the targets were the troops and later the police before the attack was finally switched to the bombing of the civilian population.

The tactic was to needle the Army into a violent reaction—in Marighela's terms to turn the political situation into a military one; beyond that, it was hoped that a 'bring the boys home' mentality might be produced in England as casualties mounted. Should the Army strike back indiscriminately the Provisionals' status as defenders of the Catholic areas would be enhanced. Bombing might be used to discredit the authorities, unable to control it as they would certainly be, and to spread an atmosphere of anarchy which would force the Government to adopt ever sterner measures in an effort to contain the terrorism and so alienate the people. The authorities must be made to look evil or inept—or, preferably, both.

By July, 1971, the bombing campaign had escalated to a monthly total of over ninety explosions. Moreover the difficulty of gaining convictions in the Courts of Law had increased as witnesses were intimidated—and, on occasion, killed. In these circumstances the British Government agreed with the Northern Ireland administration, though with apparent reluctance and against the advice of the Army—or so the Press intimated—to introduce internment without trial. On Monday, 9 August in the early morning, the usual time for such operations, suspects were rounded up. The 'latest grip of repression' as NICRA chose to call it, had begun. There were 342 arrests, including, claimed the Army, 80 IRA 'officers'. Reaction was swift; a campaign of civil disobedience was started and moderate Catholic leaders asserted that it was impossible for them to talk with the Government while interment continued. In order to demonstrate its staying power the IRA stepped up its campaign. Allegations of brutality in capture and interrogation were immediately made. The subsequent Compton Report led to the dropping of some techniques—long periods of wall standing (hands on wall, legs apart), the hooding of prisoners, continuous noise to induce disorientation, bread and water diet and sleep denial among them. IRA members improved the propaganda hour by 'betraying' innocent people to the Army (which achieved the dual purpose of keeping the troops fruitlessly occupied and alienating the population) and by faking injuries (cf. the techniques of Grivas).

To the bombings (for example the Belfast Electricity Board, 25 August, 1971, one dead, thirty-five injured), the ritual attacks on girls accused of associating with soldiers (one picture of a victim tied to a lamp post and tarred and feathered became notorious) the 'Officials' added the dimension of assassination, killing a Senator; members of the Ulster Defence Regiment (a bi-sectarian force of part-time volunteers) were attacked, one of them being murdered in front of his family.

The turn of the year, as before, brought another 'hinge point'. Sunday, 30 January, 1972, represented (whatever else may be said of it) a massive propaganda victory for the IRA. Incidents spread over a mere thirty minutes became the subject of two enquiries—one under Lord Widgery, the other 'under' the *Sunday Times*, and many pages of print. Some eighteen months' later the inquest on the thirteen victims, all men of military age, shot by the Parachute Regiment, brought all the controversy back to life as the Coroner accused the Army of 'unadulterated murder'. From the point of view of the urban terrorist of course the truth is irrelevant, it is what people outside Ireland—especially in Britain and the USA—*believe* that matters. The Widgery Report says that the Army did not fire first, the *Sunday Times* considers that it did. Whatever the truth of the affair the bombing continued with unabated ferocity; on 4 March there occurred the Abercorn restaurant explosion in which two girls were killed and several others maimed for life. The result was that when the British government announced (on 24 March) that it would in future rule Northern Ireland directly through a Secretary of State the

181

immediate Catholic reaction was to turn away from the Provisionals.

Most moderate Catholic opinion, including the Social Democratic and Labour Party, welcomed Direct Rule. Since the Provisionals believed that it was they who had forced the decision on the British Government they announced that their campaign would continue. In the security context the development was highly desirable; the guiding principle in counter-insurgency is unity of political and military effort and the uncertain division of responsibilities between Stormont and Westminster had made this difficult to achieve.

Following direct rule the Provisionals expected and did their best to provoke a Protestant backlash. Caught in the middle would be the Army which, they hoped, would be unable to hold the ring. Reaction in the rest of the United Kingdom to the Army's being assaulted by both communities would then force the Government to withdraw the troops.

Initially those hopes received some confirmation in Protestant forays into Catholic areas, especially by the 'Tartan Gangs'. Working-class Protestantism, however, preferred to demonstrate its solidarity by holding a massively supported strike. Leaders in the Protestant community also pointed bitterly to the resistance of 'Free Derry', the Creggan and Bogside, where the Queen's Writ did not run. Protestants eventually felt bound to demonstrate their strength by setting up their own 'no go' areas. Before this, however, there occurred what may well turn out to have been the high point of Provisional IRA political influence—the truce of July, 1972.

Paradoxically the meeting of Provisional IRA leaders with Mr Whitelaw and Mr Wilson in London sprang as much from a loss of popularity as from an unwonted degree of agreement between the Northern and Southern leaders of the movement that the political line might be worth a try. For the Officials too this was a time of waning popularity, stemming from their murder of a Catholic Derry boy on leave from the British Army. He was hooded and shot while those who disapproved were called 'slobbering moderates'. Partly due to the local out-

8. Weapons may be concealed anywhere; here men of the King's Own Regiment check for hidden grenades with a mine detector at the Sheikh Othman checkpoint in Aden

9. A snap frisk and search carried out by the Argyll and Sutherland Highlanders in the Crater area, Aden

10 and 11. (*Above*) British troops wait for the approach of a hostile crowd in Aden and (*below*) disperse it successfully. Note the competing NLF and FLOSY signs daubed on the wall.

cry that met this killing the Officials declared a qualified truce (which did not preclude 'defensive' activity).

The Provisionals' truce and the demonstration of control which it involved placed that body in a position of some political potential.

Mr Faulkner acidly observed that the truce 'had come 378 lives, 1,682 explosions and 7,258 injuries too late'. Nevertheless the Provisionals' leaders (MacStiofain, O'Connell, Twomey, McGuinness, Bell and Adams) had their day in London on 7 July. Before Mr Whitelaw, Secretary of State for Northern Ireland, could even discuss the arguments put forward with the Cabinet the truce had been broken; while the Provisionals reverted to terrorism, the Officials continued with the truce. The latter, as a Marxist movement, must be concerned at the risk of civil war since that would clearly postpone the working-class solidarity on which both ideologically and empirically they must rely. Despite the loss of one of their most prominent leaders, Joseph McCann, shot by the Army some months earlier, they might, had the truce continued on all sides, have emerged as a political force of some consequence. To date they have maintained their truce, though reserving their right to fight 'defensively'; they have, nevertheless, occasionally been involved in gun battles at street level, especially with rival Provisional groups.

Whatever the reason for the end of the ceasefire—an internecine dispute within Provisional ranks or a reflex resort to violence by now so automatic that a truce could only be seen in military terms (as a breathing space)—the Provisionals, once having returned to violence, did so with redoubled ferocity. On 19 July a five-month-old baby was killed by a bomb, on the 20th a newsagent was shot dead and his wife shot in the back as she went to his aid.

On the 21st in the centre of Belfast, at railway and 'bus stations and on a bridge, nineteen bombs exploded, killing nine and wounding one hundred and thirty people; there was no warning. Any in the Provisionals who had hoped to adopt a political stand now found that their own wild men had made such a position untenable. In Eire as in Belfast and London denunciation of such actions was absolute and unequivocal.

'The scene which met those who saw the building was almost indescribable. Pieces of flesh and broken bone, bearing no resemblance to the human body, lay on the road and what had once been the forecourt of the station. Pools of blood were on the pavement outside the 'bus crews quarters and a pile of intestines had draped itself obscenely over part of a broken wall. Police walked around trying to gather the remains into polythene bags.'

Thus the correspondent of *The Times*. Mr Whitelaw affirmed in the House of Commons that he would never again talk with the Provisional IRA. Toleration of the 'no go' areas was ended; on 31 July *Operation Motorman* was carried out and all such areas, Catholic and Protestant, were occupied by the Army. In Londonderry Centurion tanks equipped with bulldozer blades were followed in by over one hundred armoured vehicles. There was little opposition, the Provisionals warned by the Army and discredited by their recent activities, faded away across the nearby border. As they went they vented their spleen on the village of Claudy, killing six people, including a nine-year-old girl.

By now there had appeared, beyond any politically logical threat of violence, beyond sense or sanity, even beyond explicable madness the darkest forces of murder—freelance gangs and individual psychopaths indulging in sadism and ritual death. To such killings there was little pattern other than a mindless sectarianism; by the year's end there had been one hundred and twenty-one of them. Although conjured up by the violence of the Provisionals these killings which continued through the ceasefire period were out of their control or that of the extreme Protestant organizations.

While on the political front the Government issued a 'Green Paper' on Northern Ireland which cautiously recognized an 'Irish dimension' and a conference was held at Darlington, the

Army pursued the military battle, enjoying, during the last months of 1972, some considerable success. Twenty-five leading members of the Provisionals were apprehended and that organization was by that time seriously depleted both in Belfast and in Londonderry. In the border areas the IRA retaliated by producing Russian rocked launchers, the RPG 7, an anti-tank weapon; in the first attack sixteen missiles were fired. Russia disclaimed responsibility. Some suspected Libya's Colonel Gaddafi who had proclaimed on 11 June that he was supporting the 'Irish revolutionaries'.

The year 1973 was to be the year of the ballot. By providing the people with a legitimate form of self-expression the British Government looked for a resumption of political activity. All previous experience indicated that given the chance of a secret vote people would reject the proponents of terror. The manifesto of the middle-of-the-road Alliance Party caught the mood; it was entitled 'Vote the Gunmen Good Bye'.

On 8 March the border plebiscite was held; the total poll of 58·6% and the high turn-out in Protestant areas indicated that the majority of the Catholic population had not voted. On 20 March the White Paper on the Northern Ireland Constitutional proposals was published. There was to be a Northern Ireland Assembly elected by the 'Single Transferable Vote' system.

Throughout this period violence continued, Protestant militancy in particular showed a marked increase, strikes being accompanied by mob attacks on Catholic areas. Churches were desecrated and a Catholic funeral procession fired on. For its part the Provisional IRA while continuing to attack the Army and bomb the civilians, once more adopted EOKA tactics when on 23 March, off-duty soldiers were lured to a flat in an 'out of bounds' area. One of the girls involved left the flat on the pretext of fetching friends; she returned with her gunmen colleagues who shot the soldiers in the back and the head while they lay face downwards on a bed. One survived to tell the tale.

The Northern Ireland Assembly Bill was passed on 3 May; the subsequent poll took place on 28 June (local government representatives had been elected on 30 May). Results showed a rejection of the Provisional demand to spoil the ballot papers while the Officials' allies, the Republican Clubs, polled a derisory 1·8%.

Thus by mid-1973 the IRA, of whatever faction, had been decisively defeated at every ballot on every issue on which they had taken a stand both in Northern Ireland and in Eire. The problem which faced the movement, many of whose leaders had been killed and captured, was how to adapt their strategy to this situation? A youthful and inexperienced leadership increased the chances of undirected and politically counterproductive violence increasing; Fianna (a kind of junior apprentice IRA) had already dragged its elders into embarrassing situations. The neo-colonial strategy which had hitherto been adopted had not been successful; the British public had yet to be persuaded that the game was not worth the candle and an 'English nationalist isolationism' had not emerged in response to the death and destruction. Clutching at straws the IRA leadership at a Press Conference outside Dublin affected to see great significance in a petition campaign to 'bring the boys home' started by a housewife in England. The advertisement inserted in the *New Statesman* (8 June) by the British Withdrawal from Northern Ireland Group must also have given them some comfort. [It was, paradoxically, to be the Protestant strike of May, 1974, which most seriously affected public opinion in the direction of possible withdrawal, rather than the terrorism of the IRA.]

The alternative strategy was to carry the attack to England. Even given the failure of a similar IRA policy in the 1930s and the risk of hardening British resolve which such a tactic might run, in the desperate position the Provisionals were then in, it may have seemed worth a try. It had the added advantage of appealing to the younger revolutionary elements associated with the IRA (as distinct from old-style Republicans) who were aiming ultimately at the overthrow of the social structure in the United Kingdom and Eire. Among Anarchist and Trotskyist youth in England there were those who excused the bombings and murders of the IRA; perhaps they might offer more active support, however poor material they appeared to hardened terrorists like the Provisionals? Ireland might become a revolutionary cause alongside the Portuguese provinces in Africa to fill the emotional gap left by the ending of the war in Vietnam. (After all Lenin himself had written in 1915, 'Marx demanded the separation of Ireland, not in order to secure justice for the British people but in the interests of the revolutionary struggle of the British proletariat'.) The Provisionals, always prone to 'splittism', might now make a virtue out of necessity by organizing into small self-contained cells which might for security purposes be kept separate from one another, in classical Blanquist fashion, and in touch only with the centre. This tactic might lead to a loss of cohesion but it would perhaps pay dividends in terms of a proliferation of small disruptive actions which, allied to rumour and hoax, might keep Security Forces stretched and foster an atmosphere of uncertainty and unrest. More Provisional recruits were now coming from middle-class areas rather than the traditional working-class strongholds of Republicanism; such people could move more freely in the English environment, especially if their Irish accent was at least muted.

Previously the IRA had mounted two attacks in England. In Aldershot on 22 February, 1972, a bomb planted outside an officers' mess by the Officials had killed five women, a gardener and a Roman Catholic padre. 'Unfortunately', said Red Mole, the then organ of the International Marxist Group in England, 'no Army Officers were killed.'

The second attack was mounted by a Belfast Provisional group which placed car bombs in central London; one person died and over two hundred were injured. The group's leader was a girl student teacher from Belfast; shouts of 'Up the Provos' were accompanied by clenched fist salutes in the trial court.

Both of these operations were 'one off' affairs; the former was mishandled since the bomb went off too early and killed civilians instead of the 'high ranking' army officers claimed by the Dublin Headquarters of the Official IRA. In the case of the London car bombs the effect was to strengthen rather than weaken the Government's hand in dealing with the IRA; some were quick to point out that Belfast had to put up with this sort of thing every day. Those who argued that to give way to terrorist demands in Northern Ireland would merely encourage extremist groups to attempt similar operations in the rest of the United Kingdom found their case helped by such demonstrations of the ease with which such a campaign could be mounted.

Nevertheless in August, 1973, the campaign in England was resumed. At least one newspaper[10] asserted that this was to be student-based; the phrase 'Weathermen tactics' was used. Letter bombs were sent to Service and Government organizations and incendiary devices planted. The provocation did not succeed in forcing the Government into the over-reaction which the terrorists looked for; while some suggested the introduction of the death penalty, identity cards for Irish people in Britain and the declaring of the IRA and its support organizations illegal, the Government kept a low profile on the matter, refusing to introduce measures which might result in the very ethnic and social polarizations which the terrorists desired.

Outside traditional areas of support the Provisional IRA has generally not forged effective trans-national contacts (other than those of propaganda support). The most public and spectacular exposure of international ramifications came over the *Claudia* affair. This 298-ton ship was found to contain five tons of arms when she was intercepted by the Irish Navy off Waterford. After leaving Nicosia, Cyprus, where she was registered, the ship took on the arms at sea near Tripoli. Proceeding through the Straits of Gibraltar, the *Claudia* arrived in the Irish Sea late in March; on the 28th of that month she was intercepted. Those arrested included Joe Cahill, one time IRA leader in Belfast. The ship turned out to be owned by a German 'merchant of death', Gunther Leinhauser, formerly imprisoned for running Czech arms to the Kurdish rebels in Iraq. Arms seized included 245 Webley revolvers, 250 sub-machine-guns, 14,600 rounds of ammunition, 100 boxes of anti-personnel mines, 100 anti-tank mines, hand-grenades, TNT and other explosives.

The International Marxist Group (IMG), a Trotskyist organization allied to one of the wings of the Fourth International, has given maximum propaganda support to the Provisionals' campaign. IMG sees itself as creating the embryo 'revolutionary cadre force' for Britain. Tariq Ali, one of its leaders, has forecast that in the wake of the Northern Ireland troubles Liverpool might eventually be the scene of armed proletarian action. The Fouth International duly set up a section in Dublin but its emissary in that capital, Peter Graham, once on the staff of Red Mole, was found shot dead in October, 1971. It was suggested that he was involved in arranging arms supplies for the Provisionals.

Other attempts were made to internationalize the Northern Ireland issue—IMG supporters went to Belgium, Fourth International Headquarters, to lecture on Northern Ireland. Northern Ireland was seen as providing IMG with another Vietnam-type 'Solidarity Campaign'; the formula was duly repeated and the Irish Solidarity Campaign was launched. IMG was also active in the Anti-internment League, being one of no less than fifty groups affiliated to that body.

Doctrinal disciples of Trotsky were also to be found among the International Socialists (IS) in whose ranks some of those associated with People's Democracy in the early days of the Civil Rights movement in Northern Ireland might find their spiritual home. The movement has supported the Provisionals and has waged a propaganda war against the Army; surprise was nevertheless expressed by IS at being subject to the attentions of the Police after the Aldershot bomb disaster. At that time (March, 1972) they declared that they gave 'unconditional but critical support for the *IRA*'. The 'Red Brigade', which appears to be a Trotskyist organization, has claimed responsibility for bombings in Belfast and, in England, for blowing up a coach taking Servicemen and families back to camp.

Beyond such organizations lie the short-lived magazines, the ephemeral splinter groups and the Maoists, all giving support, some muted, most at least verbally aggressive, to the terrorists in Northern Ireland. The far Left magazine *Time Out*, for example, remarked prophetically in 1971, 'We must bring the war home where it belongs—to Whitehall and the City of London.' *Workers' Fight* loftily observed, 'Incidents like Aldershot are not terrorist exercises in any Marxist definition of terms.' These organizations gained their support almost exclusively from students and their leadership, especially that of IS, was heavily weighted with intellectuals.

Others sought to further the national interests of the Soviet Union; there were reports in the Press of KGB representatives conferring not only with the Marxist Officials, which they could do via normal contacts through the Communist Party of the Soviet Union, but also with the allegedly 'fascist' Provisionals, and in particular at the time of a Provisional meeting in October, 1972.

Further contacts were with the Basque ETA, the small Breton Nationalist movement (two of whose leaders are resident in Dublin) and with the Popular Front for the Liberation of Palestine whose representatives visited Eire in May, 1972.

Much of such support was verbal; the bulk of Provisional money, apart from protection rackets and bank raids, comes from the United States. The Northern Ireland Aid Committee has donated something in the region of £1 million, according to one estimate.[11] Arms have also been smuggled from the USA and from Canada, while contact was made with the Soviet Union's chief arms entrepreneur state, Czechoslovakia. (Protestant extremist groups have also acquired arms from this source.)

International influences have had but little impact on the Provisionals' mode of organization which has continued in a traditional IRA manner. Battalions responsible for an area were sub-divided into Company units; operationally the small 'active service unit' containing perhaps half a dozen men was preferred. In Belfast there has been, at least in theory, a Brigade Headquarters and three battalions under Twomey and Adams while in Londonderry there were also so-called 'battalions'; as the Provisionals have come under increasing pressure from the Security Forces this paper order of battle has corresponded less and less to reality.

Post-Autumn 1973 reorganization was simply a recognition of fact. The breakdown of the command structure with the imprisonment of so many leaders and the lack of contact (and often sympathy) between Belfast and Dublin forced a decentralization and a formal reduction of unit size in an effort to re-establish the security situation. Provisional activists frequently seemed 'all chiefs and no Indians' as captured terrorists were invariably described as 'Officers'. These 'Officers' moreover became ever younger as the years went by and the attrition rate increased. In a Republican family the task would be passed down from father to son, from brother to brother; Northern Ireland has seen an increasing involvement of the very young in terrorist activity. In June, 1973, for example, three boys (aged 15, 16 and 17) were charged with the murder of three British soldiers who were killed inspecting a booby trap in the Divis Flats in Belfast. In the first six months of the same year over forty young people (under 17) had been involved not merely in rioting, where youngsters had always been sent as a provocation to the troops and a cover for the terrorists, but directly in terrorist acts. The Diplock Commission pointed to the lack of special provision for young offenders and called for a secure unit for boys aged 14 to 16.

Provisional methods of control have been savage and designed to prevent potential informants even contemplating contacting the Security Forces. Similar methods have been used for internal discipline and in the intermittent warfare with the Officials as well as in interrogation of tribal enemies. In the mid-1973 period the decimation of the Provisional leadership led to a suspicion that the Officials had perhaps tipped off the Security Forces and, even if they hadn't, that they were using the discomfiture of the Provisionals to reassert control over areas seized from them. James Bryson, a Provisional leader, was killed in a three-way shoot-out, also involving the Army and the Officials; after his death the Ballymurphy and White

Rock areas of Belfast slipped from the Provisionals' grasp. The result was increased friction both outside and inside jail. Official prisoners were moved at their own request and for their own safety away from the Provisionals. The number of incidents of disciplinary brutality (always a good index of morale—the more there are, the lower it is) once again rose. Methods used by the Provisionals have ranged from head shaving, tarring and feathering through razor slashing, shooting through elbows and/or knees (the bullet through the kneecap is a favourite device) to burning with red-hot pokers and, of course, the finality of death.

In the dismal course of events in Northern Ireland it is possible with the benefit of hindsight to identify a number of turning points around which the catalogue of terror and heroism has revolved. One expert[12] sees these as the initial failure of the RUC to prevent the Burntollet Bridge incident (a reaction to which pushed the NICRA into the hands of its extremists); the June, 1970 arms searches and the subsequent turning of the Catholic community further towards the IRA; the introduction of internment and, finally, the two most violent incidents—Bloody Sunday and Bloody Friday.

Internment in particular carried with it some military as well as political penalties. A number of suspects were rounded up who were not in fact IRA activists; the impact on Catholic opinion was thus doubly damaging. Both Long Kesh and the detainees section of the Crumlin Road jail became training centres for terrorists. In these 'prisoner of war' surroundings campaigns can be planned, indoctrination completed and training sessions, complete with 'visual aids' carved from wood or made from soap, held in bomb-making and weapon techniques. Some who went in as but lukewarm activists may well come out convinced terrorists, with no trade to offer but that of killing and nothing to give to life but death. A further 'hinge point' may be identified in the failure of the Provisionals to capitalize on the truce. Their shortcomings in that respect and their loss in numbers may leave the Officials in the ultimately stronger position, particularly as their members are on average more mature, both chronologically and politically, than those in the Provisionals. It was hoped that the elections would also prove to be a crucial development; certainly the successful holding of those elections and the failure of terrorists either to prevent or to influence them was a major setback for the Provisionals.

No other urban terrorist campaign was conducted with such a weight of explosive and such a concentration of bombing as that of the Provisionals during 1972, yet throughout its operations the terrorist arm of the movement has appeared to dictate the overall strategy and, when that is the case, the result must be that, instead of being a political instrument, the violence becomes an end in itself. Tim Pat Coogan in his book on the IRA[13] relates how in a training camp there was no one able to bring himself to kill a sheep for supper and how, on a raid against a British Army camp in the 1950s, attempts were made to silence a sentry by hitting him over the head instead of knifing him as ordered; the result was that the sentry raised the alarm and the attack failed. Things have certainly changed. They were changed by the example and the literature of international terrorism; Taber's *War of the Flea*, with its fostering of the myth of guerrilla invincibility, and Marighela's *Mini Manual of the Urban Guerrilla*, to provide the technical detail, were allied to a belief that the British would once more withdraw, as they had done in Aden and Palestine, if only things were made hot enough for them. To the Provisionals' theorists it seemed that the British were on the run; 'terrorism had worked elsewhere, it must work here'—the conclusion seemed simple; some thought that thirty-six British soldiers dead would do the trick.[14]

After five years of terrorism, quite apart from the casualty figures, the result has been that to the wounds inflicted by poverty on the children of Ireland there have been added those of violence and fear.

The Provisionals in late 1973, though by no means completely destroyed in the cities (their strength was down to under four hundred), had reverted to the pattern of border raids which characterized earlier IRA campaigns plus sporadic bomb attacks in England. By using the border as the base the Provisionals may additionally seek to extend their influence in a series of geographically semi-circular areas; these may for specific operations join together and form a base for deeper penetrations. Numbers at present prevent the full implementation of such an approach.

Whatever may emerge in Northern Ireland the detainees of Long Kesh, representing a complete generation in some areas, politically and militarily indoctrinated, are going to pose a threat to any government in Ireland, north or south of the present border for many, many years to come.

NOTES

1   Gann, *Military Review*, March, 1966, p. 44 et seq.
2   q.v. Chapter 5.
3   Quoted W. Byford-Jones, *Grivas and the Story of EOKA*, Robert Hale, 1959, p. 183.
4   Grivas, *Memoirs*, Longmans, p. 204.
5   Grivas, op cit, p. 150.
6   Quoted Byford-Jones, op cit, p. 57.
7   Quoted Hodges and Shanab, *National Liberation Fronts*, Morrow, 1972, p. 145.
8   NICRA later reverted to a more orthodox Marxist control.
9   The split became formal on 10 January, 1970.
10   *The Christian Science Monitor*.
11   *Ulster: Politics and Terrorism*, Institute for the Study of Conflict, 1973, p. 18.
12   Clutterbuck, *Protest and the Urban Guerrilla*.
13   Tim Pat Coogan, *The IRA*, Fontana, 1970.
14   Maria McGuire, *To Take up Arms*, Macmillan, 1973.

CHAPTER 11

Viva la Muerte![1] The Terrorism of Desperation

A Government which blocks all the political exits must expect to have them blown open. If a group feels its very existence to be under threat then it will naturally resort to terrorism. Such violence is neither 'Right' nor 'Left', 'Nationalist' nor 'Proletarian'; it is the defiance of the cornered animal. In Eastern Europe after the Second World War the resistance offered by underground movements was, objectively, hopeless. Manipulation of the local Communist Parties backed by the reality of the Red Army soon convinced most patriots that the most they could expect from Stalin, provided they grovelled to his satisfaction, was to be allowed to exist. No help would be forthcoming from the West. Groups which fought on in Poland and the Baltic States did so because they preferred to die in arms rather than in chains. Minority groups which do not possess the necessary power base or international connections to underwrite their separatist demands are similarly conscious of the probability of their own eradication; some still choose to fight.

An alternative version of this condition may come to characterize a majority group or section of it which feels that the 'traditional way of life' is being sabotaged by the Government's undue concessions to 'revolutionary elements'. This then becomes a counter-revolutionary situation which may end in a *coup d'état* by groups which feel that they embody the threatened national genius. Members of such movements may seek to deal with what they see as the terrorist threat, actual or potential, directly, i.e. without waiting for due process of law. In the case of extant terrorism counter-groups will usually be freelance, though some may be adopted officially or clandestinely by the Government. Once this process is begun the spiral is self-perpetuating and there follows a proliferation of progressively less and less 'respectable' terrorist sects engaged in hunting one another down.

If the terrorism is, in the eyes of the majority group, merely latent, then it may seek to pre-empt a terrorist strike by mounting one of its own. Acting in the name of the 'silent majority' such bodies will seek to root out the 'cancer in our midst' before it spreads and 'infects the whole body politic'. Movements discussed in this chapter were not the product of intellectual theorizing nor was there any 'revolutionary consciousness' present at their inception. Any ideological trappings in which they decked themselves were acquired after the events precipitating the terror had occurred. Theory tended to get made up as the terrorism went along.

The OAS—Secret Army of the pieds noir[2]

In no case has ideological inprovization been more striking than in the rise, decline and fall of the Algerian Secret Army Organization which grew out of a military's sense of betrayal and a minority's fear of immediate economic and ultimate physical extermination. Attempts to present the OAS as a bastion of anti-Communism, or of the West and its civilization against the barbarian hordes of Asia, while a genuine enough reflection of some attitudes in the Organization, cannot hide the essentially visceral nature of the motivation behind it. Identification of the OAS with the extreme Right in French political circles did its cause no good and, given the nature of the French political scene at the time, conspiracies to overthrow the Fifth Republic in favour of some corporate system served to rally both Communist and moderate, at least on this issue, behind de Gaulle.

It was, however, only after alternative roads had been blocked that OAS became active. De Gaulle had made it clear that *Algérie Française*—a phrase he had once been rash enough to utter himself—was no longer a possibility. At Evian the Conference between the French and the Algerian Nationalists was due to begin; de Gaulle had betrayed the pieds noir.

The attempt to overthrow de Gaulle via the putsch of Generals Challe, Jouhaud, Salan and Zeller from 22–26 April, 1961, had failed; only a minority of the Army in Algeria itself had become involved actively on their behalf. No troop transport aircraft dropped *les paras* on the capital. In West Germany the armoured columns did not move. Challe (probably the most successful General of the Algerian War against the FLN) wanted a 'legal putsch' without bloodshed. He was unsure of popular support in France—as well he might be since the Communist-led Unions were clamouring for arms with which to fight him.

So the putsch failed; the hopes of the pieds noir for a saviour from the dilemmas of Gaullist policy were for the time being dashed. The OAS had, however, already been formed before the putsch; its roots lay in an organization called the Front for French Algeria under whose aegis there existed various underground groups. During the putsch OAS remained quiet. One of Challe's errors lay in his failing to arm the civilian population. Such a tactic was outside his particular rule book of the *coup d'état*. Had he done so he would have faced those units which were prevaricating with the choice of throwing in their lot with him or firing on the pieds noir.

After the collapse of the putsch a number of army officers and NCOs were 'on the market'; many were simply running from the prisons which awaited them but some were convinced that their oath bound them to defend Algeria and were seeking for a way in which they might continue the struggle. De Gaulle and the FLN had between them killed any hope of integration (though the early OAS continued for a time to pursue this mirage); the lull before the negotiations at Evian got under way saw the reconstitution of the OAS and the laying of plans for further resistance.

The authorities mishandled the aftermath of the putsch, treating Algiers like an enemy city, with none too gentle cordon and search operations. In Metropolitan France the Press jeered at the pieds noir. At the moment of decision the Army too had let the pieds noir down; perhaps it might be persuaded to redress matters later—or so some of the OAS leaders thought—if the Moslems could be provoked into a violence that must draw the troops on to the streets to protect the Europeans. Basically the events of the putsch demonstrated to the pieds noir, however, that if they wanted a resistance they must make it themselves.

Technically and professionally the OAS leadership was well equipped to organize a campaign of terrorism. Access to arms and explosives was assured by the collusion of the European population. Moreover the OAS could count among its adherents officers and civilians who had made a study of guerrilla warfare and, in the former case, had themselves fought in anti-terrorist campaigns. In particular Colonel Godard, ex-Algiers Police Intelligence, had an intimate knowledge of the organization and tactics of the FLN.

While they could count on the support of the pieds noir population which predictably closed ranks in the face of the common threat (the Communists abandoned international proletarianism and reverted to pre-existing tribal loyalties) the characteristics of that population were not well suited to clandestine activity. Discussion and gossip were part of the life style. Additionally there was a bureaucratic mania for writing things down. Neither of these habits was likely to contribute to the security of an underground organization. Psychologically too a population accustomed to leaving the propagation of French Algeria to the Army was ill prepared to undertake a protracted struggle. What could the OAS then hope to achieve?

There were a number of possible outcomes; these, in order of pieds noir desirability (and reverse order of likelihood), were:

1. The overthrow of de Gaulle and the replacing of his Republic by another dedicated to the colonial rather than to the European glory of France. This would require a revolution.
2. A sufficiently dramatic poisoning of the atmosphere so

that the Evian Conference could not get under way or, were it to do so, a sabotaging of its chances of success.
3. The paralysis of the French administration in Algeria so that the implementation of any agreement became impossible.
4. In the event of independence becoming a real and immediate prospect a consideration of partition (this was initially ruled out by the OAS and only reappeared as a desperate throw when all else seemed lost).
5. Finally the forlorn hope that the FLN might be moved towards a more pro-Western attitude, even involving pieds noir participation in the Government.

The OAS had to prepare quickly; they were well aware, following Maoist principles, that they needed time in order to create the necessary political will in the European population. What was needed was a slow-burning fuse of mounting pressure—but the impending French withdrawal and the nature of the pieds noir alike demanded immediate and explosive action. Time was always the dimension working against the OAS; they were trying to hold back a tide of events which rushed inexorably in on them. At Evian the conference began on 20 May; OAS reorganization had hardly begun. Great hopes, however, were placed in the charismatic figure of General Salan. His prestige among the Europeans was enormous. Frenchmen (unlike the Anglo-Saxons) are still occasionally prepared to put their trust in a 'man of destiny'. For French Algeria Salan fitted the bill.

Generalizing from the experience of the French wartime resistance, the Viet Minh and the FLN, the OAS leadership concluded that a safe base outside the country was essential; Madrid was chosen.

On the question of tactics, some favoured a *maquis* in the countryside, others (including Susini, the most politically sophisticated member of the leadership) thought in terms of a Haganah-like army of self defence. In the event the decision was made by Godard, militarily experienced in the type of struggle that lay ahead, now gamekeeper turned poacher. The organization adopted owed a good deal to the FLN: a popular base (the Organisation des Masses), which could bring the people on to the streets when required, a psychological warfare section (a kind of insurgents' SAPI),[3] and finally a terrorist arm. Algiers was to be the hub of the OAS and, at least to begin with, its campaign was to be predominantly urban.

In the OAS' activities may be observed the escalation of means and degradation of motive fatally inherent in urban environments; although the OAS might defiantly declare, 'neither coffins nor suitcases' there was, in fact, no other way beyond death or emigration and, without a credible political aim which alone could have given some logical boundaries to terror, deterioration to mindless destruction was inevitable.

The beginning was quiet—plastic bombs designed to warn rather than to kill. In June the Evian Conference broke down. For the next nine months the OAS waxed stronger. Bab el Oued, a 'poor White' enclave (formerly a Communist stronghold), became its Casbah. In the view of some commentators Salan could have taken Algiers in the winter of 1961.[4]

In the summer the terrorist arm began to make its presence felt. Degueldre, a ruthless ex-Legionnaire in charge of the Bureau d'Action Operationelle, meant business. His group became known, after his initial which they used as a sign, as the 'Deltas'. On 31 May they killed a Police Inspector.

Meanwhile Susini busied himself with the creation of further Front organizations, recruiting from extreme Right Wing groups. From them he also attempted to form potential fighting units. He was building his own power base and there was no love lost between him and Godard. Dissension had also appeared between OAS-Madrid and OAS-Algiers. In general these clashes involved those who were concerned about the political direction and those who were 'in the field'; the 'schemers' versus the 'doers'. Despite all this the fight went on; indeed given the dismal record of factional strife characteristic of all such movements, the volatile nature of the OAS membership and the shortage of time, the wonder is that there was comparatively so little argument.

In the early stages some efforts were made to recruit Moslems, mainly from among ex-Servicemen; to do so was to court a risk of infiltration and their numbers were never very great. In Oran the Europeans of Spanish extraction naturally fought with the OAS while the Jewish community formed its own Haganah for self-defence. (The latter should have known better since they were advised from Israel as early as 1960 that their position was hopeless and that they ought to get out.)

In August the psychological warfare experts in the OAS brought off a brilliant coup. Algerians watching their television sets one night saw the screen go black then, dramatically, came the message ... '*L'OAS vous parle*'. Having blown up the TV transmitter the OAS had broadcast from the hills surrounding Algiers on the same wavelength. Pieds noir morale rose. OAS posters appeared in the streets, OAS pamphlets were passed from hand to hand. In September Salan left his hide-out in the back country and returned to Algiers. The basis had been laid. Now the aim was to press home the advantage and to carry the fight to Metropolitan France.

The effort in France failed, however, to become politically significant—except against the OAS. This was due partly to the ineptitude of the OAS and partly to the refusal of the authorities to be deflected from their main task of putting down that organization in Algeria. Salan's attempts to unify pro-Algeria factions in France foundered on the rocks of personal animosities and inadequacies. Emissaries from Salan found their predecessors unwilling to give up their authority—and prepared to back their position by force of arms. Poor communications meant that the prime aim of co-ordinating the Algerian and French efforts was never achieved. Attacks were mounted on Communist Party headquarters, police stations and FLN meeting places. There was also some industrial sabotage. Initially the police displayed little enthusiasm for chasing the OAS since the former had suffered six years of the FLN; on the principle that 'my enemy's enemy is my friend' they were not disposed to be over-zealous in their investigations. Yet the OAS rapidly used up whatever goodwill it possessed in France. The Communist Party refused to be provoked into armed action and held impressive and massively supported demonstrations instead. An OAS attack directed at Culture Minister Malraux badly miscarried when the bomb smashed glass into the face of a four and a half year old girl; she lost the sight of one eye. Cries of '*OAS–ass–ass–ins*' grew not only louder but more credible.

Unfortunately on the question of the assassination which mattered the OAS were too little and too late. They only attempted seriously to hit the main target, Charles de Gaulle, when all was in fact lost in Algeria; such efforts were thus merely matters of personal vendetta and devoid of any political utility as far as the fate of Algeria was concerned. The one strike at de Gaulle which might have made a difference—that of 8 September, 1961, at Pont-sur-Seine when a bomb blew a hole in the road a split second after de Gaulle's car had passed —was not carried out by an OAS Commando but by a small group of free-lance anti-Gaullists.

In Algeria in the autumn of 1961 the terrorism continued with attacks on Moslems and the police. The Army pronounced a unilateral truce and pulled back from the countryside; in September the C-in-C announced that the Army would, if necessary, fight the OAS. Since such a proposition (at that time at least) was somewhat lacking in total credibility it became clear to those in authority in France that, if the OAS was to be fought, it would have to be challenged by forces additional to and separate from those then in Algeria. In November, 1961, the killings increased. People became habituated to the daily shooting of policemen and of innocent Moslems. The anti-OAS unit of Colonel Grassien was brought home—they were sent off with a fusillade of shots from their adversaries which killed Grassien's deputy.

'*Les extrêmes se touchent*'; now semi-official hired killers were to face the OAS. The Government began to organize, or at least stimulate, a counter-propaganda group and, loosely allied to it, Mission C—a trained but autonomous group of police officers. Still further 'way out' were the barbouzes (a slang word variously translated as 'police thug' or 'spook').

These last were Gaullist freelances, well paid and lethal, including some Vietnamese—a fact not likely to win the hearts and minds of the pieds noir. The Government could claim, at best, that it was looking the other way. Opponents simply replied that these assassins were hired to enable the authorities to disclaim responsibility for the dirty work they were about to carry out. On balance the barbouzes were unsuccessful; they garnered useful intelligence but were swiftly tracked down by Degueldre's Deltas and in effect imprisoned in their villas. Their quarters were shot up—and eventually blown up. By February, 1962, the barbouzes had been eradicated.

Inside the OAS those who had the wit to see that Algérie Française was becoming less and less politically credible began to talk again of the possibility of partition. This caused disagreement which ended when the heretics were shot; there was little further talk of partition. Inside such movements the gun usually becomes a substitute for debate, the result being that violent but politically inept elements take over, and the OAS was no exception.

By early 1962 there was a renewed likelihood of more Government/FLN negotiations while in Algeria the ethnic battle lines were being drawn with greater geographical precision. Moslems moved out of mixed areas and the Europeans too drew more closely into their strongholds. Street killings increased—casual lunchtime murders with targets identified merely by pigmentation.

In Evian there were more negotiations and on 18 March agreement was reached. There was to be a ceasefire in Algeria, with a referendum to follow. For the pieds noir there was no reassurance—'guarantees' were subject to a three-year time limit.

Algeria took the news quietly and waited for OAS reaction. Two responses were offered; firstly to continue to attempt to provoke the Moslem population and secondly to seize control of European enclaves from the authorities, setting up 'no go' areas. These measures achieved no success; Moslem areas were bombed but the expected backlash did not materialize. In Bab el Oued the authorities were challenged and the police and army told to get off the streets or be attacked; the challenge was met, riot control troops of the *CRS* (q.v. Chapter 12) moved in with the gendarmarie while armour and air strikes were used against rooftop snipers. Resistance was crushed; gendarmes rampaged through the area smashing up homes and man-handling their occupants. Not only CRS and gendarmes had fired on the pieds noir—the Army had also turned on them.

On 25 March the lesson was driven bloodily home when a demonstration organized by OAS leader Vaudrey, in defiance of a government ban, moved on the shattered Bab el Oued. Moslem infantrymen, inexperienced in urban tactics, barred the way. The crowd swept round them and the troops, panick-ing, fired indiscriminately. Eighty people were killed, two hundred wounded. From the Right in France there was an out-cry; pieds noir children (one had been killed) apparently did not matter as much as ones injured by OAS bombs. To Susini it was a disaster on another count; the Army had once more acted against the people. The population, though bitter, was now thoroughly cowed.

Desperately the OAS tried another tack. Colonel Gardes tried to set up a maquis organization in the countryside, enlist-ing the aid of a pro-French local chieftain and seizing three small forts. No army units showed any interest in joining his adventure, however, and the Air Force strafed his troops. Lack-ing training, equipment and physical fitness the OAS was ill prepared for a rural guerrilla war; the maquis was a flop.

By now the OAS was finding it more and more difficult to stem the flight of capital and people from Algeria to France. Politically it was on the run. In France de Gaulle mustered support for his policy by further use of the subtly worded referendum; he received a massive 'Yes' to what amounted to a demand for a *carte blanche* for his Algerian policy.

On 20 April, 1962, Salan, the personification of Algérie Française, was arrested.

For the pieds noir now two courses only remained—Flight or Death. Some military men in the OAS were for fighting on.

Susini might turn this way and that, clutching at one political straw after another, but none was of any substance. A rapprochement with the FLN? But within the FLN men of compromise were already being shouldered aside now that independence was near. If any OAS remained after the day of independence Ben Bella would have wiped them out. The idea of a pro-Western group in the newly independent Algerian Government was never practical politics.

In the first week of May there were 203 murders. It was no longer 'OAS' but fury and sadism, a blind nihilistic destruction of property and life. It was the day of the psychopath. Swaggering teenage hoodlums prowled the streets. In the same week a lorry blew up in the docks, the scattering crowd being fired on; sixty-two died. The FLN planned a retaliation which would have decimated the remaining European population but were persuaded by the French Prefect of Police to hold their hand.

So the pieds noir left, burning their belongings and setting fire to installations as they went. By the end, of the one million who had set out to fight for French Algeria only some 150,000 were left. (By 1968 the number had dropped to 80,000, most of them too old to start a new life elsewhere.)

The secret OAS radio made its last broadcast in Oran: '*Tout est fini. Adieu, Algérie*'.

Of the OAS leaders captured by the French Government the lower ranks were shot. The Generals lived to be released as counterweights in 1968 when the Left in its turn threatened revolution. The rest slipped away into exile.

What conclusions may be drawn from this tragic and hopeless affair?

That the leadership was divided and had no aim in common with the pieds noir? (For while the former dreamt of a new anti-Communist France or an integrated, national socialist and pro-Western Algeria all that the latter desired was to be left unmolested in their inheritance of property and home.) Yet FLN and Irgun had not always displayed unity and they had not been defeated.

That there is an anti-Imperial and anti-European tide in the affairs of men and nations against which any battle must be in vain? Yet against all the odds Israel had survived.

That lacking a firm base and friends outside Algeria OAS was unable to make any effective impact inside France? Perhaps; certainly Spain jailed some of the OAS-Madrid group (in return for de Gaulle's making life uncomfortable for Franco's enemies in France). The lack of an external patron power was a serious drawback.

Yet from the beginning the cause seemed doomed unless some very extraordinary Act of God should intervene. Given the very small resources of the OAS compared to those available to the Government it is surprising that the former came as close as it did to the seizure of Algiers. OAS numbered under a thousand, perhaps as few as five hundred. If any demonstration were needed of the power of dedicated and desperate men in the modern urban environment the OAS certainly provided it. On the other hand such a group, though it may destroy a great deal and kill a great many, cannot outface a determined Government resolved to hold to its course; only if the political aim is well defined and their political support widespread can such terrorists have a positive impact on policy. Yet at the end of this affair Frenchmen had grown sick of the OAS, the FLN, the barbouzes and the whole sorry and convoluted mess; at one time there were upwards of five 'secret' organizations shooting it out on the streets of Algiers.

There are lessons for governments as well as for insurgents. OAS was not taken seriously until it was almost too late; de Gaulle's contempt for the pieds noir was only exceeded by his judgement as to the political stupidity of the Army. Just as formerly he seemed to forget that the Army he was dealing with was not the traditional force of pre-1939 but a middle-class, technically competent and politically aware group of which a significant proportion regarded Algeria as a crusade, so he saw the pieds noir as a bloody-minded minority which stood between France and the world.

In a more general sense politicians might note that minority groups will fight, or support those who do, regardless of how 'senseless' such a course may appear from a safe emotional and physical distance. To use 'third force' units—such as the CRS or the barbouzes—is likely to provoke such a population to further acts of desperate self-immolation. The psychological and political position of the Northern Ireland Protestants is in some ways similar to that in which the pieds noir found themselves.

Northern Ireland Protestant Groups

'Desperation terrorism', whether conceived as indicative of 'Ulster Nationalism' or 'Protestant Extremism', was always probable in Northern Ireland once the security situation deteriorated. British Government reforms could always be seen as a product of IRA terrorism; the conclusion drawn would then be that only a countervailing violence would defend Protestant interests. Yet Protestant activists have always faced a number of dilemmas.

Violence, if directed against the Catholic population, would only strengthen the claims of the IRA to be the former's necessary defenders. To attack the Army would distract it from the task of dealing with the Provisionals and contribute to the breakdown of law and order which was an IRA objective. Intransigence on the part of the Protestants might also lead to an English mood of a 'plague on both your houses' and a growing impatience with the 'Irish'; both sentiments which played into the hands of the Provisionals. Yet notwithstanding such arguments the Protestants might feel that they had been cast in the role of 'poor Whites' and provide a classic backlash. Potentially they have always represented a force which if united and unleashed could present the Security Forces with a militarily impossible task.

Such dilemmas have led to the break-up of traditional Unionism. Loyalty to the Queen sits ill with attacking her Army, even if sent by what might be regarded as a traitorous government.

Three traumatic events have strengthened the hand of the 'Ultras' on the Protestant side in Northern Ireland—the dissolution of Stormont, the temporary toleration of IRA 'no go' areas and the 'power sharing' arrangements introduced in 1973 with the associated tentative recognition of the possibility of Irish unity.

In the wake of direct rule of the province from Westminster Mr William Craig formed, in March, 1972, his Vanguard movement. He noted that one day it might be necessary, if politicians failed to liquidate, the enemy; by this, he subsequently explained, he meant the 'removal from the scene of terrorist organizations'. Vanguard found common cause with the Reverend Ian Paisley's Democratic Unionists after the 1973 elections in opposing the new Assembly and 'making it unworkable'. Vanguard has numbered among its supporters the powerful Loyalist Association of Workers and the Ulster Defence Association (UDA).

During 1972 the UDA proved to be the leading para-military organization on the Protestant side. Its original conception as a Protestant Home Guard assisting the Security Forces gave way to more aggressive modes of behaviour. During May of that year both the Shankhill and Woodvale areas of Belfast became temporary 'no go' areas. In September the UDA claimed that two of its men had been shot dead by the Army (during an attempt to set up a UDA 'Command Post'). Rioting followed and by October there was a policy of calculated confrontation with the Army with hand-to-hand fighting. Tommy Herron of the UDA, then emerging as a leading spokesman, claimed that the Protestant population was totally alienated from the British Army. At this time the UDA asserted that it has 50,000 adherents trained in guerrilla warfare; it certainly had several thousand on the streets.

Yet the UDA soon began to show signs of dissension within its ranks. Both the traditional Ulster Volunteer Force (UVF) and some of the new extremists produced by the fighting distrusted a number of the UDA leaders. There were rumours of profiteering and protection rackets, with criminal elements moving in. By January, 1973, the rift was out in the open.

In June Herron's brother-in-law was shot in the former's house. Internal Protestant disputes were said to lie behind the affair. Businessmen, especially publicans, in Protestant areas complained of extortion. The West Belfast UDA suspected the East Belfast group of criminality; the corrupt and psychopathic were apparently once more being drawn in by the prospect of easy pickings or warped emotional satisfaction. In September Herron himself was shot dead and his body found in a ditch; Protestants were again suspected of the murder.

By this time there were several groups, some ad hoc, some with pretensions at 'organization' indulging in sectarian killings. Some operated on a geographical basis, picking their victims from a certain street or public house, others aimed at Catholic movements such as the 'Ex-Servicemen's Association'. Much activity was on a gangland basis the aim being to gain or maintain a hold over a certain locality or street. Just as similar activities on the Catholic side were beyond the control of the Provisionals so the UVF was similarly placed.

The UVF reappeared in 1966 in Belfast and has been dominated by one man, Augustus 'Gusty' Spence; Spence was jailed in 1966 but absconded while on parole in June, 1972, remaining at large until November of that year. UVF funds have come mainly from crime and its numbers are probably in the low hundreds. Although armed with old Second World War weapons—and some even more ancient—the UVF are still capable of seriously affecting the security situation.

June, 1973, saw the emergence of another Protestant extremist group, the Ulster Freedom Fighters (UFF). The UFF claimed responsibility for several killings of 'informers' as well as those of SDLP Senator Wilson and his (Protestant) lady companion. At a Press Conference held in the Europa Hotel in Belfast two masked UFF men attempted to explain their position. They claimed to be afraid that Ulster would fall; their historic example was the 'Jewish Freedom Fighters' and they asserted their determination to retaliate in the only way in which the IRA 'animals' would understand. Thereafter UFF responsibility has been claimed for several bombings in Catholic areas; warnings are not given.

By the end of 1973 both the UFF and another fringe organization, the Red Hand Commando had been outlawed.

The extension of the bombing campaign to England in 1973 brought vague threats from 'English UDA men' that they too were willing and able to use violence in that country as well as being prepared to go and fight in Ulster. There is some support for the UDA in Scotland and explosives and ammunition have been discovered in the hands of the '1st Ranger Battalion of the UDA' in Glasgow.

The course of armed confrontation and aggression as distinct from that of defence, however explicable, has done nothing to strengthen the case of the Northern Ireland majority. Violence once unleashed has, as on the IRA side of the fence, proved self-perpetuating and soon out of control; murder and crime flourish in the shadow of political motivation in Loyalist as well as in Republican areas.

If, on the other hand, the majority of the Protestant population are prepared to stand together they can effectively hamper any arrangement of which they disapprove by a campaign of non-co-operation and passive resistance. Ultimately they can simply withdraw their labour. It is militarily and politically impossible for a democratic British government to commit its Army to running the province indefinitely. In the hands of a determined majority the general strike is, especially in the liberal democratic context, a more potent weapon than terrorism—which remains a technique most effectively used by those who start from a position of weakness.

NOTES

1 'Long Live Death'; a battle cry and slogan in the Spanish Civil War.

2 The derivation of this term is uncertain but is possibly due to the burning of scrubland by early settlers.
3 The Psychological Information and Action Services of the French Army.
4 e.g. Paul Marie de la Gorce quoted Paul Hennissart, *Wolves in the City*, Hart Davis, 1971.

CHAPTER 12

The Response

Ultimate success against urban terrorism is possible only when Governments and people remain calmly committed and behave normally in the context of their own traditions. In countries where there are few civil liberties their suspension in the face of terrorism is necessary if the Government is to survive (leaving aside the question of whether or not one considers that such a Government ought to survive) and failure to act ruthlessly would lead inevitably to further outbreaks. International pressure group criticisms are seen by such Governments as concerned not to alleviate the suffering of the people but to persuade the Government to go soft on anti-guerrilla measures so that the insurgents stand more chance of success. Ideologies, concepts, strategies and techniques of response must thus be articulated in a manner consistent with the popular traditions of the country concerned. In states with a liberal democratic tradition matters are more complicated; to be true to themselves such countries have to run greater risks.

The Ideology of Response
One of the problems facing governments in Western liberal democracies is that there is no coherent and generally accepted philosophy in the name of which force can be organized against the violence offered by the terrorist. Overt use of government force is seen by significant portions of liberal opinion as in itself illegitimate—its use as 'bullying', 'harassment' or 'provocation'—while the violence of the terrorist, especially when couched in 'revolutionary' terms, is regarded as 'heroic' and 'understandable'. To a large extent the semantic battle which precedes the activities of violence has already been lost. The

importance of this battle is well understood by extremists; Stokeley Carmichael put the matter succinctly by quoting from Lewis Carroll:

> 'The question is,' said Alice, 'whether you can make words mean so many different things.'
> 'The question is,' said Humpty Dumpty, 'who is to be master, that is all.'[1]

The 'definers of terms' and hence the 'masters', are increasingly the extremists. So pervasive is the notion of 'class conflict' that it is part of the accepted discourse of the media and the contemporary 'edmass'. Alternative explanations are not discounted, they are simply not known. Since education and economics are discussed in the terms of a crude and naïve class analysis it is not surprising that other phenomena, those of protest and violence, are seen in the same terms. The result is that the mere proposition of counter-force is perceived in the language of exploitation and aggression. As the West's international conscience is selective so a similar double standard is observed internally; 'protest' is good *per se*, to be regarded as an advocate of 'law and order' is to be equated with Fascists. A prime task facing liberal democracies is therefore to go onto the intellectual offensive; they must not, as T. E. Lawrence put it, 'Let the metaphysical weapon rust unused.'

The dimensions of the classic liberal dilemma in urban terrorist situations are by now well enough known; the terrorist is attempting to provoke an over-reaction and thus to make the Government appear repressive. Yet if the Government is to pursue the terrorist effectively it may be forced to take strong and unpopular action. A resolution of this dilemma is held to be possible provided the Government acts through the normal processes of the Courts and is not panicked into a hasty suspension of civil liberties. In particular the holding of elections enables the people to show their sympathies with regard to the terrorists' political allies and serves to give the Government a mandate for any subsequent emergency legislation which may be necessary.

At the same time the Government must examine and deal with those grievances upon which the terrorist is attempting to capitalize; it must also be prepared to negotiate with and support those elements which have pursued the alleviation of problems in a constitutional manner. Both the 'supply' and the 'demand' side of urban terrorism must be met.

Such orthodox formulae are unexceptionable but leave out the small print. The difficulty lies not in stating how governments must proceed but in putting these principles into operation in a specific situation.

Strategies and Concepts of Response

Orthodox wisdom, generalized from the rural guerrilla context, emphasizes the importance to the insurgent of popular support; the guerrilla is seen, as in the Maoist thesis, as being like a fish, with the people among whom he moves constituting his natural, life-giving environment. Counter-guerrilla operations must therefore either remove the water, i.e. physically move the population so as to segregate them from the guerrillas, or carefully take out the fish, trying at the same time not to 'muddy the water' by ruthless methods which will alienate the population. Most armies have in fact based their doctrine on rural, colonial situations; the danger is that the challenge of revolutionary war in a western urban setting will be similarly viewed, both intellectually and in terms of the physical response. In particular it is vital in the domestic context to *plan for peace*, that is to prepare for the handing back to the civilian authority of areas and functions which have temporarily become the concern of the military. Internally, as well as externally, the use—or even the display—of military force is a political act. Inside his own country the soldier must, if he is successfully to carry out his security tasks, be totally integrated with the people whom he serves; he should be no more 'separate' than is the miner, the teacher or the plumber. The soldier is operating in a total and continuing political situation from which he will not be able thankfully to escape once his 'tour of duty' is complete;

12. British police in the formation used to drive into and split up a demonstrating crowd

13. Men of Alpha Company, Police tactical unit at the ready in Hong Kong

14. The technology of response: a soldier in Northern Ireland with a variety of riot control equipment

he is in fact part of the problem as well as part of the solution
to it.

It is therefore dangerous to transfer received anti-guerrilla
wisdom to the urban terrorist environment without modification.

Of course to the urban terrorist popular support is initially
highly desirable and ultimately, in the revolutionary context,
essential—doors left open to facilitate his escape through the
lines of houses; crowds ready to close round him; individuals
prepared to hide him and his weapons. Such support is not
however essential in the initial stages; a public unprepared
positively to aid the police is the only ally the modern urban
terrorist needs. Public panic is even better. So sensitive is the
technological environment and so anonymous the city crowds
that unless the whole community co-operates with the authorities there will be sufficient targets and cover for his operations.
Panic will magnify the terrorist's power a thousandfold; a calm
contempt for the terrorist and a positive co-operation with the
police will on the other hand eventually isolate and expose him.

It is also received wisdom that the 'urban terrorist cannot
win'; as Oppenheimer puts it:

> 'No writer from conservative to radical anywhere suggests
> that an urban insurrection can be anything but wiped out
> once the rebels are geographically isolated and the govern-
> ment is in a position to move against them in a unified
> fashion.'[2]

Such comments are unhelpful since it is precisely the purpose
of the terrorist to prevent the Government moving against him
'in a unified fashion'. To talk in terms of 'winning' and 'losing'
is inappropriate both in the colonial/separatist and in the revolutionary contexts. Urban terrorist logic is to apply a degree of
violence to persuade the Government via the pressure of its
own public to alter its position. In the colonial context it can
be—and has been—an element in hastening the withdrawal of
the colonial power. For the separatist, while he is unlikely to

215

be successful in his main aim against a modern state, there is the possibility of altering the political framework in the direction of greater autonomy.

In fact urban terror movements have not to date generally been distinguished for political acumen; over time they have tended to split and fall into the hands of their own extremists. They have used violence fanatically and nihilistically rather than logically. However, in the 'revolutionary' as distinct from the colonial/separatist situation the misconception about 'victory being impossible', given certain conditions, is more serious; it implies a degree of complacency and inevitability about the defeat of such movements. The revolutionary urban terrorist is not necessarily seeking 'victory' in some narrow military sense nor even anticipating the escalation of his efforts in the direction of 'People's War'—though he will devoutly hope that the latter will occur. On the contrary, to the extent that he is politically sophisticated he will not be naïve enough to consider such an outcome as likely. What he seeks is an increment in a gradual process of erosion, the hastening of the forces of history as he sees them. 'Revolutionary gymnastics' will on this thesis strengthen the resolve and expertise of the insurgent while undermining the morale of the authorities. What is envisaged is a series of skirmishes, not a single definitive battle; concessions wrung from the Government are regarded as war booty, not 'acceptable compromises'. Thus the use of violence, articulated with other measures—industrial and psychological—may over a period of time so erode the cohesion of a society that it will simply cave in on itself, its structure no longer able to support the weight pressing on it. Should the terrorist achieve a modicum of success external help will swiftly be offered to him; arms smuggling will occur, perhaps necessitating the interception of foreign shipping, small incidents will lead to accusations of 'atrocity' and international commissions will arrive to investigate.

Successful action against urban terror groups remains primarily a matter of prior intelligence; if that intelligence is to be effective it must be gleaned from a population aware of the problem and willing, not merely to stand aside, but actively to co-operate with the police and Army right from the start. It is no accident that most successful urban terrorist movements—in Cyprus, Aden, Uruguay and Northern Ireland, have been able, one way or the other, to destroy or seriously embarrass the police intelligence network. Once surveillance breaks down the terrorism is almost certain to reach military proportions and, in that case, the authorities and the population are in for a long and bitter haul. In times of peace and apparent internal stability the temptation to neglect the intelligence function usually proves irresistible; democratic governments find such matters distasteful and there is the ever-present need for financial economy to rationalize those acts which they find ideologically attractive. Intelligence is, however, a process, not an event, and ground lost through niggling economies in manpower—as for instance in the withdrawal of military intelligence officers—will later prove doubly expensive to recover. Extremist movements, if they are not to cause bloodshed, must be crushed once they commence overtly violent and criminal acts.

Emphasis, in orthodox anti-guerrilla doctrine, placed on winning the 'Hearts and Minds' of the people has tended to obscure the equal necessity of attacking the morale and allegiance of the terrorists. Hard-core fanatics may be beyond redemption but the peripheral elements can be convinced of the hopelessness of the struggle and of the usually selfish, corrupt and disunited nature of the movement's leadership. 'Psychological warfare' in the contemporary environment needs also to acquire some sociological perspective in order to understand, identify and exploit the social and political characteristics of subversive movements even as they seek to do to the system of established authority. The implications of terrorist demands must be clarified and the smokescreen with which they try to obscure their true motives and allies removed by a vigorous public relations campaign; the control of this process is however, a matter of political sensitivity.

Kitson, in particular, has called for a greater use of psychological warfare to combat the terrorists' use of it and points to the paucity of expertise on this subject in the British as compared to that available in the American or West German armies. While there indeed seems reason to pay more attention to this aspect of countering terrorism it would be better carried out within the United Kingdom directly by the Government rather than through the Armed Forces. Governments which do not keep a tight control of their psychological warfare apparatus are likely to find themselves embarrassed by it—as was the case with the French in Algeria.

Even if the terrorist should ultimately be defeated the scars he leaves, once allowed to adopt a military approach, will take generations to heal; the prisoners deprived of their youth and the bitter memories on both sides will require vast and lengthy programmes of rehabilitation.

Once urban terrorism is on the streets the tactical problems of meeting it are acute, especially in the United Kingdom, and decisions of choice among the available options cannot long be delayed.

It is clear that an Army cannot continue to act as an anti-terrorist force over a long period of time without there being repercussions on training, efficiency and political outlook. The characteristics which soldiers need to develop for conventional warfare are not necessarily appropriate for anti-terrorist operations. The strain on the families of soldiers of constant change-over of units is bound to tell in morale and recruiting. Britain's contribution to the defence of Western Europe as a whole is weakened. The flanks of the Atlantic Alliance are generally held to be vulnerable enough without withdrawing elements which might be used for their defence in order to chase terrorists. Nor will expansion of the Army, even if politically and financially possible, meet this problem unless some part of that expansion becomes specialized in anti-riot and anti-terrorist techniques. There is no doubt that any Army used on the streets for a long time with no prospect of this role ending will become 'politicized'. This is not something about which politicians and the public ought to become frantic as though a military conspiracy were involved; it is an inevitable result of the carrying out of some of the functions of government—as any effective counter-terrorist must. Such 'politicization' does not necessarily imply a desire to interfere in the workings of constitutional government. Sensitivity to the possible political consequences of actions which might appear militarily desirable is essential if a counter-terrorist campaign is to stand any chance of success. Unity of political and military effort is axiomatic in such situations but if the military side of the equation has constantly to make sacrifices to atone for the mistakes of its counterparts then relations are likely to become strained. In Northern Ireland the desirable continuity of military response has been hampered by the changing political perception of the threat. Initially the Protestants were seen as posing the challenge and the Army found itself in an uneasy alliance with Republicans in defending Catholic areas. Then Protestant support from 'Loyalist' elements was welcomed as threat-perception switched to the IRA, only to revert to 'Ulster nationalism' at the time of the May, 1974 strike. The ever-present representatives of the media incalculably increase the risks of mistakes on the part of the military, presenting them to the eyes of millions of viewers and readers. Such exposure makes soldiers, whether they like it or not, instant politicians.

Paradoxically the desired 'democratization' of the Officer corps increases the chances of politicization rather than the reverse. Officers who are better read, better qualified and more professional are likely to apply an alert and informed intelligence to the activities of their political masters. Such officers are committed to the Army—and this is particularly true of the Infantry and the Artillery, both used in counter-terrorist operations (the latter as makeshift infantry) whose officers do not always have skills which are readily marketable outside the military environment. Contemporary army officers are not, with a steadily declining number of exceptions, the scions of noble houses, nor do they have private incomes, estates or commercial contacts which will provide them with an assured and comfortable retirement. While the bravery and integrity of the army officer may be praised, his knowledge and intelligence are not. Establishment intellectuals, with a few exceptions, are Gaullist in their contempt for the intelligence of the Army.[3] Young university students have no contact with soldiers, except via the television screen and the Press, and still live in a world of military caricature.

Whether Armed Forces become politicized in a stronger sense, i.e. of interfering in politics, will depend on the coincidence of a number of factors. The traditions of the country and the Army concerned, the degree of ineptness displayed by the politicians and the intensity of the terrorism will all be variables affecting the outcome. In most West European contexts—and certainly in the United Kingdom—more is required; 'the Armed Forces in such countries are very unlikely, except in the case of France, to take any political initiative by themselves. Only in the event of extreme public disillusion with politics, coupled with a breakdown of the economy and of law and order, would any intervention by the Armed Forces be even remotely likely.

The use of the Army, while a means of holding the ring for a time, does not appear an ideal way for meeting the urban terrorist threat; it gives to internal conflict the dimensions of 'war' and enables the terrorist to play upon liberal fears of the military while at the same time going some way to giving such fears some substance.

Both politically and militarily the Army is a crude instrument for dealing with internal disorder. For the Government to use troops grants to the terrorist a kind of 'combatant status'. The confrontation takes on a different nature and leads to terrorist demands to be treated as political or military prisoners rather than as criminals—demands which sections of internal and international opinion will be predisposed to regard as legitimate. Army involvement heightens public tension and leads to a feeling that the situation is 'getting out of hand'. Troops are not policemen—their reactions must be more vigorous; for them to retreat before rioting crowds is a sign of weakness they cannot afford to display, yet to disperse those crowds, if petrol bombing and sniping is involved, may mean bodies on the streets. Military deployment, given the backgrounds of the soldiers themselves, becomes a matter of difficulty; one cannot risk putting family and local loyalties against the requirements of duty. Once military force is committed it must, in the physical sense, be successful; since the troops are the last resort open to the Government a major failure on their part would be psychologically disastrous.

It can therefore be argued that troop commitment should be pushed further back in time by the insertion of a further rung or rungs in the ladder of escalation. A 'third force' especially trained and equipped for riot control would allow such a graduated response; within that body there might be further unit sub-divisions allowing a more sophisticated organizational reply to the provocations offered. This graduation may additionally be achieved by the development of offensive and defensive operational equipment. Internal conflict response would thus be limited, flexible and more amenable to political direction.

In the French system for example there are four stages of response before the Army need be called in. If the local police cannot deal with the problem then special intervention companies of riot police in their black uniforms and equipped with plastic visors, shields and rubber gloves can be used. Beyond them lie the Compagnies Républicaines de Sécurité (CRS), 15,000 strong, under the Minister of the Interior—a specialized anti-riot organization. If further support is needed then there is the national organization of the Gendarmarie Nationale, controlled from the Ministry of Defence. Local 'brigades' in each canton ensure accurate low level intelligence; mobile groups can be brought in to a support role anywhere in France and the 'special agencies' include sections dealing with security and interrogation. This force is equipped with machine-guns, helicopters and scout cars. The Army's loyalty and honour is not therefore to be risked in any but the most extreme circumstances. The May, 1968 disturbances in Paris demonstrated the difficulties facing even so comparatively sophisticated a system; para-military forces are still theoretically dealing with a violent citizenry rather than a revolutionary guerrilla. If in the judgement of the Government the situation has so far deteriorated that the 'provocation' of using troops can be discounted then it might be better to signal governmental resolution by deploying troops while they still have the initiative. Political judgements of the motivational and organizational factors at work are crucial. In the Paris incidents the police found rioters who were, apart from firearms, as well equipped as themselves. Opening fire in such circumstances on young students, while an option open in a totalitarian country, is not part of the acceptable pattern of response in a Western country (unless the rioters open fire first). Nor are the police and para-military forces necessarily convinced in such confrontations that the Government is blameless. It remains true, however, that it is wasteful and inefficient to use a high status, technological army as a counter-terrorist force. Similarly in Holland, Japan and Italy there are specialized forces—though in the case of Italy their mutual competition is sometimes damaging to the security effort.

If the idea of a 'third force' is rejected as politically unacceptable then the advantages of a graduated response may be gained by training the police, instead of the Army, in a dual role. In West Germany, while theoretically the 'Basic Law' allows the Government to use the armed forces to deal with an imminent threat to the liberal democratic existence of the state or a constituent 'Land' within it, in practice no Government would consider such a move unless there was a war. The existence of a well-equipped Police Force (possessing anti-tank weapons, rifles, machine-guns and mortars) with its own armoured cars and special riot squads available in most towns, saves the Government the embarrassment of having to involve the Army.

By giving all policemen anti-riot training the advantages of a 'third force' might be obtained without suffering the political and psychological penalties of employing 'riot specialists'. In this respect the modus operandi of the Hong Kong police is instructive. Should the ordinary policemen, singly or in small groups, be unable to cope with a riot situation then the Company on stand-by can be called in. Initially this Company will deploy from its vehicles in normal uniform and attempt to disperse the crowd by persuasion and a relatively gentle display of force (linking arms, etc). Should such actions be unsuccessful the police withdraw, only to reappear within minutes equipped for riot control. Within that riot control pattern the idea of 'minimum force' is still carefully and demonstrably maintained; while all the unit wear helmets only the rear rank will have firearms while those immediately in front will have gas and the front rank only shields and batons. A pattern of response rather than provocation is thus established; the onus of escalation is placed on the rioters' leaders (if any). In a situation of extreme unrest more men can progressively be withdrawn from their 'beat' duties and assigned to their alternative role. With the police trained in this manner it becomes easier to withhold troops until a later and more serious stage. Troops can then be brought in as extra manpower to set up cordons and man roadblocks, leaving the search and arrest operations to the police. Only in the event of a complete breakdown of order and the exhaustion of all these gradations of response will troops become actively involved; thus it should be possible to act in line with public concern rather than cause it by too hasty a reaction.

In the United Kingdom the police are naturally unwilling to sacrifice their traditional role as citizens in uniform; their use in crowd control involves large numbers of men being used as a human wall to contain and divide a mob, channelling it away from its targets. If the police wish to retain the 'bobby' image then they clearly cannot be used in a dual role, part citizen, part military.

In the case of the United Kingdom the 'third force', though possibly the lesser of the evils, also contains serious disadvantages. The very existence of such a force would be seen as a provocation and an incitement to riot by extremists. Memories of the 'Black and Tans' would be aroused, and emotive cries of 'Gestapo' raised in some quarters. Recruits to such a force and their families would be targets for intimidation. Politically in a liberal democracy like the United Kingdom such a force could not be raised until matters had reached such a pitch that its intervention would be ineffective—the correct time politically would be, from a security viewpoint, too late.

There remains the possibility of using reserve or Territorial Army units. They would not, on the evidence,[4] be effective in the highly sensitive riot control and anti-terrorist role but could act as a back-up and relieve regular troops of the routine jobs, for example, roadblocks and patrols outside the area of immediate confrontation.

The problem is at root, one of intelligence—and in that respect the Territorial unit has a more vital function; were all Regular Army Officers to be required to do at least one (possibly short) tour of duty with a Territorial Army unit and to maintain their contact with that unit by periodic visits, attendance at camps and conferences, etc, then there would be, for every area of the country, at least one Regular Officer with local contacts and knowledge. In the event of any area becoming a focus of unrest the Regular Officer concerned could be attached to the operational unit involved and liaise between it and the local TA, police and civil authorities. In this way the advantage to the terrorist of knowledge of the local terrain and population might be to some extent negated. Only good and early information will enable the Security Forces to check terrorism; once it has proceeded to a campaign of bombing and shooting sustained over a matter of months then the confrontation is bound to be long and arduous. Lenin's advice to his disciples was never to play at insurrection; the reverse is also, on all the evidence, true—never play at putting it down. Frightened people want to know if the Government is really determined to succeed.

In the immediate future these matters will doubtless continue to be the subjects of debate but it seems in the meantime that the Army, at least in the British context, could be used at one of the following four levels; it is important that it be committed at the correct level for the particular situation and does not over-react by going, e.g. for a *Level 3* response when a lower level tactic would have been adequate for containing the challenge:

> *Level 1* would involve liaison with the police and use would be made (by the latter and under their command) of army equipment, such as helicopters and armoured cars, to meet particular short-term terrorist threats as, for example, possible attacks on Airports.
>
> *Level 2* would commit army personnel in order to release the police for more specialized duties; soldiers might man road blocks or, in the case of the Military Police, take over traffic control duties.
>
> *Level 3* would describe a more serious situation of direct military involvement, if necessary with weaponry, in crowd dispersal and would also imply the assumption of many other police duties by the Army, probably under the over-all command of a military Director of Operations.
>
> *Level 4* would only be reached in the case of Limited War and would involve what would, in effect, be a period of military government with the imposition of a curfew, identity checks, etc.

Clearly there would have to be a situation of, by European standards, catastrophic civil upheaval before any Army could be committed beyond *Level 2* and, if it were so committed before the challenge justified such a reaction, military intervention would merely make matters worse.

Some, indeed, in their eagerness to pre-empt terrorism have suggested measures which would be almost as bad as the terrorism itself and would certainly invite it. Not building the Channel Tunnel because it would make a good target for terrorists or reinforcing all public buildings by having, for example, no windows on the ground floor are surely counsels of despair and surrender. The adoption of a 'fortress mentality' and the decline of the State to a permanent Sparta for ever watching its extremist helots merely presents an image of the society the terrorist would impose were he successful. Time and

money would be better invested in keeping the public informed
of the dangers and dimensions of the problem so that the panic
and fear of ignorance can be avoided. It might call for a more
vigorous defence of the virtues of peaceful change and a more
critical approach to romantic notions of revolution prevalent
among certain sections of contemporary youth culture.

> 'We have to clear our minds of romantic ideas of revolution
> making. The poetic glamour of the revolution of barricades
> belongs to the past, and not even the recent past, as cer-
> tainly as does the *frischfrölicher krieg*—the brisk and jolly
> war.'[5]

It might require a more frequent and forceful reminder that
compromise with today's terrorism merely ensures a more
virulent epidemic tomorrow; that those who climb to power by
terror, by terror will maintain their control.

> 'The only way to guarantee constitutional liberties is to be
> provided with the apparatus for psychical immunisation.'[6]

Attempts have been made to use counter-terrorist squads, i.e.
police or army (or sometimes 'independent' but government
sponsored) units operating in plain clothes. This tactic makes
good sense in the jungle where the unit can come to think like
its quarry and eventually 'out-guerrilla' him. Counter-gangs
were used effectively against Mau Mau in Kenya. In the city
the tactic is politically risky; firstly because by using it the
Government appears to abandon its claim to legitimacy and
descends to the same level as the terrorist, secondly because it
enables the terrorist to commit violent acts and blame them on
to the counter-squads. Such counter-terror units are difficult to
control and thus may prove politically counter-productive; they
tend to pursue vendettas without regard to the overall situation.
They also constitute a standing temptation to their members to
indulge in freelance robbery and extortion of their own, thinking that they are above the law. In the end the people do not

any more know who is shooting or bombing them and conclude that 'they're all as bad as each other'. Some Republicans in Ireland are convinced that Special Air Service killer squads are operating widely; however out of two hundred murders investigated by journalists Dillon and Lehane[7] only one, they felt, could be blamed on the Army. It remains true that the use of such plain clothes armed units is highly sensitive and politically dangerous. Where the allegiances of the people still hangs in the balance the efficacy or armed counter-gangs in the urban environment is doubtful. (See the Case Studies at the end of this Chapter.)

Urban terrorist organizations suffer from a number of prevalent weaknesses each of which constitutes a possible leverage point for the authorities. Such weaknesses are relative to the degree of popular support enjoyed by the terrorist and the number and strength of other favourable contextual factors.[8]

Terrorists, separatist, revolutionary and racialist, have to date tended to overestimate the impact of their tactics on the population both directly and via the media. Attacks on a professional (as distinct from a conscript or National Service) army are unlikely swiftly to lead to a widespread demand to 'bring the boys home'. Television coverage soon loses its initial impact. People become anaesthetized to horror. Even the population directly involved has the capacity to absorb a tremendous amount of physical and psychological punishment without breaking down, as Northern Ireland has demonstrated. In the absence of mass discontent governments generally have the resources to sit out a campaign of terror if needs be. (Unfortunately while this may objectively be the case the groups likely to use terror do not see things in those terms.)

Terrorist political direction is unlikely to be very sophisticated and the political wing, especially in separatist movements, is likely to lose in any dispute with the militants. This is particularly the case where the political directorate resides outside the operational area. When under pressure, terrorist movements are likely to splinter into a number of disparate, and frequently warring, factions. Ideological fringe groups will seek to ride to prominence on the coat-tails of the terrorist cadre; the infiltration and dissension involved in this process is likely further to divide the leadership. Terrorism quickly gets out of control and hoodlum elements use the style and the name of the terror for their own ends. Such copycat methods are attributed to the original group and the political thrust gets lost as the violence spreads into a free-for-all. Identification of the insurgents with orthodox criminality is fatal to the logic of political terrorism and eases the task of suppression. It is this consideration, among others, which leads to a postponement of emergency legislation and to the attempt to deal with terrorism by the ordinary processes of the law. The aim of the Army in Northern Ireland, for example, has been to assist the civil authorities, to restore public confidence in the rule of law and in the Security Forces as protectors of the peace. 'Restoring public confidence' implies a campaign of psychological warfare. Public knowledge about terrorist methods and weaknesses robs their tactics of their impact. Specific techniques of countering terrorism are harnessed to the overall strategy and seek to capitalize on these weaknesses.

Techniques
Techniques are only as good as their political impact. Even when 'low profile', however, they must be indicative of a will to win and a determination to maintain the psychological and moral dominance of the terrorist.

Operations which produce no results merely annoy the local population; 'cordon and search' is only worthwhile if there is a 75% chance of netting something or somebody; if that is not the case then such operations are merely propaganda victories for the terrorist. Such affairs conducted 'rural style' with a concentration of army vehicles and personnel are of doubtful utility in the urban context; they are both noisy and provocative, thus succeeding in alienating the population by the same means as they warn the terrorist. Clandestine operations by plain clothes operatives in civilian cars are undoubtedly more effective militarily although they carry considerable political risks. It can be argued that if the population is in any case actively supporting the terrorist then nothing can be lost by 'hunch' operations though even in this case much will depend on whether or not it is considered possible to reverse the position and on the evaluation of negative effects on national and international public opinion. In the usual situation where the terrorist is feared rather than positively supported or where public allegiance is in the balance the probable effect of such activities needs careful appraisal.

Public opinion considerations remain paramount in the case of crowd and demonstration control and they apply particularly acutely where specialist riot control squads are not available. Barricades are usually set up in streets, preferably narrow, which have open spaces near them into which the crowd can safely disperse. 'Snatch squads' to seize individual law breakers are backed by 'arrest teams' who can swiftly process these prisoners in accordance with the law; all activities should ideally be recorded on videotape, either by hand-held or fixed-position cameras. Controlled escalation is difficult to achieve, especially when there may be upwards of several hundred press men and dozens of television crews—some of whom will be looking for 'army/police brutality' and who, publicity guaranteed by their very presence, constitute a provocation to extremists to cause incidents.

Since the terrorist relies for his impact on public opinion on the dissemination of his views and activities by the media there have been suggestions that such free publicity should be denied him or that the Press should be required to print a kind of 'authorized version' of what happened. Censorship in fact encourages rumour and the deliberate planting of rumour and fringe publications would undoubtedly seize upon its imposition as a means of increasing their sales by claiming to ignore it—thus achieving the opposite effect from that intended. 'Authorized versions' will almost certainly be read, if at all, only with extreme suspicion. Censorship, apart from its repugnance to democratic traditions, is thus only to be considered *in extremis*.

Reporting which is inaccurate is on the other hand damaging to the morale of the troops—as are incidents 'stage managed' for the benefit of the cameras. Only in the event of the media actively supporting the terrorist or wilfully ignoring evidence against him can action be taken; countervailing information via a vigorous government public relations campaign is the orthodox—and to date apparently the most effective—answer. Some aspects of mass media coverage and instant reportage remain open to criticism; the practice of thrusting a microphone under the noses of army or police officers during or shortly after incidents is both politically and morally reprehensible. Politically because it places the officer in the role of apologist for a policy which he had no part in formulating and morally since it casts him as defendant with the interviewer as inquisitor. In the Northern Ireland context army personnel have become demonstrably better at microphone and television technique, partly because they have been prepared for it, during the course of the Emergency; however laudable this may be it is not their primary function. It is necessary that they be able to explain their roles to themselves and to their subordinates and that they are knowledgeable about the political situation in which they are operating; it is no part of their job to justify themselves on television.

With the breakdown of normal 'law and order' a vacuum is created which can be filled either by the terrorist or by the Security Forces. Terrorist and soldier compete for the support of the population and whoever is successful will become, in fact if not in theory, the Governor of the area in question. This competition will involve a programme of civic action on the part of the security forces and of terror to dissuade participation from the opposition. Clubs and camps for teenagers, aid projects to the civil community—in housing, in help for the aged and handicapped—all represent a genuine attempt by the security forces to integrate themselves into the life of their host community. Their success will be limited by the fact that they may only be spending a comparatively short time in the area— the terrorist will be a longer term consideration. If units stay for longer periods than normal in order to combat this tendency they will tend to become identified with 'their' area, there will be marriages and integration may be taken to the point where objectivity is lost and hostility felt towards the civil administrators who 'do not understand the people'.

A Note on the Technology of Response[9]
Mao Tse-tung asserted that 'technology' was irrelevant in a 'People's War'; except in a propaganda sense this was never true. If technology is used as a substitute for politically directed action then it will mislead the counter-insurgent force into costly errors; conversely as the servant of policy it is indispensable in contemporary anti-guerrilla warfare, and doubly so in the urban context. Since the terrorist is using the Government's technology as one of his targets and his own access to it as a weapon he must be met by a qualitatively superior response. In addition to smuggled high velocity rifles, mines and rocket launchers the terrorist will use unsophisticated home-made devices such as crude guns and mortars (the latter sometimes killing their own operators). Common-sense measures such as tighter control of explosives by monitoring and registration need to be supplemented by innovations in the fields of weapons and equipment.

Good communications are at a premium in urban surroundings where visual contact is limited by buildings, smoke and confusion. Such communications must be secure from interference and interception; troops equipped down to patrol level with two-way radios operating on UHF and protected by scramblers meet this requirement. The terrorist also needs these facilities and he may seek to use both radios and the public telephone system, both of which are susceptible to monitoring by the security forces. Voice prints may lead to swift identification of callers, especially if the system uses computers.

Television cameras and videotape recordings may be used for surveillance and identification of known terrorists. They have potential uses in interrogation, in court proceedings and in training. Videotape is less objectionable than voice recording as evidence since clandestine editing is extremely difficult to achieve.

On the personal level light body armour and shields made of plastic render riot control and, in the former case, patrolling somewhat less hazardous. If soldiers are to be used in future against urban terrorists in Western Europe they must be equipped with personal weapons better adapted to that role than the standard NATO rifle. A lightweight rifle is essential if the situation of the terrorist being able to bring his weapon more quickly into action in a sudden confrontation is to be avoided. This requirement may be met by the new police L39 A1 which is being produced at the Royal Small Arms factory. Effective gas masks (in the early days in Northern Ireland the then issue gas mask was useless) are essential. Combat kit designed for an urban background of greys and blacks is needed rather than the olive green desirable in a country setting.

Riot control technology is currently a subject of much sensitivity. Such devices as 'Nightsun', powerful helicopter-mounted floodlights, or 'Skyshout', enabling information and instructions to be passed to large crowds, cause little controversy. Gas and disorientation devices not unnaturally arouse very different emotions. Ideally a riot control weapon should discriminate between the criminal and the innocent bystander and, while it should incapacitate in the short term, it should have no lasting effects. Both the CS gas and rubber bullets in current use fall short of these requirements. CS developed at Porton is classified as a 'harassing agent' and causes coughing, tears, tightness in the chest and a feeling of nausea. Since CS is dispensed in aerosol form it creates fumes which can enter nearby houses as well as affecting 'innocent bystanders'. Late in 1973 it was reported that the Ministry of Defence in the United Kingdom had authorized the use in 'certain special circumstances' of a new gas, CR. CR is, it is claimed, no more harmful than CS and is less indiscriminate since it can be dispensed in liquid form, for example by water cannon. Rubber bullets are considered dangerous; 1 in 16,500 have killed, 1 in 1,900 caused permanent disability and 1 in 800 serious injury. Two further devices have yet to be used and at least in Western Europe are unlikely at the moment to be authorized.

The 'squawk box' which could be mounted on a helicopter or a vehicle produces two slightly different frequencies which are almost inaudible but which, in the ear, combine to create two other frequencies, one their sum, the other their difference; the result is fainting, nausea and spreading panic as those affected run away or collapse—the device is directional.

The 'photic driver' uses strobe lights as well as noise to produce giddiness, sickness and fainting; there is the danger that it will also cause epileptic fits among those who are susceptible to the 'flicker fit' phenomenon.

More generally acceptable are gelignite 'sniffers', whether mechanical or canine, and the remote control trolley, 'Wheelbarrow', developed by the British Army to place explosive charges in suspect vehicles. There is also the possibility of a discharger being produced to spray plastic foam to blanket the effect of bomb explosions.

In all these contexts it seems inevitable that a technological spiral will set in as governments will have to assume that the terrorists will acquire some of these aids themselves, either by seizing them or through being supplied from a friendly country. Experiments to overcome the 'humane barrier', i.e. to produce a chemical agent so short term in its effects as to overcome the natural repugnance against gas warfare will doubtless continue. A 'knock down' (or 'out') agent which would prevent the individual from standing upright or anaesthetize for a short period might meet some of these criteria and has been the subject of experimentation in the USA, as have riot control agents based on lysurgic acid (LSD).[10] In any event there is a case for arguing that more resources should be switched to anti-terrorist research and development.

The Tactic of 'Counter Terror'—Case Studies

Guatemala

Guatemala attempted to fight Left Wing guerrillas by using counter-terror groups; the idea appears attractive—simply inject a similarly structured antibiotic in order to eradicate the infection; unfortunately such treatment is liable also to kill the patient. These para-military groups are considered to have been originally organized by Colonel Arana who later (1970), due to his success in fighting the insurgents, was elected to power. Of the three original such organizations (the White Hand, the New Anti-Communist Organization, and the Anti-Communist Council of Guatemala) the first, Mano Blanco, became the most well known. Such groups, without having to observe any code—military or civil—were prepared to fight, as one of their splinter groups put it, 'Ojo per Ojo'—an eye for an eye. They threatened to kill ten 'leftists' for every soldier, policeman or anti-Communist killed. These squads operated with the tacit approval of the authorities and were alleged to contain junior army officers. Together with the US-trained Army they achieved considerable success in harassing the guerrillas.

Violence increased as such groups used their power and anonymity to initiate a vendetta of their own against all liberal elements even suspected of Leftist sympathies. While on the Left kidnappings continued (the seizing and murder of the West German Ambassador was the most notorious but two local businessmen were only freed after a total of 750,000 dollars ransom had been handed over) the Right resorted to assassination. 'Institutionalized violence' took over from government. While the Left Wing received setbacks—guerrilla leader Yon Sosa was killed by a Mexican Army patrol on the border (19 May, 1970)—it was calculated that rival para-military groups were killing four or five people daily. Guatemalan Press estimates put the number of violent deaths in 1971 at over 1,000, with 171 kidnappings and 174 persons missing, almost all in Guatemala City.

The Government of Arana introduced a programme of reform and, while it had been forced to declare a state of siege in an attempt to deal with the violence, it felt strong enough to hold elections in March, 1972. These were at municipal level and Arana's National Liberation Movement polled 70% of the vote. Left Wing terrorists struck back in June and July when Paiz, a Vice-President and one of the leaders of the anti-Communist campaign, was assassinated in a cafe in Guatemala City. On one day in July (13th) the guerrillas eradicated four other prominent members of the ruling MLN.

Counter-terrorist operations in Guatemala indicate the dangers of encouraging para-military freelancing. The rise of Left Wing terrorism led to the toughest and most able army colonels being used against it; such officers when successful gain political influence and then take over. Neither Right nor Left 'wins' but the chances of a moderate régime coming to power are nil. So the Left, especially when holding naïve views about the efficacy of armed youth, merely conjures up the very devil it set out to exorcise.

Brazil

A variation on the counter-terror theme is to be found in Brazil. Terrorist attacks so inflamed the police that they formed their own Death Squads to track down and kill those whom they suspected. They feared delay and acquittal should they have to go through what they regarded as the tedious and corrupt processes of the law. From 1964, when the Death Squad was formed, until 1973 the security forces in Brazil were faced with a campaign of urban terror. Ruthless Brazilian response has been successful in the short term in destroying those terrorists. Government forces killed the theorist of urban warfare, Carlos Marighella, and his successor, Ferreira, 'died of a heart attack' after being captured by police. Small urban terrorist groups carried on their activity, principally through bank robberies and kidnappings.

Government counter-measures aroused considerable criticism

and allegations of torture; one of Marighela's original band died on the mis-named 'Flower Island', it was said from the effects of such treatment. The Roman Catholic Church became divided into 'progressive' priests, especially members of the Dominican Order, accused of supporting the guerrillas and 'conservatives' who defended the Government. Mgr Helder Camara become internationally famous for his denunciations of the Brazilian Government's methods. In contrast the Sao Paolo Police Chief declared that even though the Church had been undermined the Armed Forces were still reliable and would do their duty in carrying out the sacred task of safeguarding national security. Right Wing extremists instituted a terror of their own and were suspected of several killings, including that of a priest on Mgr Camara's staff, Father Neto.

The Death Squads, their activities 'signed' by their skull and crossbones trade mark, were held responsible for over 1,000 murders from 1964 to 1970. After a Police Inspector was killed in July, 1970, he was avenged by eleven reprisal murders. Among those killed was a Left Wing leader, Nunes, suspected of the Inspector's murder.

Most of the remaining urban terrorist groups were eradicated during 1972 and 1973. (Carlos Lamarca, an army deserter who had achieved some reputation, and had operated as a rural guerrilla in Sao Paolo State, had been killed in September, 1971.)

Brazilian methods although much criticized have thus proved for the time being successful. Urban-based movements have been prevented from moving beyond the stage of sporadic terrorism. The Government has been prepared to bear the burden of international disfavour. Marighela's thesis did not, therefore, receive support in the experience of his own country. Once again the quarrels endemic to the Latin American Left divided and weakened the efforts of the guerrillas. In particular Marighela and his successors failed to build up the 'urban tactical front' to a pitch sufficient to enable the opening of a 'rural front' which might co-operate in a strategic offensive. Armed Forces fighting for their survival in the face of the implacable opposition of revolutionary elements may be relied upon to show a marked degree of enthusiasm and efficiency. However consistent on ideological grounds the attitude of revolutionaries to the Armed Forces may appear, it is tactically disastrous; movements which have come closest to success (e.g. Venezuela and Uruguay in the early stages) have all made an appeal to the Armed Forces and attempted to reassure them.

NOTES

1 Stokeley Carmichael in *The Dialectics of Liberation*, Cooper, Pelican, 1968, p. 153.
2 Martin Oppenheimer in *Riots and Rebellion*, ed Masotti and Bowen, Sage Publications, 1968, p. 429.
3 De Gaulle once remarked that the Army was incapable of seeing further than the nearest hill.
4 e.g. of the American National Guard and of the use of militia in British history—at 'Peterloo' for example.
5 Hermann Rauschning, *Germany's Revolution of Destruction*, Heinemann, 1939, p. 10.
6 Chakhotin, *The Rape of the Masses*, Routledge, 1940, p. 127.
7 Martin Dillon and Denis Lehane, *Political Murder in Northern Ireland*, Penguin, 1973.
8 See Appendix B.
9 See 'New Scientist' generally and especially March and September, 1973.
10 For further details, see the author's article in 'Battle' magazine, Ian Allan, No. 5.

CHAPTER 13

Postscript—A Market for Terror? The Prospect for Western Europe

Civil war has been regarded throughout history as a particularly terrible experience, dividing communities and families and leaving wounds which fester for generations. Today this understanding has been replaced in some quarters by a romanticization of internal violence provided that it is presented as 'revolutionary'. There is a tendency to perceive the torture, mutilation and death of the 'Counter State' as less reprehensible than such matters would be if used by the State being attacked. Bandit figures have in the past been subjects of folk story and myth but their mantle sits ill on the shoulders of the assorted psychopaths and criminals who become involved in modern terrorist operations.

The first problem for Western Europe lies therefore in the realm of values and perceptions—particularly those of a generation which has known war only at second hand, its experience of it filtered through the media and its interpretations provided ready made by the commentators' instant expertise. Such a generation must be made to understand that there are no brisk and jolly revolutions to be had. Urban terrorists, whether they call themselves 'guerrillas' or 'freedom fighters', exist to kill and then to rule by fear and hatred. Intellectuals and politicians who romanticize such people must be made individually to face the infliction of suffering which their statements sometimes encourage. A few may be prepared to pay that price; it should at least be made clear what it is.

There are some signs that a few of these lessons have been grasped. The nineteen-sixties were the decade of revolutionary optimism—but also of disillusionment. 'Revolution' proved unsuccessful as an event, disappointing as a process and frustrating as a way of life. Revolutionary romanticism, whether on the campus or in the jungle, received a number of salutary awakenings. In Bolivia, as in Paris, the hopes of activists were dashed. Yet the problems and conditions which gave to the movements of that time, however misconceived, at least a plausibly objective rationale, have become not less, but more, acute. Unless social engineering and piecemeal reform can achieve tangible progress against urban decay and pollution then the temptation to seek the single cataclysmic solution will return doubly strengthened by gradualist failures and the impatience of the young. In that situation were a 'revolutionary' course to be followed it would not be by the mechanistic application of traditional models which are discredited by their failure to provide any solutions to the contemporary versions of the classic dilemmas.

The antithesis between nationalist/separatist ambitions on the one hand and international class solidarity on the other continues to divide those opposed to the continuation of current social and political systems. In the context both of race and of poverty the question of choice between being poor but proudly independent (e.g. black cultural nationalism and working-class counter-culture) or fighting for equal ease of entry to the rewards of the dominant culture is no nearer resolution. Intellectuals have been unable to decide whether they wish to liberate the working class or to join it. Contemporary 'revolutionaries', and more especially those in the West who come from middle-class backgrounds, have consistently undervalued the continuing importance of racial, ethnic and cultural divisions. In Western Europe too, in the mutual competition to become middle class, the myths of proletarian brotherhood are seen to have less and less relevance. Students, far from being allies, are often seen by workers as a pampered minority, strong on rhetoric but organizationally flabby outside the defence of their own particular interest.

There is no doubt however that economic and demographic

changes are producing an environment increasingly sensitive to the use of terrorist techniques.

Some urban planners have seen the future of Western Europe in terms of massive conurbations, ranging in size from the mere metropolis of two million or so to the megalopolis of one hundred million and the urban region of seven hundred million, where for every twenty-five miles of countryside there will be a thousand square miles of buildings. In the United Kingdom the line from Lancashire through the Midlands to the south east will constitute a megalopolis and, by the end of the next century, one quarter of the land will be under urban use.[1] In West Germany the rate of urban extension is even greater.

Such developments will necessitate technological innovations which will themselves be highly sensitive to interference. Such matters do not lie merely on the wilder shores of conjecture nor does the ability to send 'pestilence through the post'[2] or for any moderately competent scientist to manufacture his own atomic bomb. Other threats can be more subtle and at a less indiscriminate level; a computer makes an excellent target since it can be made to yield confidential information, can be fed with alien instructions by anyone skilled enough to break into the system or, more crudely, can be destroyed or held to ransom. Costs of reassembling the information held in a computer might be enormous. Electronic experts can 'bug themselves in' to global telephone systems by copying coded signals and can then dial any statesman anywhere in the world, not excluding on the 'Hot Line' between Washington and Moscow.

Politically the situation in Western Europe has stress areas which may produce civil upheaval or be used by external powers to that effect, nor are these confined to the problems likely to face Spain and Yugoslavia when their respective leaders die. Even in the heartland of Western Europe affairs are from a KGB point of view not unencouraging.

In Italy the revival of the Right is stimulating a militant reaction from the Left; the reappearance of a type of 'Fascism' in that country under the auspices of the MSI Party and the activities of peripheral extremist organizations such as 'National

Vanguard' and the 'Mussolini Action Squads' have led to clashes with the police and Left Wingers involving bombings and gun fights. In Germany the Social Democratic Party is a target for infiltration both from the 'New Left' and from the German Communist Party, which makes a practice of trying to split the SPD. It has been found necessary in France to ban both a Trotskyist and an extreme Right organization ('New Order') after violent clashes over the immigration issue. To the KGB and its masters these manifestations indicate a certain potential. In such a situation the Soviet State can continue to present the aspect of benevolence and détente. In public the Russians have no need to dirty their hands; secretly they can supply the arms and propaganda or use the disaffected as part of their espionage network.

Modern communications facilitate a system of mutual assistance among extremists—the phenomenon noted by some observers of 'trans-national terrorism'.[3] Thus training facilities have been supplied by Arab guerrillas and the Basque ETA allegedly receives help from the IRA and the Breton Nationalists. Any effective response must thus itself also be trans-national; in December, 1972, the North Atlantic Treaty Organization members discussed proposals for meeting the threat of international terrorism. It is unlikely however (although not impossible) that an organization which contains countries with such differing ideological and political views as for example Greece, Turkey, Holland, Norway and Portugal would be able to exhibit an effective degree of co-operation in this field.

Each new technological advance will be utilized by those who are skilled in the Leninist techniques of social destruction for the time honoured purposes of manipulation and exploitation—as they were by Lenin himself and by his admirer, Joseph Goebbels. Tariq Ali of the International Marxist Group in his book, *The Coming Revolution in Britain*, sees four areas of 'revolutionary potential': radicalized youth, black workers, women's liberation movements and, inevitably, Ireland.

At the moment there is in the United Kingdom a general

disinterest in the kind of extremism which he advocates—which is reinforced by the disadvantages under which many of its leaders labour; originating from outside the country they lack local credibility. Internal dissensions have resulted in a proliferation of mutually recriminatory splinter groups. Only if economic conditions deteriorate markedly will some of Tariq Ali's potential sources of revolution become activated. The most sensitive pressure point would then be, not Ireland, nor radicalized youth (which in general shows no signs of a willingness to make the necessary sacrifices) but in the coloured community.

Much has been written about the problems facing that community and in particular about the question of police—immigrant relations.[4] Despite the efforts to train the police in community relations and the provision of specialist officers in that field it is an illusion to suppose that the police can in some way compensate for society. Policemen cannot be expected any more than soldiers to bear the burden of sorting out the results of political and economic decisions taken by governments. Even if governments do formulate realistic policies there will be problems enough calling on all the resolution and training of the police; without such policies the forces of law and order, however well intentioned, will simply appear as 'white oppression'. If unemployment amongst black youth is allowed consistently to rise above that of comparable whites then trouble will follow. If a situation like that in the United States develops where black children lose one IQ point every year after they go to school, where half the young men are unemployed and where drug abuse is high, then urban violence involving weapons, ripe for politicization, will occur. Subsequent formation, expansion and decay of urban ghettoes, physical and emotional, will on the evidence to date be succeeded by a period of urban warfare both from coloured and from poor white elements, whipped into frenzies by their respective and mutually supportive demagogues. Such a scenario would envisage an extremely depressed economic situation, with industrial unrest widespread; demonstrations in ghetto areas would be used as a cover for bombing and sniping. Others, claiming to be 'nationalists' in Wales and Scotland would then join in while the bulk of the population formed self-protection squads. Much of the upheaval would be caused not by genuinely nationalist elements but by small extremist groups, some externally supported, which would act in their name, hoping to drag both them and others into the fray.

It can also safely be assumed that industrial disputes will be made the occasion for physical challenges to the police and if possible the Army. In particular both the police and the Army, the bulk of whose men now serve in the United Kingdom, will increasingly become the targets for infiltration and subversion from all the elements which have been considered in this book—Anarchist, Communist and Trotskyist; the aim will be to reduce military effectiveness in responding to the challenges which may be posed by racial, separatist or 'proletarian' violence.

In November, 1973, the Communist Party of Great Britain at its Congress considered a resolution which called for a drastic reduction in the size of the Armed Forces and for the 'disbanding of the Special Branch and counter-insurgency research units, the ending of "crowd control" and counter-insurgency training and the dismissal of all Officers associated with such work.'

The (Trotskyist) Workers' Revolutionary Party has said that counter insurgency experts must be 'eliminated' and the 'structure of the Army broken' by means of 'mass meetings in the Barracks' (9 November, 1973) while other extremist groups, such as the International Marxist Group and the International Socialists are similarly committed.

In the event of serious civil strife it can be expected that extreme Right Wing movements will attempt also to infiltrate and corrupt the Armed Forces.

Urban terrorism thus represents and will continue to represent part of the anti-democratic thrust of twentieth-century totalitarianism, whether of Left or Right. It seeks to identify or grows out of the divisions in a society and then uses these leverage points to split apart the fabric of social cohesion and destroy it piecemeal. In particular it uses and will continue to use the technological and liberal sensitivities of democracy in order to destroy it. The question of the freedom of speech and its abuse is vital. Just as Vietnam provided the first full-coverage TV war, so the Provisionals' is the first protracted full-coverage TV terrorist campaign. Both will be seen in the future as having been fought primarily for the emotions and loyalties of the population via the TV screen and the newspapers, with disgust, revulsion and fear as the principal weapons. In the end, as T. E. Lawrence remarked, the battle is 'for the minds of men'.

NOTES

1 See, for example, Best, *March of the Concrete Jungle*, Geographical Magazine, October, 1972.
2 As has already been threatened in West Germany.
3 Especially Brian Crozier of the Institute for the Study of Conflict (ISC). See *Annual of Power and Conflict*, ISC.
4 e.g. Derek Humphry, *Police Power and Black People*, Panther, 1972.

APPENDIX A

IDEOLOGICAL BACKGROUND OF GROUPS USING OR LIKELY TO USE URBAN TERROR

Type	Background	Tactics	Examples
Anarchist	Bakhunin	Violence as destroying an evil system; based on a view of man as naturally social, and of authority as enslaving him.	Angry Brigade, Anarchist groups in Spain, Italy
Moscow-oriented Communists	Marx and Lenin	Terror as a tactic when 'revolutionary conditions' (i.e. social and political environment) are right.	CPs that have not gone over to 'front' tactics, e.g. recently Guatemala. Potentially Official IRA
Nationalist groups 'sectional chauvinism'	History, Culture, Language	Terror to discredit government and influence public opinion (in what is seen as a neo-colonial situation) to give in to separatist demands.	Prov. IRA FLQ—Canada ETA—Basques USTASHE—Croat
Composite and eclectic groups. Generally 'Socialist', anti-US; independent political line	Socialism Nationalism Examples of other movements Marighela	Urban terror to discredit government, encourage climate of collapse, leading to strikes, opportunity for political arm of guerrilla movement to pose as only viable alternative and accede to power, possibly by armed action, possibly through elections.	Tupamaros ALN (Brazil)
Maoist Peking-oriented splinter groups	Mao, Giap	'Urban Brigades' to support main activity of peasant guerrilla war.	CP of India (M-L) (Calcutta '70/71)
Black racist	Fanon	Terror as catharsis for the individual and as reinforcing and creating racial group identity and self-respect.	Black Panthers before 'constitutional' phase

'New Left' student-based middle class	Marcuse, Fanon, Bakhunin	Terror seen as protest and as weakening capitalist system in general; freeing individual from 'alienation' and 'de-personalization' of capitalist society; influenced by Anarchist thought and history.	Weathermen in US
Castroite	Guevara, Debray	Urban activity related to and under control of rural 'foco'. Elite to 'create revolution', self-consciously 'hairy-chested', guerrilla force as 'the party in embryo'.	Cuban Revolution (in theory). Unsuccessful Guevarist movements in Bolivia, Venezuela
Trotskyist	Trotsky, Guillen	'The creation of a new revolutionary leadership for the world proletariat'; in Europe less likely to initiate violence than seek to exacerbate and, 'politicize' it once started.	Argentinian groups Support for IRA
Right Wing Reaction	National history, threatened majority group identity.	Counter terrorism, sometimes independent, sometimes government inspired.	'Death Squad' (Brazil) several groups in Guatemala. UVF UFF **KKK**, 'Minutemen'(US)

NB: The list is not exhaustive; Palestinian terrorist groups do not fit easily into the above categories, and are obviously likely to continue to pursue terrorism against Jewish interests anywhere.
The situation is even more complicated than the table would suggest:

(a) within any group there may be sub-groups/individuals who do not share the dominant motivation (e.g. 'New Left' middle-class youth in Prov. IRA).

(b) such groups are, especially in Latin America, volatile in the extreme.

(c) there are psychological/sociological motivations which are sometimes merely justified by political labelling.

(d) groups are liable to infiltration and takeover, especially by international movements and particularly when under pressure.

(e) the increasingly 'trans-national' nature of contemporary terrorism blurs ideological categorization.

(f) criminals and psychopaths utilize political upheaval and terror to pursue their own ends.

APPENDIX B

CONDITIONS CONDUCIVE TO URBAN VIOLENCE

If two or more of the following factors are present in an urban environment then there is likely to be an outbreak of urban violence which if (6) is present, will be politically significant and not merely anomic.

Factor	Example
1 a self-conscious, segregated, ethnic, cultural or religious minority.	Catholics in Northern Ireland IRA French Canadians in Quebec FLQ Basques in Spain ETA Racial groups: 'Black Power', Puerto Ricans in US.
2 which feels itself to be economically deprived or politically oppressed (a feeling exacerbated by the effect of modern communications) with poor job opportunities, lack of voting rights: but has been encouraged to believe that change is coming ('rising expectations') and then disappointed.	Blacks Slum dwellers in South America Catholics in Northern Ireland Middle class in Uruguay (Tupamaros) Catholics in Northern Ireland
3 in a situation of unemployment/inflation	
4 externally encouraged	from Peking, Moscow, Havana or international extremist movements
5 with an historical 'THEM' to blame	the 'Church', the 'Whites', the 'British', the 'Capitalists', etc.
6 and with frustrated élites to provide leadership and to overcome the natural distaste (of all save the psychopathic fringe) to initiate violence by giving it an ideological justification.	radical students extremist agitators

APPENDIX C

SOME NORTHERN IRELAND ORGANIZATIONS

A. POLITICAL

Name	Notes	Prominent personalities
UNIONISM split in January, 1974, into:		
Official Unionists	opposed to any 'power sharing' and any 'Irish dimension'	H. West
Assembly Unionists	supported 'power sharing'.	B. Faulkner
(Both the above claim to represent 'main stream Unionism')		
The UNITED ULSTER UNIONIST COUNCIL, formed to fight the February, 1974 General Election comprised:		
Official Unionists		
Vanguard Unionists }	hard-line Protestant working-class movements largely dependent on the personalities of their leaders.	W. Craig
Democratic Unionists		Rev. I. Paisley
Note: Groups of Protestant trade unionists, the Loyalist Association of Workers and the Ulster Workers' Council, are closely associated with the above movements; it was the Ulster Workers' Council which organized the general strike in 1974 after the 14 May Assembly vote in favour of the Sunningdale Agreement.		
SOCIAL DEMOCRATIC AND LABOUR PARTY (1970)	aims to achieve social progress and Irish unity by constitutional means.	G. Fitt
NATIONALIST PARTY	the traditional Catholic party; now almost defunct.	
REPUBLICAN CLUBS	run by the political wing of the Official IRA.	M. McGurran
(Provisional) SINN FEIN	political wing of Provisional IRA; policy of non-participation.	
ALLIANCE PARTY (1970)	moderate bi-sectarian party; largely middle class.	O. Napier
NORTHERN IRELAND LABOUR PARTY	bi-sectarian working-class party; strong trade union ties.	

249

B. PARA-MILITARY AND TERRORIST ORGANIZATIONS

Name	Notes	Prominent personalities
PROVISIONAL IRA	formally appeared January, 1970; aims to escalate the cost of military presence in Northern Ireland to the point where public opinion in the rest of the UK brings about withdrawal.	David O'Connell Seamus Twomey Sean MacStiofain
OFFICIAL IRA	'defensive activity' to protect Catholic areas. Marxist 'war of national liberation' when objective conditions are favourable.	Cathal Goulding

Note: several freelance squads, more or less licensed by the Provisionals, operate in England.

Name	Notes	Prominent personalities
ULSTER DEFENCE ASSOCIATION (August, 1971)	large Protestant working-class para-military organization with contacts in England and Scotland.	Charles Harding Smith
ULSTER VOLUNTEER FORCE (appeared in present form in 1966)	traditional para-military Protestant force; announced in August, 1974 that its 'political wing' would contest elections.	Augustus 'Gusty' Spence
ULSTER FREEDOM FIGHTERS (June, 1973) RED HAND COMMANDO (mid-1973)	anti-Catholic terrorist and murder squads; have carried out bomb attacks, particularly on Catholic public houses.	

Note: there have been Press reports of a small neo-Trotskyist terrorist group operating in Northern Ireland.

BIBLIOGRAPHY

Selected Further Reading (this list is additional to books already referred to in Chapter footnotes)

HISTORY
Adamic, *Dynamite*, Chelsea House, 1969
Bernstein, *Auguste Blanqui and the Art of Insurrection*, Lawrence & Wishart, 1971
Clarke, *We All Fall Down*, Pelican, 1968
Ebermayer and Meissner, *Evil Genius*, Wingate, 1963
Halperin, *Mussolini and Italian Fascism*, Van Nostrand, 1964
*Hanser, *Prelude to Terror*, Hart Davis, 1971
Hibbert, *Mussolini*, Longmans, 1962
Hitler, *Mein Kampf*, Hutchinson, 1969
Orlow, *The History of the Nazi Party* (2 vols), David and Charles, 1971
*Page, *Lenin and World Revolution*, McGraw Hill, 1959
Schapiro, *The Communist Party of the Soviet Union*, Eyre & Spottiswoode, 1960
Schapiro and Reddaway, *Lenin: the Man, the Theorist, the Leader*, Pall Mall, 1967
*Smith (ed), *Trotsky*, Prentice Hall, 1973
Sykes, *Cross Roads to Israel*, Collins, 1965
Vagts, *Hitler's Second Army*, Infantry Journal, Washington DC, 1943
Wiskemann, *Fascism in Italy*, Macmillan, 1969

POLITICAL/IDEOLOGICAL BACKGROUND
*Arendt, *Crises of the Republic*, Penguin, 1969
Brzezinski, *The Soviet Bloc*, Harvard, 1971
*Caute, *Fanon*, Fontana, 1970
*Cranston (ed), *The New Left*, Bodley Head, 1970
*Crozier (ed), *We Will Bury You*, Tom Stacey, 1970
Franklin, *From the Movement Toward Revolution*, Van Nostrand, 1971
Lerner and Lasswell, *World Revolutionary Elites*, MIT, 1965
Mackenzie, *Secret Societies*, Aldus, 1967
*Oppenheimer, *Urban Guerrillas*, Penguin, 1970
Pomeroy, *Guerrilla Warfare and Marxism*, Lawrence & Wishart, 1969

* indicates a book that is recommended for initial reading.

CASE STUDIES

Cooper, *Colony in Conflict*, Swindon Book Co., Hong Kong, 1970
Mitchell, *Having Been a Soldier*, Hamilton, 1969
Morf, *Case Studies of the FLQ*, Clarke, Irwin, Toronto, 1970
O'Ballance, *The Algerian Insurrection 1954-62*, Faber, 1967
Paget, *Last Post: Aden 1964-67*, Faber, 1969

TACTICS

McCuen, *Art of Counter Revolutionary War*, Faber, 1966
Mallin (ed), *Terror and Urban Guerrillas*, University of Miami, 1971
*Methvin, *The Riot Makers*, Tom Stacey, 1972

INDEX

253

255

257